Terrorism and International Relations

Edited by
Daniel S. Hamilton

Hamilton, Daniel S., ed. *Terrorism and International Relations*.
Washington, DC: Center for Transatlantic Relations, 2006.

Calouste Gulbenkian Foundation
Av. de Beina 45—A
1067-001 Lisbon
Portugal
Tel. (+351) 21 782 3000
Fax (+351) 21 782 3025
Email: info@gulbenkian.pt
http://www.gulbenkian.org

Center for Transatlantic Relations
The Paul H. Nitze School of Advanced International Studies
The Johns Hopkins University
1717 Massachusetts Ave., NW, Suite 525
Washington, D.C. 20036
Tel. (202) 663-5880
Fax (202) 663-5979
Email: transatlantic@jhu.edu
http://transatlantic.sais-jhu.edu

ISBN 0-9766434-8-0

Table of Contents

Part III: Media and Terrorism

Part IV: Law and Terrorism

Part V: Responding to Terrorism

Acknowledgements

On behalf of the authors and of the Center for Transatlantic Relations at the Paul H. Nitze School of Advanced International Studies I would like to thank the Calouste Gulbenkian Foundation, especially Emílio Rui Vilar, President of the Board of Trustees, and Rui Goncalves, my partner in this effort, for the initiative to launch its cycle of conferences and books on Conflict and Cooperation in International Relations, and to examine in this volume the nature and implications of terrorism for international relations. I would also like to thank the authors themselves for their own engagement and insights. Particular thanks go to my colleagues at the Center for Transatlantic Relations for their continuing energy and support. Each author writes in his or her personal capacity; the views expressed are those of the authors and not their institutions.

Daniel S. Hamilton

Foreword

Terrorism and International Relations

Emílio Rui Vilar

The Closing of a Cycle

With this volume we close a cycle of books and conferences initiated in 2003, the underlying theme of which was the paradox of conflict and cooperation in international relations. This is a paradox that epitomizes the cohabitation of threat and risk with which we live in our times, with the hope that "the defense of liberty and the hope for justice" can win ground every day.

The first conference in 2003, on *Transatlantic Relations Europe/USA*, sought to frame transatlantic controversies that were exacerbated by the Iraq crisis and by the divisions that the crisis generated within Europe.

In 2004, we reflected both in a conference and a resulting book on *The New Frontiers of Europe—The Enlargement of the Union: Challenges and Consequences*, in a period marked by many events with a decisive impact on the rhythm and direction of the process of European construction. One year ago we still had positive expectations about the Treaty establishing a Constitution for Europe. Today, the call to reinvent the European spirit is necessary and urgent because it is indispensable to find our direction again and reconcile the citizens with the European project.

The international scene is not short of themes that cause concern, that demand reflection and that will enliven our debate. These include the energy crisis, with the long-lasting increase in gasoline prices, and its many implications for our economies and our geo-strategic equilibrium. There are also critical areas of tension and conflict, without an end in sight, such as in Iraq. There is the intolerable persistence of levels of poverty and underdevelopment as a result of the slippage in the realization of the United Nations Millennium Development Objectives. There is also reflection about reform of the United Nations itself in this year in which it completes 60 years of existence and in which we celebrate the centenary of the birth of Dag Hammarskjöld, the Secretary General who died in the service of peace and who so deeply marked the "personality" of this office.

I would like to thank our authors and, in particular, Daniel Hamilton, who again accepted our challenge to edit and launch this book in the United States hence expanding the impact of the debate we promoted in Lisbon in the Fall of 2005. I would like also to thank the participants who despite their valuable contribution, for various reasons, are not in this volume: André Gonçalves Pereira, António Vitorino, Artur Santos Silva, Diogo Pires Aurélio, Jean-Louis Bruguière, José Loureiro dos Santos, José Manuel Fernandes, Rui Pereira and Teresa Gouveia. Finally, I would like to dedicate this volume to the commissioner of this Conference, Professor Fernando Gil, from l'École des Hautes Études en Sciences Sociales (EHESS), Paris, who unfortunately passed away in March 2006.

Terrorism and International Relations   *stupefaction*

For this volume we have chosen international terrorism as a theme. The world is not the same since the morning of September 11, 2001. Our stupefication and incredulity were palpable, and a brutal absurdity turned itself into a permanent risk that can happen anywhere and in any country. The sentiment of a new and enormous vulnerability began to accompany us in our daily lives and the revolt against the absurdity began to take on the bitter taste of disbelief and impotence.

Four years after, the list of attacks to add to New York and Washington is impressive: Bali, Moscow, Mombassa, Riyadh, Casablanca, Istanbul, Madrid, Beslan, Djakarta, London and Sharm-el-Sheikh. A rational presentation, systematic and without ideological compromise, is required. However, the question continues to be sensitive and complex—it is enough to say that a commonly accepted definition of terrorism does not exist—and it is a source of perplexity for humanity confronted with a phenomenon of an enormous dimension, which persists, which changes itself and is reborn.

In trying to deal with this theme, we must recognize the mutations that can be seen in a historical perspective and in the various manifestations that, over time, have characterized the action of the various terrorist groups.

A common trace is evident, however: the use of indiscriminate violence, which is today enlarged to include the deliberate intention to affect the way of life and the politico-institutional structure in many regions of our planet, by individuals or groups who spread out across a significant number of countries or geo-political areas. It is not terrorism for national liberation or to affirm the right to be different. Today's terrorism is nihilist terrorism, it is destruction for destruction's sake, more violent and more lethal. We are talking about a new terrorism, globalized and offered for franchise, as someone has described it.

It is often associated with the invocation of religious motives and we can see in it, in the words of Craig White, a "willingness not to make concessions, not to accept compromises and a preference for total destruction instead of defeat. In this way, violence has ceased to be a means to achieve an objective but an objective in itself."

Its range is global and not sporadic or circumstantial. It is "theological-political," as Professor Fernando Gil describes it. It reveals itself within a pragmatism without limits. It knows how to explore, with great benefit, the new technologies and the global information systems that facilitate its organizational structures in networks that, in turn, amplify the effect of the actions and make combating it more difficult.

To combat terrorism, adequate forms of dissuasion are needed and the knowledge to bring together, not only all the instruments available to states but also an indispensable international co-operation that allows us to aggregate all the efforts that are needed to be successful in the anti-terrorist fight, as well as the rational perception, without preconceptions, of the phenomenon, to teach public opinion the form in which to structure the resistance of our societies.

The United Nations

Without overlooking the responsibilities of states and of regional organizations, as well as of each community, terrorism being an international phenomenon, the United Nations is, or should be, the primary legitimate platform for taking strategic positions in this field.

The UN can act as an outreach center in relation to its member countries, whether it is for human rights, such as humanitarian laws and the protection of refugees, or to facilitate finding a balance between the specific sensitivities of each of us and the global problems of security. Moreover, it promotes cultural and religious dialogues between the Muslim and Western worlds, and has underlined what exists as shared values between both, in such a way as to better educate the public in general about the perils of terrorism in the world.

In September 2005, at the World Summit of Heads of State and of Government of the United Nations, in New York, on the occasion of the 60th UN General Assembly, the draft of the final document set out proposals to identify the essential elements of a strategy to combat terrorism.

Lamentably, the final results were of limited scope, including concerning the proposal for the approval of a definition of terrorism, and as far as the recommendations to governments for them to act in a concerted manner to maintain the measures against terrorism compatible with international human rights standards or, in other words, to subject the fight against terrorism to international law and to humanitarian law.

However, it is to be hoped that on the basis of what was finally approved, the United Nations will remain, even so, in a condition to continue to promote dialogue and the wider understanding of the problems that come within the orbit of the fight against terrorism.

The European Union

The crisis of the emergence of terrorism when it enveloped both sides of the Atlantic could have been an occasion for deepening transatlantic relations, which the unilateral intervention of the United States in Iraq has unfortunately to a large extent precluded. It could also have been an opportunity to frame a true re-founding of NATO, a structure that must not lose itself but today needs a clear mission.

As Gijs de Vries, the present European Union Co-ordinator for Counter-Terrorism, has noted, Europe is not any more only a support base for terrorist attacks to be carried out in other areas. It is itself "the origin and target of terrorism."

Since 2001, the Member States of the Union have developed and adopted an extensive body of policies against terrorism. In June 2004, the European Council adopted an Action Plan containing more than

100 initiatives to be developed by Presidencies of the Union up to the end of 2005. Updated every six months, this plan covers various priority areas: information-sharing and cooperation between police forces, combating the financing of terrorism, civil protection and the protection of critical infrastructure and action on the causes of radicalization and terrorist recruitment.

Despite evident progress at the level of European cooperation, difficulties persist, given that this involves an area still relatively fragmented in relation to the forces of law and order and that it is, on the other hand, an area that is physically and socially permeable.

Indeed, the suppression of national frontiers has left European states exposed to new vulnerabilities and faced with challenges that tend to be global and transnational and which require responses of the same type. The trends in the security sphere are not different from the consequences of globalization in other areas.

Beyond this, the measures which are being considered or proposed are by nature particularly sensitive: either because they touch on the hard core of sovereignty or because, even though it is recognized that they are indispensable and urgent to guarantee the security of the citizen, they cannot help but to raise difficulties for the respect of individual rights and guarantees.

In this direction, the model of the nation-state upon which our democracies are founded—weakened by being turned more and more into a market state, as Philip Bobbit has said—seems to be overtaken in its capacity to manage responses capable of dealing with the new threats and finding innovative and stimulating proposals, particularly in designing solutions for communities that resist integration in the societies which welcome them.

So, there is a long way still to go to promote reciprocal confidence and strengthen cooperation.

Civil Society

In the area of fighting terrorism—which is also an attack on democracy—we cannot forget the importance of the role of citizens and civil society organizations.

Both have a fundamental role in the promotion of dialogue between different communities, in the circulation of reflections about the causes of terrorism, in the exercise of responsible and tolerant citizenship, and in the launching of educational and social projects that contribute to inclusion and sociability, such as the diffusion of knowledge and of the experiences of the meeting of cultures.

Conclusion

A political, economic, social, cultural and religious phenomenon, with old and complex roots, but exacerbated by contemporary displays, terrorism demonstrates with dramatic evidence that "culture matters." To promote dialogue between distinct cultures is not always easy; but we cannot stop trying. The possibility is open to all of us to intensify the cultural interchanges and to carry on the dialogue between distinct faiths (the so-called *interfaith* dialogue) and to stimulate different communities through a common effort aimed at diminishing the conflictual perception of the differences between "us and them."

This fight, which must be resolute and without quarter, must however avoid responding to radicalism with more radicalism, or repeating simplistic or simplifying stereotypes. As Jean-Marie Colombani has mentioned, "nothing would be worse in the battle against terrorism than that we renege on our own values."

For our way of living and facing up to life, terrorism appears as a brutal and absurd cataclysm. We are a few days from the completion of 250 years since another brutal event, the Lisbon earthquake of 1755, which left the Europe of Enlightenment in a state of shock. Then we will be able to say, as Voltaire in his "Poem on the disaster of Lisbon," which he dedicated to the event:

Our grief, our regrets, our losses are numberless,
The past is only a sad memory for us,
The present is frightful, if there is not to be a future,
If the darkness of the tomb destroys the being who thinks,
One day everything will be all right, that is our hope.

Chapter 1

Terrorism and International Relations

Jorge Sampaio

Terrorism represents a significant threat. It must be condemned unequivocally. It is necessary to fight it in an intransigent manner; this is a certainty for us all. To conquer it we need a strategy. And to draw up this strategy, we need to understand the terrorist phenomenon.

I want to stress that to understand terrorism does not mean to justify or to pardon it; but without this effort at comprehension, it will be difficult to combat it in an intelligent manner.

Terrorism is a political weapon with a long history. Traditionally, it has been used—sometimes with success—in the service of revolutionary or nationalist causes, in localized conflicts. One of the distinctive features of the present terrorist wave is the fact that it has an international character and objectives. In this way, international terrorism, as it manifests itself today, is also a phenomenon of globalization, making use of its possibilities and means, with efficiency and profit, in its operations.

A second distinctive feature of the present terrorist wave concerns the dimension of threat. In effect, September 11—which caused thousands of deaths and incalculable material damage—alerted us to the possibility of terrorist attacks of catastrophic dimensions. The use of weapons of mass destruction by terrorist movements is, as a consequence, a danger that we must consider, even though, fortunately, we should not underestimate the technical difficulties of developing and using this type of weapon, which, up to now, only a limited number of states have succeeded in overcoming.

We do not know with precision to what extent this terrorism is coordinated and centrally commanded. Nevertheless, it seems legitimate to suppose that the war in Afghanistan has disrupted, to a considerable extent, the chain of command of al-Qaeda, which was responsible for the September 11 attacks and for previous attacks in

Kenya, Tanzania, Yemen and in Saudi Arabia. At present, the elements that have come to light point to the existence of a decentralized network, spread out to the four corners of the globe, with informal contacts between their members, who at times act on their own initiative. These characteristics make the fight against terrorism more difficult.

Notwithstanding the apparent absence of a centralized direction, it seems clear that the attacks of the last four years—and here I want to recall, after New York and Washington, Bali, Moscow, Riyadh, Casablanca, Istanbul, Madrid and London, to refer only to the most important points in the geography of terrorism—these attacks form part of a coherent strategy: they are not isolated phenomena.

They all have the signature of radical and fundamentalist Islamic movements, inspired by doctrines known as "salafista" (radical extremist). All lay claim to the spirit of *jihad* and share common objectives: to introduce and deepen an irreparable cleavage between the West and Islam, in such a way as to isolate Islam and thus, as a result, to put it under the yoke of these fanatical and retrograde doctrines. In this sense, international terrorism is itself revolutionary and profoundly ideological.

The difference is that, instead of operating in a national framework, it operates at the international level; it is not set within a rigid hierarchy but operates in a decentralized form; its objectives are not localized, but transnational. Instead of gaining its inspiration from political and social doctrines, it operates—in an abusive way, if you will excuse me for saying so—in the name of religion.

We are faced with a phenomenon that is probably going to accompany our lives for some years to come. However great our efforts might be to combat the terrorist menace in the field—and these efforts have already succeeded in preventing and thwarting dozens and dozens of conspiracies and of planned attacks—it is best not to harbour illusions: we have to reckon with the occurrence of new attacks in the coming years, the dimensions of which we cannot predict.

Having made this summary diagnosis of the nature and the political objectives of the terrorism conducted or inspired by al-Qaeda, what conclusion can we reach about the terrorist campaign initiated in the mid-1990s and the efforts made to fight it up to now?

There can be no doubt that this campaign has provoked an environment of tension in relations between the West and Islam and had important direct and indirect consequences.

I refer, first, to the military interventions in Afghanistan and in Iraq, which have profoundly altered the political situation in the Middle East and whose repercussions continue, and will continue for a long time, to make themselves felt in a powerful and, up-to a certain point, unpredictable manner in the whole context of relations between the West and Islam. In contrast to the intervention in Afghanistan, which was widely supported by the international community, the war in Iraq opened up great breaches in the international consensus. This is not the moment to analyse, in all its complexity, the situation that exists in that country, and the prospects for its evolution. In relation to our theme, it is perhaps enough to point out that one of the consequences of this intervention was to open up a new front in the fight against international terrorism. In the context of Muslim countries, Afghanistan and Iraq belonged to separate worlds. Now, they are part of the same set of problems. Because of this, whatever the starting positions were in relation to the question of Iraq, it is in the interest of the whole of the international community that the United States is successful in that country.

I will mention, secondly, that the example of September 11 and its sequels seem to have widened the recruiting base of the terrorist movements and inspired a new generation of activists ready above all to commit new attacks, even though, up to this moment, none has had results comparable to the attacks against the Twin Towers and the Pentagon.

It is particularly worrying that some of the individuals who make up this new generation of terrorists have originated in the vast Muslim community resident in Europe. This a question which needs to be raised with particular care to avoid that the great majority of Muslims resident in Europe, who energetically repudiate terrorism and the ideologies from which it draws inspiration, might be unjustly affected.

The terrorist campaign launched by al-Qaeda had important consequences. However, if put in the perspective of this campaign's widest political objectives, one is forced to recognize that its effects have not met the ambitions of its mentors and executors.

For the Western countries—and it was they who, until now, bore the most violent attacks—it does not seem that terrorism is capable of putting in doubt the solidity of their democracies and their economic system. Even if the fight against terrorism means, or comes to mean, some trampling—never justifiable—of human rights and the freedoms and guarantees of citizens, it seems exaggerated to say that this campaign of blind and indiscriminate violence puts our democracies in danger. On the contrary, our political systems have demonstrated a notable capacity for mobilisation to resist and fight terrorism.

As in the Muslim countries, whose political regimes, even if indirectly, are the main targets for this campaign, the objectives are far from being attained: the regimes denounced as "apostate" did not fall; on the contrary, it was the Taliban who were overthrown in Afghanistan.

The most recent results of the Pew Global Attitudes Project show that support for the extremists and for their violent methods is declining in the Muslim world, and in a particularly pronounced way in countries such as Morocco and Indonesia, that were victims of suicide attacks.

As I have noted, at the international level the ultimate objective of the terrorist campaign seems to be to isolate the Muslim countries from Western influence, in order to subject them to a new form of religious totalitarianism. The attacks are an instrument to sow hatred and mistrust and to provoke a cycle of reprisals that might feed and consolidate these sentiments. To this extent, they have attained their objectives at least in part, having provoked an environment of tension and mistrust between the West and Islam, as much in the international field as in relations with the Muslim communities in Europe. The situation thus created causes concern but it is not irreversible. What should then be the elements of a strategy to fight terrorism efficiently?

First, the logic of confrontation between civilizations is the one which best serves the terrorists interests. It is of crucial importance to avoid it. To succumb to the xenophobic urge, to identify Islam with terrorism, to retaliate indiscriminately—there is nothing better than this to stimulate resentment, hate and incomprehension. Because of this, it is right to measure our responses and not to get the target wrong. We must at all cost avoid falling into the trap of contributing to achieving the ends that the terrorists are seeking to attain.

Second, we need allies in the Muslim world to fight this scourge. It is necessary to prevent the establishment, in the minds of people, of an erroneous identification between Islam and terrorism; but for this perception not to harden, it is also necessary that the Muslim world actively collaborate in this battle. I am fully convinced that a large majority of Muslims do not see themselves reflected in the fanatical concepts from which the terrorist movements draw inspiration. On the contrary, they have a moderate concept of religion and aspire to a future of economic and social progress and of liberty, with respect for their own cultural identity. For these Muslims, terrorism represents a threat at least as great as for the Western countries.

Because of this, we need to hear the voice of the moderates in the Muslim world denounce terrorism loud and clear. The religious leaders have a particular responsibility in this area, because of the authority invested in them to refute the interpretations of the Koran invoked by the extremists to justify the indiscriminate and mass assassination of civilians. It is, above all, in the Muslim countries that terrorism must be discredited politically, isolated, overthrown and eliminated, by the action of their governments and by the pressure of public opinion.

Third, to help this happen, we must seek to resolve problems that also contribute to the present state of tension in the relations between the West and Islam. One of the factors that has contributed most to spreading hatred of the West in the Muslim countries is the conflict between Israel and the Palestinians. To move forward with a solution of this conflict, which represents a focus of permanent tension that has dragged on for so many years, would make an important contribution to turning this relationship more fluid and more peaceful.

Fourth, we must continue to mobilize the international community for this fight. Cooperation is a determining factor for the success of this battle. In the last four years, the European Union has made enormous progress in this field. We must now extend this cooperation to the whole of the international community. Even though it has not been possible to obtain a consensus definition of terrorism in the 2005 United Nations Summit, the terms of the adopted declaration represent an important advance. In effect, it was possible, for the first time, to arrive at a firm and unanimous condemnation of terrorism. It is now necessary to advance towards a Global Convention on this issue.

Fifth, on the police and military level, we cannot lower our guard. It is necessary to keep the practical and ideological support networks for terrorism under constant vigilance and pressure. At an internal level, we must not tolerate the activities of supposed religious leaders who abuse freedom of thought and expression to preach hatred and to incite violence.

In the medium term, it is in the political and ideological realms that we must win this battle. September 11 was important not only for its immediate impact but also for having revealed that extremist ideologies possess a surprisingly extensive basis of sympathy and support in the Muslim world. To overthrow extremism definitively, and all the terrorist movements that find inspiration in it, it is important therefore that we not only mobilize all those who oppose them but also to bring back many of those who actually subscribe to them to more moderate positions.

It is difficult to ensure that this will happen in political systems that have been blocked for a very long time and have had great difficulties offering rapidly growing populations prospects of life compatible with their expectations. These political systems will therefore have to evolve. This evolution will probably be turbulent, but it is inevitable. To force this evolution through external interventions does, however, carry great risks.

In effect, these interventions tend to generate powerful perverse effects, especially when they are undertaken without taking into account the historical and cultural specificity of the countries in which they take place. It would therefore be preferable if these evolutions were to result from internal dynamics.

Islam and democracy are not incompatible. In the dialogue of the West with the Muslim countries, we must not hold back from advocating liberty, democracy, human rights and the emancipation of women, which we ourselves secured with so much effort. But we must do it in full consciousness that these values can only thrive in a lasting way if they correspond to the independent and genuine will of each people and if they are expressed and are lived out in the idioms of their respective cultures.

I want to conclude this contribution on a confident note. Even though the road might still be long and difficult, and despite some options at least debatable, I am fully convinced that the West has the means, the determination and the political intelligence to contain the threat of international terrorism, without putting in doubt its values and principles. The fight against terrorism and the ideologies from which it derives inspiration will require patience and determination and will certainly involve some reverses. But it is a battle that was imposed on us, from which we cannot run and which, I am certain, we will finish as victors.

Part I:
Terrorist Itineraries:
Causes, Networks
and Biographies

Chapter 2
The Terrorist Setting

Daniel Sibony

The logic of Islamic terrorism is much more clever than we might believe. Moreover, it fascinates Western authors who see in it a "subversive" setting. This setting consists in inflicting violence but not on the enemy (which is too strong), but on anybody, including its "brothers." A suicide attack can kill good Muslims, and the cars that burned in France were anybodies, including those of Arab workers. The important thing is to provoke those responsible for law and order, to stimulate them to respond in ways that are unfair or without justice (in a suicide attack, the guilty party is already dead).

It is also the logic of a hostage taking: you take a precious object (the life of people or their possessions) and you provoke unfair acts, which prove that the enemy is as unfair as we have always said (and as it is written in the founding Text). And that fact is then used to justify attacking him afterwards. And that then brings to the terrorists the sympathy of all those who, for other reasons, do not like this enemy. This enemy is America or Israel (al-Qaeda has not written in its statutes that you must kill the French and the British, but the Jews and the Americans). The United States has many enemies, above all in Latin America, and the cause of Israel is relatively badly-known: what are all those Jews doing down there in an Arab land? Moreover, if the media show pictures of the responses to attacks, responses which are obviously unfair, the mistrust towards *this enemy* is reinforced and also, thus, the sympathy for those who fight it.

Sometimes, people use the psychological argument: "if people are ready to give their life to hit the enemy, it is because they hate it, and this hatred must be well-founded." This is a well-founded argument, all the more because the reasons can always be found to justify it. However, someone can hate you because that hate gives sense to their life, it re-assembles their identity, which, otherwise, would fly into fragments under the blows of reality. And it is perhaps the case for the extremist identity: fundamentalist Islam has created a strong identity, which has reigned in its space for centuries but which, more and more, is coming up against reality: it finds it difficult to live with it, to evolve with it. Because in one way, this identity is too perfect: it puts forward in its founding text, the Koran, that the others, "the people of the Book" (Christians and Jews) are traitors or perverts and that the only worthwhile way is *submission* to Allah, which is precisely Islam. It does this in such a way that, in this identity, evil does not so much come from life or history but from other people. Certainly, the real Muslim identity is enriched by a wish for conviviality, a wish to live with others: but when the "fundamentalist" call is heard, this wish for conviviality appears to be, for this identity, a betrayal.

It seems that Islamic terrorism may be the tactic best adapted to an identity that experiences difficulty in coming up against its weakness and its limits. Weakness and limits which come up against all other identity and which can even help it to evolve. The identity in question finds it difficult to say goodbye to its initial, fundamental richness; on the contrary, it has difficulty to accept that those who are cursed by Allah succeed. These are the people of the "Book," the "Book" being the Bible, from where, for that matter, the Koran has drawn its positive elements, before rejecting the supporters of the Book as being on the side of insubordination and of arrogance. It has a grudge against them succeeding, while the Arab Muslim world, rich with enormous resources, remains behind. The terrorist tactic expresses a *mortification*: It will not conquer but the *other* will not live in peace.

This tactic produces paradoxical effects. By hitting at the heart of New York on a certain September 11, it has produced a response that, beyond its rather naïve rhetoric about the battle between Good and Evil, seems to have produced a precise result: this response breaks down little by little the extremism in its totalitarian structures (Afghanistan, Iraq . . .), it is approaching the great homes of the system (Arabia and Iran) and seems not to shake the Muslim world or even cut it in pieces as if *to better integrate it in the global game*—as if, in the same way, it was too big or too fixed to join in the global game in a coherent and peaceful manner.

This integration will take some time just as it seems difficult for certain Muslim minorities in European societies. Besides, this reference to Islam is not a religious one but one of identity: this is also the case for most religions today; they count more as poles of identity than as precise beliefs.

Another factor for complexity is Israel; I have demonstrated in a recent book, *Psychoanalysis of the Near-East Conflict*, that the existence of this state is a weakness in Muslim identity, all the more because, in its textual fundamentals, the borrowings from the Hebrew Book are massive. Everything takes place as if the resurgence of Israel was *the return of a frustrated person* that had been frustrated by the Islamic identity over the centuries and which comes back either in reality or "in" its founding Text. And even there, it is not an effect of religion: the Jews have talked about this land as theirs for almost thirty centuries and that has made this land as if "possessed" by them, haunted by them. Even though the Arabs might have conquered it and converted it to Islam, as they have done in so many lands, one could say that this Jewish "possession" has finished up by finding its sinuous way across the centuries to come true but also to recall to the Islamic identity the rift that it believed it could deny.

One can thus understand that the logic of terrorism might have imposed itself. It can only end when enough "moderate Muslims" will have done their mourning for the original richness and accepted the rift in identity as inevitable, as it is for every other identity.

One can also understand that the logic of terrorism leaves Western leaders perplexed—or exasperated, when they try to apply their rational and organized logic to it. Of course, they fail: they cannot understand that there are certain people who have as their tactic to kill anybody, even from their own community. These leaders do not take into account the major *symbolic* problems such as the mourning and the mortification. If someone mortifies himself in his mourning and beats himself (or beats the social body), it will not do any good to tell him "That does not serve any purpose." It is not the order of service but the symbolic inscription. The radicals want to mark in blood, no matter whose it may be, their pain at losing their identity in all its fantastic splendour.

From this point of view, Islamic terrorism is a *painful symptom, but from a positive phenomenon* : a symptom of mourning for the loss of the all-embracing identity, that of the Umma; the positive phenomenon being the integration in time of this Umma in the planetary game, when it will have finished its mourning for its supreme fantasy. Let us suppose that it achieves this. Because, let it be said in passing, there are hard-core elements in the Umma which refuse integration because they see only too clearly the risk that it brings: dissolution inside the space of the others.

In the meantime, the terrorists and those who organize them are like the "black sheep" of an honorable family: they bear the weight of the non-said, of the suppressed rift, of the family secret. (This secret concerns, for example, what the Koran says about the Jews and the Christians; these are very hard remarks, and it seems that nobody wants to hear them, the matter remains secret).

These secrets and this unitarian fantasy of the Umma cannot be boiled down to their religious content. Today, it is through the aspects of identity that religions express themselves. People do not confront one another about their respective beliefs, but rather about themes of identity. The problem is that Muslim identity is constructed, above all, in opposition to that of the others, these "people of the Book"-from which it has taken the message of rejecting them for their treachery. (More precisely, it has taken in the great Hebrews of the Bible, from Abraham to Jesus passing by Moses, David and Solomon, setting down that these are the submissives of God, which is to say of the Muslims; but it has mobilized a large condemnation to distinguish itself from their Jewish and Christian descendants: The Jews have perverted the message and the Christians have betrayed it because they are idolatrous.) When the extremists read these things in their Book, if they do not have permanently at their side calm and reasonable people who can "explain" to them, they can become rather violent.

It is because of this that one cannot simply qualify the terrorists as "sick:" we must ask ourselves about the "how" and the "why" of this illness. My hypothesis is that it takes its root in the fact that the founding Text, which constructs a complete identity, without a fault line, so to say—the rift and the defect being the work of others—*this Text functions like a living being*: when it feels that we are moving away from it, that we seem to be "betraying" it, it creates the zealots who rise up to defend it, to give back to it the richness which belonged to it at the outset and which lasted for centuries. A richness, which, today, is given the lie by the proof of reality, where one observes that those who are cursed by Allah, the upholders of the Bible (but, once again, we must take this as a reference to identity rather than to religion), these "people of the Book" then, far from failing, seem rather to be succeeding. Moreover, in the extremists' fantasy, they are represented by two countries with a strong biblical connotation, Israel and the United States (Let us not forget that in Catholic Europe, reading the Bible was frowned upon for centuries, it was even almost forbidden). And when these people succeed, it revitalizes the identity wound of the extremists. It is they—radical extremists, terrorist sympathizers— who most strongly resent this wound. Even if they have not read the founding Text, they are as if "read" by it, bound or recaptured by it, called to come and defend it. They become the fanatics of a certain identity, of which the fantasy has now suffered many cracks.

What makes things worse is that they find themselves confronted by a Europe full of guilt. This guilt, which in Europe represents a code of ethics, cannot be boiled down to colonial guilt. It includes another, farther away, which derives from Christianity. I have shown in *The three Monotheisms* in what sense the Christian ethic, founded on grace, has been unable to avoid the feeling of error, in the following way: if Jesus died as a result of our errors, every time that we err, and it happens, we become guilty for his death, we become the cause of it.

In any case, the guilt, which represents an ethical issue in Europe, finds itself multiplied by the fact that the terrorist logic is constructed to make us guilty: every time that we fight terrorism, we are perforce guilty, because we provoke the suffering or the death of innocent people that terrorism has taken hostage and thanks to which it protects itself. In passing, let us add that a certain terrorism operates at the level of speeches: if Europeans ask questions of themselves about the integration of Islam, they can find themselves put in the wrong, accused of xenophobia or of "racism," when they are not being malevolent but find that there is a problem and that we need to discuss concrete questions about cohabitation with "immigrants," practical questions which can only resolve themselves if we speak about them. This terrorism of the word is very sensitive in France and feeds a "politically correct" atmosphere, which is a little too rigid.

Happily, the convivial line is important: most people want to live together, eat, laugh and build together. The problem is that the two "waves" that characterize the Islamic world, that is to say the *fundamentalist* wave and the *convivial* wave, are not separated by a very clear frontier, as some would like, which would like to put to one side the moderates and to the other the radicals so that we know who are good and who are bad. It is not as simple as that since the radical wave can reach anyone according to the occasion, just as the convivial wave can. It is thus more complicated but it is more interesting.

The terrorist strategy, whether physical or verbal, is to make America and Europe guilty on the basis of the errors and injustices that they commit. It is thus to pass off a fundamental identity condemnation under the sign of an objective reality, observable, in which the injustices and abuses appear clearly. Now these abuses and injustices are also found in the Arab-Muslim world, among the oil magnates or in the feudal structures. It is not a reason to deny them, on the contrary. Europe and America must assume their mistakes and try to correct them. At the most they could say to the violent radicals: "We have and we are committing faults, but you will not be our dispenser of justice!"

This is why they are in charge of fighting terrorism, without counting on the UN, which has not yet been able to define it. This means that the states that "understand" Islamic terrorism have wanted to include in the definition the action of certain states, such as America or Israel, who fight it militarily and who, because of this, commit injustices and unavoidable serious faults.

I insist on this: the wish to live together will necessarily prevail but it will take some time for preparation so that Islam itself can overcome a distance in relation to its founding Text and so that its faithful may distance themselves from the Text without having the impression that they are betraying themselves.

It is clear that there is a blockage for the one as much as for the other. However, if we hide the origin of the blockage from ourselves, we cannot free ourselves from it. Nobody can be freed from a chain if it does not recognise that it is in chains.

I hope that my comments will help this recognition. And reality that will work so that every identity seeks *to integrate its weakness* without imputing it to others.

Chapter 3

Al-Qaeda—An Expanded Network of Terror?

Magnus Ranstorp

I have interviewed many Islamic Movements—Hamas, Hezbollah and others. I would caution anyone to put the current phenomenon of al-Qaeda in the same basket as Hamas or indeed Hezbollah, which are legitimate movements that integrate horizontally and vertically into Palestinian society, and whose approaches are based on resistance (social resistance, political resistance and, of course, military resistance). This creates problematic comparisons with terrorism.

What is al-Qaeda? What does it represent?

It is useful to reflect on what Abu Al Kareshi, one of Osama Bin Laden's closest advisers, said in early 2002. Al-Qaeda, he argued, had embraced what he called fourth-generation warfare: future wars, embraced and inspired by al-Qaeda, would be small scale. They would emerge in various regions across the planet against an enemy, like appearing and disappearing like a ghost.

After 9/11 al-Qaeda argued that it had destroyed the three underlying pillars of US strategic defense: early warning, preventive strike and the principle of deterrence. Al Kareshi said that "Al Qaeda had entered the annals of successful surprise attacks, perhaps the most impressive as the pain it cost put every individual, in American society, on constant alert for every possibility, whether emotionally or practically." He argued that the 9/11 attacks "also undermined the American preventive strike capability due to the flexibility of the [al-Qaeda] organization and the fact that it had no permanent bases." He ended with a rhetorical question: "How can people, who strive for death, more than anything else, be deterred?"

Since then the 9/11 attacks have been followed by a series of additional attacks. The list is long, from Bali and Casablanca to Madrid and London. Al-Qaeda's original core has adapted and evolved into a fluid and self-organizing global galaxy of Salafist jihadist insurgency.

The original leadership has shown a remarkable degree of adaptation in the face of adversity, burying itself into the deep tribal underground in Pakistan, within the dense urban fabric of Pakistani mega cities and even across the Arab world. There they have regrouped and remained secretly concealed to act periodically as a clarion for the broader Salafist Jihadist movement, amplifying the violence very skilfully through psychological warfare.

Of course, over time, some of the core al-Qaeda leadership has been seriously decapitated with the capturing or killing of key senior operatives. Many have been forced to spend more time on their own security than on planning and plotting new attacks. Moreover, from interrogations of those captured we now have a more refined sense of their planning cycle, their target range and operational rhythm. But we must not write off those who are still at large, because they represent a strategic threat in terms of larger acts they still may be able to perpetrate.

They have extraordinary patience. They drive very complex operations. They believe that time is on their side. They have a strategic vision that extends far beyond what they are capable of independently.

This is true not just of al-Qaeda but of all Islamic movements. When I was in Gaza interviewing Sheikh Azim, I asked him: when will you realize your vision of an Islamic Palestine? He looked at me and he said: "2022, 2023." To my amazement every one in Palestinian society had this same time vision.

When I asked him: "How will you realize this?" he said: "Well, we cannot accomplish this on our own. An Islamic Revolution in Jordan, in Egypt and perhaps elsewhere will assist us in this venture. Demography is on our side. Time is on our side."

In short, when assessing how well we are doing, we have done somewhat well, but we should not forget that we are dealing with a radical extremist adversary that sees history as being on its side.

How do we characterize Al Qaeda?

We in the West like to think in boxes, we like to box in our adversaries. But it is a mistake to focus solely on structures, even a network of networks, at the expense of failing to recognize that al-Qaeda has always been as much a movement and an ideology as a constituted hierarchical organization. It is a polymorphous threat.

How has this movement reconfigured? What are some of the trends and patterns?

First, 60% of the foreign *jihadist* insurgency in Iraq are from Saudi Arabia. *Jihadists* have flocked to wage battle in Iraq, and they are recruited not from the periphery of Saudi society, but from the mainstream.

Moreover, an unknown number of European Muslim youths have been rapidly radicalized, recruited and deployed, usually on idealistic one-way missions, to die as martyrs and to kill as many Americans as possible. We estimate that there are probably around 70 individuals from Britain, and a slightly higher number from France, who have flocked to Iraq. The evidence tells us that many of these have never been to the traditional training grounds in Afghanistan, Chechnya, or Bosnia. Money is raised in mosques for their travels and they spend some time in Syria in Koranic schools before crossing into Iraq to join in the insurgency.

It is not clear whether the insurgency in Iraq, will create a blowback effect in which battle hardened foreign *jihadists* will return to Europe or other Muslim societies and carry out terrorist attacks. It is, however, clear that the blurring effect of the Iraqi war expands exponentially the recruitment base and global reach of jihadi terrorism.

The second issue is the complexity of the European arena. The March 2003 Madrid attack was a real wake up call in this regard. According to the previously sealed Spanish court documents, the Madrid attack was not carried out by a single group, but by a complex constellation of groups, ranging from *jihadist* veterans, younger religious extremists and drug dealers, all crystallizing together more by chance than by design.

How are terrorist cells forged? 70% of cells are forged around friendships with an additional 20% based on kinship relationships. They thrive on a complex mixture of radical mosque milieus and informal "peril associations" and structures that function in parallel to the Mosque milieus. Prison experiences, for instance, are very important in terms of radicalization and recruitment. Converts and criminals seek atonement for past sins, recruiters are adept at exploiting crisis events in individuals' lives. Other radicalization processes range from social alienation, personal crisis, failure or even self-radicalization in which susceptible individuals or influenced by radical literature, videos and chat rooms in cyber space.

This takes me to the third trend: the expanding role of cyber space as an active and passive media for propaganda and recruitment, and a means to deepen the social interaction between the local and the global Jihad environment.

It is in this sphere that al-Qaeda is winning the propaganda war. Al-Qaeda forces in the Arabian Peninsula, particularly from Saudi Arabia, have been particularly active in establishing on-line magazines, which carry directives and interpretations of al-Qaeda and are used for Islamic studies and research.

Let me just mention one particularly interesting study (there are many) as an example of how al-Qaeda acts to orchestrate the priorities of this self-organizing galaxy. The document is called the *Management of Barbarism*,[1] a 113-page online document published by the Center of Islamic Studies and Research, (an al-Qaeda affiliate) that offers an outline of the project of using terrorism as a tool to reignite social upheaval in such priority countries as Saudi Arabia, the Arabian Peninsula, Jordan, Pakistan, and Nigeria. The document provides important insights into the direction and strategy that drives al-Qaeda related terrorist tactics in many parts of the world.

Cyberspace is a challenging area for Western intelligence services, since al-Qaeda's adept use of the tools of globalization require those tracking them to monitor a wide range all forms of electronic communication, including encryption of computer files, CD-ROMs, and untraceable SIM cards. Pressures on Justice Ministers in the European Union to retain more data highlight the growing difficulties Western societies face in striking the right balance between civil liberties and security.

---

[1] Editor's note: This book, by Abu Bakr Naji, is posted on the al-Ikhlas jihadi forum (http://ekhlas.com/forum). For an English summary, see the outline by the Jamestown Foundation at http://jamestown.org/news_details.php?news_id=100.

In short, these groups have proven themselves to be ingenious in the many different ways they have been able to operate and to organize themselves. One area where they are not particularly ingenious, however, is that of their financing. Infinite constellations of mechanisms have been devised to finance these groups, including the use of charities or the profits from sales of counterfeit products. But Western officials have forged equally responsive networks to track down and close down these financial streams. The inability of terrorist networks to hide their financial trails is providing to be an Achilles heel of these groups. Governments are working quite vigorously in order to bring groups and different networks to justice.

In the past, understanding terrorism was simpler. We knew who the terrorists were, where they were, and what they wanted. But the 9/11, 3/11 and 7/7 attacks painfully brought home to us the power of asymmetric constellations of small groups and deterritorialized and transnational networks driven by an exclusionary ideological subculture, that are capable of remarkable adaptation, self-healing, dispersal, reassembly and innovation. It has forced the international community, especially the intelligence services to engage in an incredible learning curve in order to cope with this international threat. Many battles have been fought and won, but in many ways we are in danger of losing the overall war. Some of this relates to the uncertainty in Iraq, which has become an ideological magnet for some and which offers hands-on battle field experience for for others committed offensive *jihad*.

Chapter 4
Terrorism in Europe

Farhad Khosrokhavar

Europe has a tradition of terrorism based on extreme left ideology (Red Brigades in Italy, Action Directe in France, Fraktion Roter Armee in Germany) or nationalist-regionalist tenets (Basque movement in Spain, Corsican movement in France, Sinn Fein in Northern Ireland . . .). The emergence of Islamist terrorism is a new phenomenon in this part of the world but some of the converts believe in the utopian role of Islam in the same fashion as middle class leftist youth in the 1960s and 1970s thought about Marxism or communism. Islamic terrorism partially feeds on the exhaustion of leftist ideologies, which mobilized part of the youth in Europe and which are not convincing any more to people in this part of the world.[1]

Muslim Immigration to Europe

Terrorism is mostly related to the immigrant population from the Muslim world in Europe, their offspring and a minority of converts. In the 1960s and 1970s Europe's industrialization attracted many immigrant workers. The offshoots of this population, from second and third generations, have many problems related to their integration within European countries.

In Europe, radical Islam has different origins, mainly related to the colonial background (France, England) or to the immigration of Muslims in the last few decades from the Muslim world (Germany, Spain). Still, each country has its specific history and its culture of "integration," and radicalization is related as well to local and regional history as to broader global trends.

---

[1] In Latin America leftist-Marxist ideology is still of some import in few countries where trafficking and terrorism go hand in hand in the name of communist tenets.

The French case

In France, radical Islam has two different roots. The external one is mainly grounded in Algerian extremist networks, particularly the GIA (Groupe Islamique Armé), directed by the military branch of the FIS (Front Islamique de Salut) after it was denied power by the military in 1992 in spite of its gaining the majority in parliamentary elections. There was (and still is) an animosity between the GIA and the French government due to the support the latter gave to the Algerian army against the FIS. But the GIA would not have been able to operate in France without the Algerian diaspora and more generally, the Maghrebin disaffected youth in the French poor suburbs.[2] Some 1.5 million people of Algerian descent (around 700,000 from Morocco and some 350,000 from Tunisia) live in France, and among them, a tiny minority has been active for the GIA. Some terrorist networks were set up in France in the 1990s and enrolled young peoples from the poor suburbs. They included people like Khaled Kelkal,[3] who was exposed to racism. A few Muslim converts were also involved. Some cells from GIA were in touch with al-Qaeda and found in this way connections within France. Otherwise, autonomous al-Qaeda networks have been exceptional in France.

Radicalism has been enhanced through links with England much more than other European countries. Religious radicalism has had a tinge of post-colonialism marked by the rancor against the former colonizers by the children of those colonized, residing in France. The people who take part in radical Islam are mostly recruited among those young people who feel themselves as belonging neither to the country of their parents (North African ones) nor to France in which they are rejected as "Arabs." They have a deep ambivalent attitude towards themselves: they believe they are hated and despised by the French and for this reason, consider themselves as free to confront this indignity with their own violence.[4] Islam gives them the opportu-

---

[2] See Farhad Khosrokhavar, *L'islam des jeunes* (Flammarion, 1997).

[3] See Dietmar Loch, "Moi, Khaled Kelkal" (Interview on October 3, 1992), *Le Monde*, October 7, 1995. In this interview, the social roots of Kelkal's Islamic radicalism are spelled out by himself. In our own interviews, many young boys of the poor Paris suburb (Argenteuil in 1997) declare that they are treated like "insects" by the French people.

[4] For more detailed information see Farhad Khosrokhavar, *Suicide Bombers: New Martyrs of Allah* (Pluto Press—distributed in the U.S. by Michigan University Press, 2005).

nity to legitimize their feeling of rejection by channeling it into a sacred cause. In this way, they take their revenge on society and at the same time accede to the salvation of their soul. They attain a twofold goal by engaging under the banner of radical Islam: they fight against a society which has never accepted them as such and they fight for Islam against the entire West. This fight raises them in their own view and provides them with a dignity that was denied them in their daily life before adhering to radical Islam. Through their engagement they gain salvation (they become martyrs if they die), they accede to a new honor and dignity and they find meaning and sense for their life which was, previously, meaningless and without any end.

There is an "Islamist affect" in many French "banlieues"[5] that predisposes part of the disaffected male youth towards the violent commitment for a sacred cause embodied in an anti-Western Islamic ideology.

Another factor that encourages this effect is the way this population feels despised by society at large. Racism is strongly felt, particularly through the advent of the extreme right[6] (Le Pen and dissident groups). This is reinforced by restrictions imposed through the Laïcité, which bans Islamic signs in the public sphere and depicts such communities as the moral negation of true and genuine citizenship. There is a "hatred" (haine) in part of the second and third generation of the people of North African origin, which finds expression in two distinct attitudes that can be combined in radical ones: one is the rejection of "Frenchness." This finds its expression in Islamic moods that define themselves not so much in an autonomous way but as "un-French" and sometimes even "anti-French." This can also be expressed by espousing attitudes related to so-called "Anglo-Saxon" versions of modernity. Many young people who travel (and sometimes stay) in Great Britain do so in order to accede to "non-French" ways of life as an alternative to French lifestyles that they feel deny them their identity. "Americanized" or "Anglicized" attitudes are sometimes displayed in a provocative way in order to show a "non-French" identity in order to impinge on the sensitivities of some French people and deny them any symbolic supremacy.

---

[5] See Gilles Kepel, *Jihad* (Paris: Gallimard, 2002).
[6] See Michel Wieviorka (ed.), *Violences en France* (Paris: Seuil, 1999).

When cultural reaction against French society becomes radicalized through Islamist extremist networks, it gives birth to a terrorist attitude. The radical Islamic groups benefit from this predisposition of young people (overwhelmingly male) of North African origin who consider themselves to be stigmatized and banned by society. In this way, they are open to radicalization. If a network succeeds in getting in touch with them, some overcome their fears of repression and accept to act against those they hate and those they believe are against Islam because they have reduced them to misery or who, on the international scene, defend Israel and anti-Islamic forces.

The confluence of identity problems, racism and economic exclusion creates a fertile ground for radicalization and violence among a tiny minority of this disaffected youth. Islamization brings a sense of existence to them and radicalization gives them a new dignity as warriors of a just cause against a corrupt and ruthless society. This generation of poor suburban inhabitants, mostly of North African origin, who live totally without structure (monoparental families, high rate of joblessness and illiteracy, absence of strong ties with the family and the community) can be easily manipulated. Paradoxically the media are the major source of their inspiration. The tragic spectacle of Palestinians dying under the attacks of the Israeli army and the indifference of public opinion to the fate of Chechens and other Muslims in the world easily convince them that the West in general is against Islam. The antagonistic attitude of some French political groups (the extreme right) towards them is easily generalized, through the television images, to the entire Western world. The deduction is peremptory: the West is against Islam and true Muslims should fight against it in order to recover their dignity and their honor.

Police repression and infiltration among terrorist group since the 1990s has brought a halt to their acts within French borders. Some of these groups went to Great Britain and the presence of a Maghrebin diaspora there (around some 40 thousand Algerians among them) helped for a while to build up the new groups. But since September 11, 2001 the situation has changed, and these groups are under police scrutiny.

Radical Islam in France began in the 1990s. From that point of view the French authorities had to address it a decade before other Western countries. The probable number of people arrested in this regard between 1995 and 2001 was the highest in Western countries (more than 200 were put in prison). Although precise data are not available, after September 11 the same statement can be cautiously made: the number of the French people of North African origin presumably involved in Islamic terrorist activities and arrested for that reason is much higher than in England, Germany, Spain or Italy. This is partially due to the efficiency of the French police, but also to the fact that radical Islamic terrorism in France is much more deeply rooted in poor suburbs, and is not only due to a group of Muslim foreigners coming to France in order implement their terrorist activities (this is the case in Germany with few probable exceptions: the Islamists who took part in the September the 11th terrorist acts and prepared them in Hamburg did not belong to the Turkish Islamic community of Germany[7]).

In the French case, Islamic radicalism is partially rooted in the disaffected youth of North African origins or converts mostly belonging to the same "banlieues," although the networks are of Algerian (and through a branch of GIA related to al-Qaeda) and more generally North African origin.[8] This makes the French case unique. The English case is much more marginal. It involves members of radical Muslim groups belonging to the association al-Mohajirun or affiliated to other networks suspected of having ties with al-Qaeda. But these people form a tiny minority, and up to now only a dozen of them have been arrested. The French case, with the high number of people imprisoned, preserves its peculiarity concerning radical Islam so far.

In Holland, one might think of some kind of "hyper-fundamentalist" Islam in the case of the Moroccan who killed Theo van Gogh and who was affiliated to a group of Muslims with no proven direct ties to

---

[7] See Nikola Tietze, *Islamische Identitäten, Formen Muslimisher Religiosität jünger Männer in Deutschlandund Frankreich* (Hamburg Edition, Germany, 2001); Farhad Khosrokhavar, Nikola Tietze, "Violence en France, le cas de Neuhof" in Michel Wieviorka (ed.), *Violences en France* (Paris: Seuil, 1999). The "Mouvement pour l'égalité" of the 1980s aimed at defending the rights of French citizens of North African origin in a secular and non-religious manner. The slogan "touche pas à mon pote," defended by a national association like SOS Racisme, did not possess any religious content and was in accordance with the French "laïcité." The failure of this movement to achieve its goals was one of the causes of the "Islamization" of part of the young generation of French young people from the so-called "banlieues" (poor suburbs) who no longer believe in equal treatment and opportunity in a society where they feel victimized.

[8] See Omar Guendouz, *Les soldats perdus de l'islam, les réseaux français de Ben Laden* (Editions Ramsay, 2002).

al-Qaeda or any transnational Muslim organization. This type of group allegedly belongs to al-Qaeda but has little to do with the real organization, which has been destroyed in its real capacity to act directly in its former structure. This new type of al-Qaeda may be called a "metaphoric al-Qaeda": the mere fact that radical Muslims refer to it shows the prestige it enjoys within the radicalized youth in western European countries.

The English case

Some 1.6 million Muslims live in Britain; among them the Pakistanis are the majority. Their case is not unlike the North Africans in France, who came there after independence in order to promote industrialization. The English model of integration is totally different from the French model: recognition of communities and acceptance of a degree of cultural heterogeneity that is much higher than in France, where every citizen is supposed to be part of society individually without the interference of any community. The only legitimate community is the French Nation, of which every citizen is a full member. This theoretical stance is of course far removed from daily reality. In the same vein, the recognition of communities in Britain does not mean respect for different ways of lives. In practice, racism in both countries feeds on the otherness of Muslim migrants and their inability to become full-fledged citizens. In both countries frustration is high among many Muslims, who feel stigmatized and rejected even though they have British or French citizenship.

The July 2005 terrorism in England was perpetrated by four people who were British citizens: three of Pakistani origin and one a convert from Catholicism of Jamaican roots. All four were raised in Britain; none was an immigrant. Like Algerians in France, Pakistanis in Britain are the target of racism. Although part of their community is successful in business or in the public sector (in the same way as part of the North African population—in France called the "Beurgeoisie"[9]—is successful), most of them feel segregated and are exposed to racism and contempt by other citizens. The rate of unemployment, like that of the North Africans in France, is much higher than the average in Britain.

[9] See Rémi Leveau & Withold de Wenden, *La Beurgeoisie* (Paris, Editions du CNRS, 2001).

The culture of tolerance in Britain allowed many radical Muslims from North Africa, as well as from other parts of Muslim world, to migrate to England, gather in such famous mosques as Finnsbury Park, and spread the message of radical Islam. The gentleman's agreement between the British authorities and the radical community in Britain was broken after September 11. The arrest of some of radical community members and the promulgation of anti-terrorist laws has led to a situation of antagonism similar to that prevailing in France. The new generation of radical Muslims had some roots in the Muslim middle classes, through organizations such as Hizbu Tahrir, whose leaders professed an anti-Israel and a pro-Palestine stance. Radicalization was fed by some links with al-Qaeda (Khan, the leader of the group which committed the terrorist act in July 2005 in London had ties with al-Qaeda leaders through his journeys in Pakistan), but the main breeding ground for it was England and the simmering discontent among some Muslim youth due to social conditions, racism and the involvement of British troops in Afghanistan and Iraq.

France began the fight against Islamic terrorism in 1993. This fight became more urgent after the 1995 terrorist attack in the Paris underground by a young Algerian living in France (Khaled Kelkal), which resulted in a dozen killings. Institutionally the framework was set with the law against the terrorist association which facilitated the pursuit of suspects and their incarceration without the usual caveats against ordinary crimes. On the institutional level the secret services and the justice department began to work closely, the judge for terrorism being a person working within a special framework, informed by the secret services inside the country as well as outside. This made arrest much easier than under normal law and circumstances and access to information much quicker. Many were arrested without sufficient warrant but some successes were achieved through prevention of terrorism. In England, this framework did not exist until 2001. The anti-terrorist laws with their complementary laws in 2004 and 2005 have been late comers. England and particularly London were looked upon as "Londonistan"[10] by Islamic radicals; until September 11 Great Britain was considered a safe haven against pursuits in France or elsewhere.

---

[10] See Dominique Thomas, *Londonistan, la voix du djihad* (Paris: Michalon, 2003).

This implicit agreement was torn apart after the promulgation of anti-terrorist laws in 2001, but the British police were not in a situation to infiltrate the Islamic radicals in the same fashion as the French. The terrorist attack on London in July 2005 rang the bell of the last "mutual understanding" between the government and the Islamic radicals. The fight against Islamic radicalism became the same almost all over Europe and the judicial framework for it is being promulgated in many countries.

The major problem in Britain as well as France is that both have populations of former colonies who suffer from racism and the de facto inequality between them and other ordinary citizens. Moreover, the suspicion towards terrorism has caused a new wave of intolerance, and this in turn feeds radicalization of a minority within their Muslim communities in the long run.

Two major problems arise: one is related to globalization and the emergence of networks which are flexible enough to be built quickly by people who do not act within rigid hierarchies and who are therefore able to hide themselves from police scrutiny in many cases. On the other hand, the simmering discontent among part of Muslim youth makes England and France fertile grounds for recruitment of future terrorists. Repressive policies in the short run and social policies that fight racism and promote affirmative action are necessary to prevent the push towards radicalization on the part of European Muslims.

In countries such as Germany, Islamic radicalization seems, up to now, mainly directed towards the country of origin of the most important Muslim community, the Turks. Turkey seems to be the target rather than Germany, but with the advent of a new generation of Germans with Turkish origin, this situation might change in the future.

Islamic Jihadism in the Age of Globalization

A major issue in addition to the social discontent felt by part of Muslim youth in Europe is the crisis of Muslim countries and the utopia of a neo-umma, all of which is reported in real time by television.[11] Two distinct groups appear on the scene. The first is a new Muslim middle class, which is a minority among the immigrants from Muslim countries in Europe. This new middle class has everything to lose if radicalization occurs among the Muslims in Europe and a more negative image of Islam and Muslims becomes widespread among the people. Still, a tiny minority of its members opt for radicalization and separate themselves from the mainstream Muslim middle class in Europe. The main reason is their identification with the neo-umma in the world at large and in Europe in particular. Seeing their fellow Muslim people downtrodden and stigmatized through racism in Europe, and viewing on TV the faith of Muslims in the world at large and the crisis of Muslim societies, they come to the firm belief that Islam is being repressed as much within Europe as outside it, and that in both cases, the oppressors are "white" Europeans and more generally, the wicked West, mainly America. Compassion, in this situation, goes to this imaginary neo-umma rather than to their compatriots: their sufferings in connection with terrorist attacks are minimized in comparison to the plight of Muslims all over the world. In a way, the identification with this imaginary neo-umma (which does not exist in the way the radical Muslims describe it) prevents a moral attitude towards their fellow citizens, whom they reject, and gives them justification for terrorist acts in the name of a radicalized representation of Islam.

For the excluded and "disaffected" youth in Europe, the combination of economic deprivation and cultural stigma makes it much easier for them to become radicalized in the name of Allah. In this case, they come to the conclusion that their sufferings and those of the Muslims in other parts of the world, Palestine, Bosnia, Iraq or Chechnya have the same roots: the Western fight against Islam. Their enrollment in terrorist networks is based on a strong feeling of victimization rooted in their dramatic situation in Europe: in France in the so-called "banlieues" (poor suburbs); in England in poor districts; and in many European countries their segregation in enclaves or ghettos (or perceived as such by many of them) and the absence of any prospect for a brighter future. All of these factors go hand in hand to make this population a fertile ground for radicalization and in few cases, terrorism.

---

[11]See Farhad Khosrokhavar, *Les nouveaux martyrs d'Allah* (Paris: Flammarion, Collection Champs, 2003); Olivier Roy, *L'islam mondialisé* (Paris: Seuil, 2002); Gilles Kepel, *Fitna, Guerre au cœur de l'islam*, (Paris: Gallimard, 2004).

Even though many do not get involved in terrorist activities due to the renewed vigilance of the police and the secret services, still their world outlook is that of deep victimization and a negative perception of the "white" man.

The two groups, either from the middle classes or from excluded categories of people, find a common language through networks and their opposition to the West. The military actions in Afghanistan, Iraq and the Palestinian and Chechen problems are reminders of the West's involvement in the fight against Muslim countries.

The predicament of Muslims all over the world is seen through the looking glass of this neo-umma: in countries such as Saudi Arabia, Egypt, Turkey and elsewhere, governments are considered as "puppets" of the West to be fought. In the West itself, the struggle should go on in order to punish both estern governments and their "lackeys" in Muslim countries. The globalized neo-umma, unlike the real Muslim communities, does not recognize either frontiers or nations, and the ideal is not so much to topple a specific government in a particular country as to set ablaze the entire world in order to promote the neo-Caliphate and bring about the neo-umma within this institution.

In the same fashion as the leftists of the 1970S were the self-proclaimed avant-garde of the proletariat, the new radicalized Muslims believe to be the vanguard of the Muslim umma (community). This creed is not grounded in reality, however, and is simply a mental and imaginary construction with no support in the real world. Therefore the majority of the Muslims who suffer from terrorist acts like Egyptians (terrorism in Scharm el Sheikh in August 2005) reject these acts to the utmost but the terrorist groups are a tiny minority who do not follow the majority of Muslims.

The paradoxical situation is that Islamic terrorism is an outlet for the sufferings of Muslims in its symbolic dimension (it is an outlet for the Palestinian plights in their unequal fight against the Israeli army or the Chechens, in their fight against a colonial Russian army) and at the same time, whenever it happens, the majority of Muslims reject its cruelty and the indiscriminate sufferings it causes, particularly if terrorism occurs in Muslim countries (the case of Scharm el Sheikh in Egypt for instance). Muslim youth finds solace in the fact that "arrogant Westerners" suffer at the hands of al-Qaeda or those who claim its symbolic paternity. At the same time, many of them deplore its ruthlessness and the lack of discerning between enemies and foes through indiscriminate terrorist acts by Jihadist groups.

Different types of organizations

There are two major types of organizations within the realm of Jihadist terrorism. The first belonged to al-Qaeda prior to September the 11 terrorist acts. The second is a scattered form of terrorism among cells that are autonomous from each other and whose members are connected either through Internet or through associations, ties of friendship or geographic proximity (living in the same district makes relations closer and more amicable among the members).

Within groups claiming a Jihadist identity, one finds three models. The first one is based on a charismatic figure who brings together different people and gives them a sense of common identity through his knowledge of Islam or his ability to make the Jihad the core of the group's religious tenet. This charismatic personality is very important in so far as he gives a new sense of belonging to the group by bringing members very close to each other and suffusing them with a common goal, which makes each person important within the group. The charismatic figure is the most important case and in many terrorist attacks this person has played a vital role.

The second type of organization is the "equalitarian group" of friends.[12] Each one shares the same radical tenets, which makes the members of the group akin to a sect with no guru (as opposed to the first model). Everyone partakes in group activities through ties of friendship and sympathy. This type of organization seems to be rather marginal. The first type, a sectarian group gravitating around a charismatic person, is far more widespread.

The third type is that of male members of a family. Brothers, the father, uncles, cousins and even more distant members of an extended family get together and found a Jihadist group. They act within the family; the core members are related to each other by bonds of kinship. This type of group is also marginal compared to the charismatic model.

[12] Marc Sageman insists on this type of informal groups. See Marc Sageman, *Understanding Terror Networks* (Philadelphia: University of Pennsylvania Press, 2004).

The Internet plays a major role. Through messages sent to others, different people with radical tenets might get together, in search of violent action. Communications through the Internet are difficult to detect, the more so as the number of exchanges worldwide are too high to be closely scrutinized. The methods of identifying communications through key words ("jihad," "martyrdom," "fight against infidels," etc.) are not always very efficient, as the senders are more and more conscious of this system of message interception. All in all, these types of organizations show their frightening efficiency through the terrorist attacks successfully achieved.

The implicit ideology

Among the different waves of terrorism that swept Europe in the 19th and 20th centuries, Islamist terrorism is ideologically the weakest. The terrorism marked by Marxist or Communist ideologies had a set of tenets that claimed direct bearing on economics. Right or wrong, this ideology could be expressed in a rational way by its proponents. The wave of anarchist terrorism originating in Russia and spreading throughout Europe and America had also a corpus of ideological schemes that could be argued and exposed in a "rational" manner. The extreme left ideologies of the 1970s were also marked by mental constructions based on the denunciation of imperialism, the fight for the proletariat, and the praise of anarchy as the best type of government on earth. All these ideologies claimed roots in social, political and economic sciences. The fact that they were tendentious and non-rational did not prevent them from having a corpus of ideological "evidence" that claimed the Enlightenment's fatherhood or the utopias of Progress as their core material.

The Jihadist ideology is the least developed of the three radical currents already mentioned. There are three major "ideas" which underline its ideological construction. The first one, already mentioned, is the idea of the "neo-umma." This is not a factual entity but a cultural construction based on a mythical Islamic community. The second ideological tenet is a demonic West.[13] This idea has a dual origin. The first is in the leftist ideology of imperialism. The second goes back to

---

[13] See Ian Buruma & Avishai Margalit, *Occidentalism: A Short history of Anti-Westernism* (New York: Atlantic Books, 2004).

the "dar ul kufr" as opposed to "dar ul islam" (respectively the House of Impiety and the House of Islam). According to jihadist interpretation, Muslims should endeavor to convert non Muslims and spread Islam all over the world. Those countries which are populated by non Muslims are in a state of war with Islam. Every Muslim should contribute, directly or indirectly, to their forced or peaceful conversion to the religion of Allah. This is the root of the third major idea, Jihad. In Islam it is traditional to distinguish between two types of duties: if Islam is in danger, every Muslim has to engage in the fight to preserve it (fardh al ayn). If the fight is to spread Islam, Muslims should contribute to it through financial means or otherwise, without having to be involved directly (fardh al kifayah). For the Jihadists, Islam is the only valid religion and one has to go to extremes to establish its rule the world over. In the same vein, Islamic radicals believe that Islam is in danger through the malevolent action of the West (particularly the United States) and therefore, Muslims should accept even martyrdom in order to fight against an enemy who is militarily and economically the most potent.

These three sets of ideas are connected to a utopian world order which is not explicit. Palestinian, Chechen and other radical actions are based on an explicit national project, the realization of which means recourse to martyrdom. The new al-Qaeda type of ideology is not fighting for an explicit goal. The Palestinian, Chechen or Iraqi predicaments are mentioned as reasons to engage in war against the West, but the ultimate goal is not explicitly political. The neo-Caliphate is everything but clearly delineated. The fight against an impious and "arrogant" West seems to be the only tangible motive which mobilizes the sympathizers of Jihadism.

The way Islam is instrumentalized shows as well the "modernity" of this type of movement.[14] It is much less the reproduction of tradition than a regressive and oppressive form of modern action based on new technologies (Internet, networks...), and a religious ideology which finds some precedents in the past but which, in its logic of action and its ways of challenging the West, is directly related to the modern world.

---

[14]See Diego Gambetta (ed.), *Making Sense of Suicide Missions* (Oxford: Oxford University Press, 2005).

European youth who get involved in this ideological enterprise can trace dual roots. They consider themselves to be non-European, non-Pakistani or non-Algerian. The generation which becomes the spearhead of Jihad is doubly stigmatized: in Europe it is rejected and considered as non-European. In the country of the parents (North Africa for the French Muslims, Pakistan or India and Bangladesh for the British Muslims) it is considered at best as foreign. In both cases this generation is denied a clear identity. It is doubly marginalized, doubly rejected.

Islam in its radical version allows this generation to take revenge against the host society where it is born or raised and against the society of the parents, ruled mostly by non-Islamic governments. The simultaneous opposition to the West and to the East gives a sense of a new dignity to the proponents of radical Islam. The disaffected youth of the poor suburbs in France or poor urban districts in Britain feel in this way a new honor against the background of their rejection by European societies. They become heroes of a sacred cause and break the ties to their past when they were nothing and nobody. They inspire fear, and this is a form of revenge against their indignity and their insignificance of the past. They recover thus a new identity in which they believe to act as the heroes of a new age.

The middle class Muslims who join the radical Islamic groups become the messengers of the neo-umma to which they believe they belong, the new identity taking precedence over their being members of the European middle classes. Compassion for their fellow Muslims in the Islamic countries and the excluded downtrodden Islamic youth in Europe becomes more potent than their sympathy for the societies in which they live. Islam becomes a new sacred identity that overshadows all the past identities to which they belonged: that of immigrant families, that of European citizens and that of middle class people.

Another category of people become Jihadists in Europe: the converts. Most of the converts adopt a spiritualist Islam that has nothing to do with terrorism. But a tiny minority of them espouses radical Islam and engages in terrorist activities in order to be part of the neo-umma at war with the perfidious and depraved West. To these people the West is treacherous and anti-Islamic in essence. Their new identity as Muslims is offended by the plight of many Muslims all over the world and the partial and antagonistic attitude of the Western countries towards their situation. They have to prove to themselves and to others the sincerity of their faith by opposing their former societies and by declaring war on the very countries where they were born and raised. The chasm between their new faith and the societies in which they were born finds a sacred legitimacy through their identification with the neo-umma. By fighting an impious West they underline their rupture with it and their ties to a new imaginary Islamic community for which they are ready to sacrifice their life and to put to death their fellow countrymen.

The al-Qaeda type of ideology creates a magic identification process through which people as different as the excluded and disaffected youth of immigrant origin on the one hand, middle class people of Muslim origin on the other and last but not least, converts act in unison against a mythical West to which they belong but to which their sense of attachment is so weak as to make it possible for alternative identities to displace and to eradicate it. The antagonism towards the West in the name of Allah and the promulgation of Jihad as the sole way to achieve the sacred goals of Islam gather very different people under the same banner. They find solace in a religion which declares the war on the "arrogant West," a West in which they feel they have no place, whether as disaffected youth, as stigmatized middle class people, or as converts who have recovered a sense of a new identity.

Chapter 5
The Moroccan Case

Aboubakr Jamai

The case of Morocco offers insights for understanding something of contemporary terrorism. I begin with the suicide attacks in Casablanca of May 16, 2003.

These attacks came as a surprise, because the received popular wisdom was that Morocco had some kind of insurance against terrorism because of its institutions. The King is the Commander of the Faithful. This is not a church, but we thought of ourselves as having protection, of having a supreme leader in terms of religion. The May 16 bombing attacks shattered this belief that having a Commander of the Faithful was in itself a protection against terrorism.

The 12 suicide bombers in Casablanca—44 people died in all—came from one shanty town in the outskirts of Casablanca named Sidi Moumen. Although the economic and social parameters of terrorism are not always the most powerful explanatory factors, in the Moroccan case they seem to have played a role. The fact that all the suicide bombers came from these slums on the outskirts of Casablanca tells us something about the interrelationship between economic and social development and terrorism.

Almost all of the suicide bombers had menial jobs, some of them had gone to university and had some academic degrees, but all of them were excluded to some degree from Moroccan society. Sometimes the front lines of terrorism are inside our own cities. After the Berlin Wall fell, one analyst said that the Mediterranean had became the new Berlin Wall. I would add that in a developing country such as Morocco the Berlin Wall may simply be between downtown Casablanca and its outskirts. This means that in addition to the meaningful effort that must conducted be done in terms of tolerance we also have an uphill battle to wage against economic and social deprivation.

There is also an important local side to the story. None of the 12 people who perpetrated the attacks had ever left Morocco before.

These were not Afghan/Moroccans who returned to apply their deadly skills or vicious ideology back in their home country. The suicide bombers never left Morocco. They were intoxicated at home by an extreme version of Islam, and decided to give up their lives for what I suspect they thought was a higher aim, a higher goal.

Now let's go to the Madrid bombings, where the Moroccan factor was also important. Spanish authorities have revealed that part of the explosives used in the Madrid bombings were bought in exchange for drugs. One of the alleged perpetrators of these bombing attacks, Jamal Ahmidan, known as *"El Chino,"* who came from Tetuan, a northern city of Morocco, and arrived in Spain through illegal immigration networks. This means that the drug industry, which is alive and well in Northern Morocco, together with illegal immigration networks, is being used as a resource gathering mechanism for terrorism. If one understands that the Moroccan drug industry can be measured in billions of dollars (although only a few hundred million enter Morocco itself), one also understands the daunting nature of the struggle against terrorism in Morocco.

Terrorists can find resources in partially failed states, in states such as Morocco that do not function particularly well and that tolerate lawless zones without any discernible system of governance. Such zones are havens in which terrorist networks can flourish, recruit, and conduct their deadly attacks.

In short, to quash terrorism it is insufficient to focus solely on the state "governance" problem by seeking to convert failed states into well—or even partially functioning states.

Aside from the economic problems, it is very important to look at public opinion. One of the positive effects of the 9/11 bombings, if there were any, is that the world is now interested in what the Arabs think. Public opinion research is now being conducted in the Arab world. The Pew Foundation polls are particular insightful. When we look at the results of these studies we find out that the approval rate of Bin Laden has dropped dramatically, from 49% to little more than 20% in Morocco. Approval of suicide bombing as a legitimate means or terrorism against civilians has dropped significantly as well.

I want to caution, however, about over-optimism regarding these results.

The first caution would be that one should be very careful about the wording of the questions. In the 2003 study the question posed was not are you in favor of terrorism against civilians, the question was are you in favor of suicide terrorism in Israel? And are you in favor of terrorism in Iraq by insurgents, by militants? The approval rate was very high. For Israel the answer was more than 70% and for Iraq it was more than 60%. I am not sure that the same question, worded in the same way, would have had significantly less positive answers.

Secondly, while 9/11 tends to overshadow much of our debates these days, it is important to recall the tremendous impact of the second Intifada and Israeli-Palestinian tensions on public opinion in the Arab world. The largest demonstration ever in the history of Morocco occurred in the context of these tensions.

The other interesting insight from these polls stems from the question asking respondants to rank eight world leaders in terms of favorability, which of 8 different world leaders is best able to solve world problems. Bin Laden received 49%, which is interesting in itself, but the leader receiving most responses by Moroccans was Jacques Chirac. He is not Muslim, he is not Islamic, he is not even Arab. I suspect that the common denominator between Jacques Chirac and Bin Laden in the minds of the people who answered this questionnaire was their opposition to U.S. foreign policy.

Equally interesting was the answer to the question: would you favor a Western style democracy in your country? "Western-style" is a very loaded term, but 63% Moroccans said yes even though 49% Moroccans supported Bin Laden on a different question.

In short, one should qualify these results in light of one another; they cannot be interpreted in isolation. It is important to have the whole picture, and what the whole picture says is that public opposition is directed against American foreign policy, not towards the West or even towards American citizens.

Another very interesting study was published in 2003 by Zogby International under the title "What Arabs think: values, beliefs and concerns." One of the questions posed was, "Given this list of political subjects which are the most important for you?" The list included economic problems, civic and civic rights, Palestine, health issues, and other topics. More than 90% of Moroccans listed Palestine first. Their own civic rights were ranked second. The Palestine issue, in short, remains an extremely important factor in shaping the views of Moroccan public opinion of U.S. American foreign policy.

Why I am citing all these figures?

Because I think that I tend to see Bin Laden as a political entrepreneur. This does not absolve him from any of the crimes he committed, that is not the point. The point is that al-Qaeda needs to have a breeding ground, a fertile ground to recruit either through franchisees, imitators, or other means, and the recruitnment message is crafted according to what public opinion is thinking.

It was interesting to see that the last message of Bin Laden, just before the American election, was a *quasi* secular message about the liberation of Palestine and Iraq. That doesn't mean that Bin Laden does not have the ambition of Islamizing the world. But, it is clear that he has to cater to a certain demand and is crafting his message to address a certain public opinion. It also means that policies crafted to address these worries would go a long way, to use a famous metaphor, towards drying the swamp of terrorism in the Arab world, and in Morocco in particular. This will not in itself eliminate terrorism, of course—one cannot prevent a sick person from conducting deadly operations simply by fostering democracy in the Arab world or by solving the Palestinian problem. But it would go a long way,

I will conclude by underscoring the destructive effects of the war on terrorism on countries like Morocco.

Morocco is a country which likes to see itself in transition. I am skeptical about this transition period; I am not sure that the Moroccan regime has a true democratization vision of Morocco. We do have a struggle today in Morocco about this democratization process, however, between democrats and traditionalists. The war on terrorism gives those people who are trying to block the democratization process in Morocco and other Arab societies a geostrategic resource with which to stifle the lively debate that is taking hold today in our societies.

We had thought, for example, that secret detention centers were a thing of the past in Morocco. And yet Human Rights Watch and

Amnesty International have published reports documenting the existence of a secret detention center where people were tortured; we believe people were even killed in the name of fighting terrorism. To the extent that this evidence indicates that the United States may have been involved in these procedures sends a decidedly mixed signal to the Moroccan people and strengthens the hand of the extremists in our countries.

Part II:
Religion, Civilization, and Terror

Chapter 6

God: Dangerous Word, Necessary Word

Florence Taubmann

There is no need to remake the history of past centuries to note that God is a dangerous word, and that religions have often been factors for violence, intolerance and wars. Even if geopolitical or economic considerations have generally been mixed up with religious arguments, this would not be enough to exonerate the word God from the blood that it has caused to be shed. Today, we are in a context in which radical Islam has, over the past twenty years, given rise to a blind and murderous terrorist violence in many countries, killing Jews, Christians and others, but above all Muslims.

This specific violence, being deployed in the name of God, contains a specific question, already put in the century of Enlightenment: that of the dangers inherent in all religion. There is the strong temptation for some enlightened spirits of our century to declare that all religion is necessarily obscurantist, intolerant and a generator of violence between men. If this radical argument is not the greatest cause of the indifference to religion that characterizes our society today, it only serves to encourage it more. On the other hand, however, any of those who remain believers and are more or less practitioners of their religion are astonished at this amalgam, affirming that their own God is not a God of war and violence but a God of love and tolerance and that he cannot therefore be confused with this God in whose name violence is preached.

In any case, these two attitudes—of rejection of religion and of defense of one's religion as being non-violent—are attitudes of protection against the paradox linked to faith in God. This paradox is that the question of God, whether one might like it or not, is intrinsically a dangerous question. This is because it touches on areas of human existence that are very sensitive: the question of truth, that of the sense of life and of death, the question of identity, of culture, of roots. . . . All of that is susceptible to generating passionate reactions. But, at the same time—and here is the paradox—nothing can be done to make man stop one day posing the question of God, which always reappears even if one age or another seems to have forgotten or effaced it. Moreover, simple intellectual honesty must recognize that this question of God has also had eminently positive effects on societies and cultures, as much on the symbolic and aesthetic levels as on the ethical level. On the contrary, atheist societies that have become totalitarian have shown themselves to be terribly murderous.

Faced with Islamic terrorism, the theological and cultural problem of Europe at the beginning of the 21st century is that of the death of God. The secularization movement, which appeared at the time of the Renaissance and the Protestant reforms, has first of all progressively generated a separation between theology and politics. However, it seems today to be coming to an end through the disappearance of God from the common social and cultural horizon. Of course, people who believe and who practice one belief or another still exist, and the religious works of the past continue to be visited, but the God of our image of Christianity, the God who occupied our social European heaven, this particular God is no longer alive. The secularization of Christianity resulted in a spiritual de-Christianization, at the same time as the Christian values judged as the most positive were absorbed by civil society.

However, we must add, on a more philosophical and theological level, that this de-Christianization has been aggravated by the devastating effects that the great tragedies of the 20th century have had on the European conscience. After the slaughter of the First World War, after the horrors of the second, the discovery of the extermination camps, the atomic bombs on Hiroshima and Nagasaki, the God Providence of the great Christian and Judeo-Christian tradition has not been able to come away without guilt from this field of ruins. It has been necessary to totally rethink "the concept of God post-Auschwitz," according to the title of the book of the philosopher Hans Jonas. In 1984, he wrote "We affirm in effect, for our image of God as well as for our entire relationship with the divine, that we are not in a position to maintain the traditional medieval doctrine of an absolute divine power, without limit." (p. 27) The all-powerful God, the God of history, is no longer defendable, and it is under the image of the suffering God, the God in evolution, the God close to Man and concerned at the creation that he appears henceforth. Jonas takes a Jewish approach, but we can also find the echo of it in Christianity, because the God that we hear being preached today in the churches is much less often the powerful God of morality and justice than the weak God of love and compassion. All the more so since the knowledge that Christianity today has some dark periods in its past history—crusades, inquisition, anti-Semitism—generates a serious bad conscience in many Christians and in Christian societies or those impregnated with Christianity.

In mentioning this, we are not entering into questions of doctrine, because the fundamental doctrine of Christianity has not changed. But we are touching on questions of interpretation and theological sensitivity. At this level, we could therefore say that a low theology has replaced a high theology.

This theological orientation can explain the profound division which revealed itself, at the time of the Iraq war, between the European and the American God, and which, if we put our trust in newspapers, might have been able to make us believe in a religious war within Christianity, rather than in a war between radical Islam and the West. In fact, the criticism of the American Government has not been concentrated in the political field, but has had frequent theological overflows: many Christians participated in the denunciation of the God of Bush and of the Americans, accusing them of fundamentalism, fanaticism and of wanting to undertake a holy war.

This is to ignore totally the complexity of American protestant Christianity, which expresses itself through a multiplicity of churches and through extremely diversified theological and political tendencies. It is to ignore still more the weight and character of the civil religion in the United States, which means that religious language can be used in the lay space without prejudging its autonomy in any way, because in the American world secularization has not led to a cultural quartering of things religious as it has in Europe. To put it another way, God still lives in the American social heaven, whether the citizens are believers or not, and the history of America still expresses itself in categories marked by the universe and by biblical thought: born out of the Exodus like a new Israel, America has a healthy mission in the world, for which it receives the benediction of God, and that gives it the force to face up to its enemies. The American God is a God present in history, not only for the fundamentalists persuaded to receive his orders directly, but also for the Christians who draw from their faith, power and inspiration to decide on the actions and their engagement in history, and more broadly for the citizens of the United States of which it is a cultural foundation, conscious or unconscious.

In respect to the American God, the God invoked in Europe might appear as a God of post-history, a God of the scatological ethic in which the only value is peace. In comparison to the Americans, for whom the binary system good/bad, friends/enemies is still structuring and dynamizing, Europeans have already passed on to a multi-polar system where the idea of enemy no longer appears admissible and where relativism appears as a measure of wisdom. The reactions in face of violent demonstrations of radical Islam show this difference. There, where an American speech will easily raise the axis of evil and the need for a crusade for democracy, a European speech will tend to withhold itself from stigmatizing Islamism too strongly for fear of provoking an amalgamation between Islamism and Islam, and it will denounce the causes of it in the misery and injustice resulting from the domination of the rich countries. Moreover, if it accuses the extremism of Bin Laden and his henchmen, this will be by comparing them to that of American President George W. Bush.

We could think that our age is experiencing a very intense crisis and that this violent collusion between God and history could only calm itself in the future by finally leaving the God of post-history, the God of peace, to have the last word. One can also imagine that nothing can stop either secularization or globalization and that in time the conjunction of the two will bring about the weakening of religion. Nevertheless, the end of religious things does not seem to be for tomorrow and the elites of radical Islamism are often good examples of the marriage between modernity, globalization and religious extremism. Moreover, periods of social anguish are propitious for the binding quest and even if periods of indifference can make us believe that there is no more God, the question always surges back. Between a return to the religion of the fathers, an unbridled syncretism and new extremist or fundamentalist temptations, it is difficult to know what tomorrows God will be made of—what this word will give rise to or provoke in terms of progress, of steps backwards, of peace or violence. The stakes for the future seem considerable.

In addition, they are of a philosophical and theological order as much as ethical. Today in our countries, people of goodwill preach tolerance, dialogue, religious pluralism, multi-culturalism. However, this openness is not always enough to calm passions, because it is often soiled by an illusion: that the so-evident virtues of universalism will win over against the particularisms, and that men will all thus recognize one day that they have the same God: the God of peace, founded in a universal ethic. However, this is a dangerous utopia because such a God is forcibly abstract, virtual and without roots. It is not a God in history and men seem to need a God in their history. In just the same way, they need a historical identity and a geographical anchor.

In the context of globalization and of the open societies that our western societies are, the stakes are to learn to play off religious identity and religious otherness. This may be seen not only from a social and political viewpoint, or in the spirit of an ethic of tolerance, but also from a theological viewpoint. Judaism presents us with a very concrete example. It, alone among the three monotheisms, has never had the ambition to convert the whole world to its God, in putting forward as the fundamental principle the accepted difference between the singular vocation of the Jewish people and the universal importance of the revelation addressed to this people. If we remain within the framework of the three monotheisms, the work in the future could be that they articulate together their vocations and their respective charismas in order to bring the best of themselves to the construction of the humanism of tomorrow. However, the first condition is to renounce, not the quest for the truth, but an exclusive vision of the truth, which is the strongest temptation of revealed religions.

Chapter 7
Debunking the Myths of Religious Terrorism

Mark Juergensmeyer

No religion has a monopoly on violence. Christians have been involved in more acts of terrorism in the United States than Muslims. Prior to September 11, 2001, the most devastating act of terrorism in American history was the bombing attack on the Oklahoma City Federal Building, which was an act of Christian terrorism. Jewish terrorists attacked Muslims as they prayed in the shrine of the cave of the Patriarchs in Hebron, and it was Jewish terrorists, not Muslims, who assassinated Israel's Prime Minister Yitzhak Rabin. Even Buddhists have been involved in acts of terrorism—in the political unrest in Sri Lanka and in the release of nerve gas in the Tokyo subways by the syncretic Buddhist movement, Aum Shinrikyo. There are also Hindu and Sikh terrorists in India. And, of course, there are Islamic terrorists, including members of the *Hamas* movement and the far-flung al-Qaeda network.

When I looked for similarities among these diverse contemporary cases of religious terrorism in preparation for my book, *Terror in the Mind of God*, I found two patterns that emerged.

One involved the purpose of the terrorist acts: they were done less for the purposes of achieving a particular political strategy and more for the demonstration effect of what I have called performance violence. These acts of religious terrorism were employed to jolt the public consciousness, to shatter complacency, and call attention to the struggle that the perpetrators perceived as lying only slightly below the surface of ordinary reality. This point was underscored dramatically in the fall of 2005 when the Baghdad hotel housing American journalists, including the headquarters of CNN, was itself the target of terrorist acts.

My interview with Mohammed Abouhalima, one of the people involved in the 1993 bombing of the World Trade Center, illustrates the point. When I talked with Abouhalima he had been convicted of conspiracy in the 1993 World Trade Center attack and was serving time in a federal penitentiary in the California. He was a tall, affable Egyptian, with freckles and red hair. He did not appear to look like someone who might be a terrorist. If you were sitting next to him on a bus you might be engaged in animated conversation for hours without being the least concerned—until the subject turned to the issue of religion and public life.

Then his eyes would narrow and glaze, and with an almost palpable sense of frustration he would say, "you people just don't get it."

He accused us of being "like sheep." Abouhalima complained that the U.S. government had fooled the public and obscured what he thought was the most important truth about the contemporary world: that there was a great war going on. It was a war between good and evil, right and wrong, religion and unreligion. In this war the US government was the enemy.

I asked him whether this war explained why people bombed buildings. I told him that such attacks did not really achieve any kind of military victory.

But, Abouhalima said, such acts shake the public awake. We need to be awakened, he explained, confronted with the reality of what was going on in the world.

This idea of great, transcendent warfare is the second pattern that I have found in the diverse incidents of religious terrorism in recent years. This is the notion that I have called *cosmic war*, a grand encounter that is more than a temporal clash of political or social opinions. It is a war that is greater than the clashes of ordinary life. It is the image of a transhistorical war between truth and evil, good and bad, religion and unreligion, about which Aboulihma spoke.

But even though this cosmic war is ultimately located in the religious imagination, it is an idea that often is also rooted in real issues of social confrontation. Most conflicts that result in religious terrorism are not only about religion; they are also contests of identities, authority, and political ideas. In many cases a temporal clash or social or political confrontation will, through a process of frustration or deep sense of humiliation, turn from ordinary struggle into cosmic war. Just as religion is sometimes used by wily politicians in a process that is described as the *politicization of religion*, in some cases religious thinkers may begin to see political events in religious terms. Hence, through an evolutionary process, a particular conflict will be transformed into religious terms. These are cases not so much of the *politicization of religion, but the religionization of politics.* Worldly conflict is lifted into the high drama of sacred war.

How is this possible? How can worldly struggles take on a religious aura, and how can political battles become cosmic war?

Let's take Iraq as a case study. Over the past few years I have become interested in the increasing Islamicization of the resistance to the U.S. military occupation in Iraq. In 2004 I went to Baghdad to try to understand how the resistance there has become religious in such an intense and strident way. Since that time I have kept in contact with some of the Iraqis with whom I met, including members of the Association of Muslim Clergy from the Falluja and Baghdad areas. These clergy were deeply opposed to the American occupation of Iraq. They also increasingly saw it in transcendent religious terms.

The situation in the city of Fallujah was a case in point. Fallujah was perhaps the most troubled area within the Sunni triangle, the Al Anbar Province of Iraq. It is an example of how resistance unraveled into religious rebellion.

One of the Muslim clergy from the region told me that the American military had it all wrong about Fallujah. He said that the Americans thought that Fallujah was a hot bed of pro-Saddam activism. But he said that was never the case. Fallujah was a deeply religious city—it was called the city of mosques and was in the heart of what might be called the "Qur'an belt" of Iraq. The mullahs had a great deal of authority within the city, both before and after the American military invasion and occupation of the country.

The mullah with whom I spoke said that the religious leaders in Fallujah had hated Saddam's secular dictatorship, and that he had hated them. Saddam despised any potential sources of power that might oppose him, including especially the Muslim clergy, the mullah said. Saddam was scared of any alternative to his own power, he ruled through intimidation and fear and he saw us as a potential threat to his own power. So, the mullah told me, he would mistreat them, he would torture them, just as he has mistreated the Shiites.

Consequently Fallujah was remarkably quiescent at the time of the U.S. military invasion. There was very little protest against the American invasion, nor, the mullah said, was there much support for Saddam's Army. So, when the Americans came to Iraq the mullah said that they were not quite welcoming, but did not seriously oppose the U.S. military presence. The mullah told me that they had seen dictators come and go and were willing to wait and see.

The mullah said that there was no looting in Fallujah as there were in other parts of Iraq. The Muslim clergy there had the city very much under control. When they saw pictures of the civil unrest and looting throughout Iraq on television, they became disturbed about their country's future.

Ten days after the fall of Baghdad in April 2003, the U.S. 82nd Airborne took up a tentative position at the edge of the city. They had heard that Fallujah was a hot bed of American hatred. In their minds they imagined that the people of Fallujah hated them and would resist the American presence.

The military was cautious and anxious. They took up a presence in the outskirts of the city. They took over a school, they sent the students home and set up their operations in the emptied school building, as often they did in Iraqi cities in the initial stages of the invasion.

According to the mullah, the people in Fallujah were incensed—not so much at the U.S. military presence but at the fact that their children had no place to go to school. So the angry citizens of Fallujah went out in the streets and demonstrated. They marched on the school demanding that it be returned to the students.

Apparently soldiers assigned to the 82nd Airborne division looked out of the window and were alarmed to see the demonstration proceed towards the school. They were certain that the marchers were determined to attack the school, and thought they were under siege.

The U.S. soldiers started shooting. Twenty people were killed. They were shot dead, their bodies lying in the streets. From that day on, the mullah said, the people of Falluja realized that the American military occupation of Iraq was not up to any good.

The mullah was describing a situation of suspicion that then soured into resentment that subsequently deepened into a sense of war. It did not take a strident Islamic turn, initially, although the resistance certainly hardened over those months until April of 2004.

The events in Fallujah in April 2004 began with an event far away. In Gaza, an Israeli military strike had killed Sheikh Ahmed Yassin, the leader of the *Hamas* movement, who was regarded by many people in Falluja as one of their own, a kind of patriot. People in Falluja identified with the Palestinians, seeing them also as occupied people. When Sheikh Yassin was killed, they went out on the streets to demonstrate. The demonstration was countered by the U.S. military which saw it as an attack on them. In response the crowds took over one of the main streets of the city and renamed it Sheikh Yassin Street.

It was this on this street, near a bridge over the Euphrates River, that some American contracted security forces came in their jeeps. The jeeps were attacked and set on fire. The bodies of the American contractors were pulled out and dragged into the streets. They were then strung up from the girders over the Euphrates River, in a most brutal and horrific way, with pictures taken for the world to see.

The American public and the U.S. government were, of course, enormously angered at this. People throughout the world were revolted. The U.S. generals at the scene did not want to invade Fallujah, they would have preferred a more cautious approach, but the command came from the Pentagon: we cannot take this outrage, we must attack.

April 2004 was the first of the two waves of U.S. military assaults on Fallujah. With these assaults the resistance in Fallujah began to take on an Islamic character. Outsiders came with their own ideologies, with a kind of transnational *jihad*, and the resistance became an Islamic Resistance.

One of the mullahs from the area explained it to me in this way: He told me that the Americans would not succeed in Iraq. Instead, he said, Islam would prevail. What struck me as odd about this accusation was not his conviction that Americans would not succeed, but rather the notion that Islam was the opposition—that Americans had come to Iraq to destroy Islam.

In what sense, I asked the mullah, could the American military presence in Iraq be regarded as an attack on Islam? As a way of answering the question, the mullah explained that he and his colleagues had come to the conclusion that the sole purpose of the U.S. invasion and occupation of Iraq was to stifle the rising political power of Islam.

I asked how this was possible. The mullah described a kind of conspiracy theory that is popular in post-Saddam Iraq. According to this theory, the U.S. government's Central Intelligence Agency had created Saddam and propped up his power in Baghdad over the years. To support this hypothesis, the mullah offered the widely-publicized U.S. support for Saddam's regime during the Iran-Iraq war. According to the mullah this was not just a temporary accommodation, it was the public expression of a longstanding relationship.

Not wanting to argue with the mullah over this point, I said that even if he was correct and the U.S. had secretly been supporting Saddam, why would they then want to invade the country and topple his regime in 2003?

The mullah patiently explained his reasoning to me as if he was describing something so obvious it need not have to be explained. He said that the U.S. government knew that Saddam was weak. It knew that Saddam did not have weapons of mass destruction, that his method of intimidating his population was to give the impression that he had more power than in fact he had. In fact, the mullah said, the U.S. knew what many Iraqis at the time also believed—that Saddam was quite weak.

According to the mullah, the Americans knew that Saddam was about to fall and that an Islamic government would take over. That is what the Americans wanted to forestall. They wanted to co-opt the Islamic Revolution. So, they had to get rid of Saddam and run Iraq directly.

The mullah said that now he and his Iraqi compatriots could fight for the revolution that they have always wanted. They were determined to topple the continuing Saddam/U.S. regime and bring about an extraordinary Islamic change.

It was a remarkable explanation, and I was curious to know if his was an idiosyncratic point of view. I asked his fellow Muslim clergy if they believed in this account, and they all affirmed that they did. In the following days I asked other people in Baghdad about this hypothesis and even modern secular Iraqis acknowledged that it had some degree of truth. They agreed that one of the reasons why America had toppled the Saddam regime was to postpone the possibility of an Islamic Revolution. Very few people in Iraq thought that the U.S. invasion was due to a perceived threat of weapons of mass destruction, and only a few more thought that oil was a major factor. Islam, however, was a different matter.

So it was no surprise that the Muslim clergy thought that the U.S. presence was aimed at Islam, and that in turn it was necessary for them to try to defend Islam against the U.S. aggression. This anti-Islam theory about why the U.S. had invaded and occupied Iraq helped to explain how the resistance to the U.S. occupation became Islamicized.

Following the April 2004 assault on Fallujah by the U.S. military, and the temporary true that followed, the city was still under the control of the mullahs. The truce brought together a renegade group from Saddam's old Army to keep the peace in Fallujah. But the resistance to the occupation persisted. Among the resistance fighters in Fallujah were indigenous Iraqi Islamic rebels as well as outsiders who followed Jordan's Al Zarqawi. But the outsiders were largely contained by the mullahs, who still had control over the resistance fighters in Fallujah as long as the city stayed intact.

By the end of the summer the truce began to unravel and the American Army returned to Falluja in November 2004. The city was virtually destroyed.

After November when Fallujah was flattened the resistance fighters were scattered throughout the country. One result of this was that this Islamic resistance movement spread throughout Northern Iraq. Another was that the young men were no longer under the control of the mullahs, whose agenda is much more an Iraqi nationalist agenda than a transnational *jihad* agenda, and instead the extreme forces of al Zarqawi gained even firmer control.

In a remarkable way the American destruction of Falluja had the effect of changing the character of the resistance and helping to transform a local Islamic resistance increasingly into a transnational *jihad* along the lines of Al Zarqawi's brand of al-Qaeda's ideology. Today, it is increasingly Iraqis, as well as the outsiders from Syria, Jordan, or Saudi Arabia, who are undertaking acts of suicide bombing on behalf of a transnational Islamic cause. The resistance has become "jihadized."

In the course of a year or so the resistance against the U.S. occupation in Iraq took on a religious aura and become magnified into a kind of transnational cosmic war. This points out to me several significant things about contemporary terrorism, and counters several prevailing myths.

One is the myth that *these conflicts are only about religion*. One aspect of the radical jihadi ideology is a political one, the notion that all the politics of the Middle East after the end of the Ottoman Empire is an European invention. When Osama Bin Laden appeared on television soon after the 9/11 attacks, he said that the U.S. and Europe had been meddling in Middle Eastern politics for 80 years. He was referring to the fall of the Caliphate, the end of the Ottoman Empire. Western style politics are contrasted with the traditions of the Middle East and portrayed as a kind of continuing colonialism within the region. To the extent that the *jihadi* movement in general, and the radical wing of the Iraqi resistance movement in particular, is countering Western influence it raises a real political issue that resonates with many Middle Easterners, even though most Muslims in the region do not yet see it in cosmic terms.

In short, the issues behind the *jihadi* ideology are not simply about religion. As Roger Pape points out on his recent book, *Dying to Win*, suicide bombing is often about the defense of territory.

But one could then race to another conclusion, which is the second myth about religious terrorism—that *the religious aspects are irrelevant*. This is seldom the case. Though it is true that religion may sometimes be used simply to a gloss over a political or an economic program, when religion enters the picture, as one sees in the case of the activists in Fallujah, it transforms the struggle. It expands timelines into eternal goals and expands the rewards of the strugglers into cosmic rewards; it transforms a realistic struggle into a cosmic one and changes the character of the battle.

The third myth is that *modern terrorism is against freedom*. In a sense, freedom is exactly what the *jihadi* terrorists are battling for. In the case of the *jihadi* resistance to the occupation in Iraq, their goal is free Iraq of American influence, and eventually to free all of the Middle East in a similar way. In another sense, however, one can argue that the presence of the American troops in Iraq help to insure fair elections and make possible the political freedom of the democratic process. Hence two versions of freedom are embraced: the American understanding of the importance of democracy and individual freedoms, and the *jihadi* understanding of becoming free from Western meddling within the Middle East. Tragically, these two versions of freedom are presented in a way that appears to be in competition with each other.

The fourth myth is that the conflicts identified with religious terrorism are part of *a clash of civilizations*. The *jihadi* terrorist attacks certainly signify a hatred of the West but it is an open question as to how widespread this sentiment is within the Muslim world. The notion that there is something deeply violent about Islam or something mystical about Islam's relationship to politics which we Westerners can never understand and never deal with, is absurd. Most people within the Muslim world want what everybody else wants, and that is to live their lives in a very simple, unfettered way without being encumbered by other people's notions of who they should be and what they should do. It's not a clash of civilizations, but rather a competition between notions of what freedom means within the Middle East.

Finally, there is the myth that *we can win the war on terrorism*. This is a myth because simply thinking in terms of war buys in to the very rhetoric and the worldview that people who are engaged in cosmic war want to promote. In this regard the very first mistake the Americans made in responding the 9/11 was to frame the conflict as a "war" on terrorism, the first war of the 21st century. The idea of war magnified the importance of the *jihadi* ideology and it magnified the importance of Osama Bin Laden as a great leader of the Muslim world. The idea of war magnified the importance of this way of thinking and, in a sense, even bought into it. The problem, however, is that as long as the U.S. is trying to fight on these terms, it cannot win.

The consequences of the U.S. adopting a militant approach to terrorism was brought home to me in a conversation I had in Iraq with a woman who was a professor in Baghdad University. She appeared very modern and was dressed in a Western style. She said, "You know, we have such expectations when Saddam fell, but, you know, all these expectations have been dashed." Then her eyes narrowed and she said, "You Americans, you became like the terrorists that you came to destroy."

The very severity of the occupation, in her mind, was a kind of terrorism. It helped to unleash the forces of insecurity that make it difficult to live in Baghdad in the post-Saddam world.

Though we can't win the war on terrorism in its own militant terms, we can contain it. We can help to dissolve the support for it, and undercut the ideology that gave rise to it in the first place. In that we can help to dissipate the notion of cosmic war, the great war between good and evil. The sooner we move beyond the language of war and return to the language of international human rights and the dignity of all people, the better our changes of winning a world without terrorism. This should be our goal, not trying to fight the terrorists on their own terms.

The bad news is that there may be more waves of terror associated with various visions of cosmic war in the years to come. The good news is that the cosmic war is an imagined war, an ephemeral thing, and it can dissipate as easily as it arose in the first place. Just as this image of cosmic war can gather like a storm cloud on a summer day and suddenly overtake a way of thinking, as it did in Falluja, it could also dissolve almost as quickly, because it is, after all, a fantastic vision, a war in the mind. It is a war that can disappear as quickly as it gathered. The key it is to deal with humans as humans, to subscribe to rules of international human rights and international law, and to treat all people with respect and dignity.

Perhaps the deepest emotion that gives rise to any act of violence is the feeling of being humiliated, of not being respected, of not being listened to, of being "dissed," in the words of American rap music. As long as people feel that they have been dishonored then there is the potent possibility of the rise of violence in response. The beginning of the end of terrorism, it seems to me, is to offer respect to the visions of all people, even people who, at least for the moment, despise us and seek to do us harm.

Chapter 8
Religion and Civilization

Daniel Benjamin

As moderns we tend to be queasy about discussing religion.

We always say, in America, that you never talk about religion, money and sex. We now live in a world in which we have to discuss, at a minimum, religion.

Religion underlies so much of our civilization and accounts for so much of its richness that we may be having a hard time recognizing that we are at one of those moments when the river of religion threatens to wash over the banks that contain it.

The challenges Mark Juergensmeyer points out so well are not just from religious violence and extremism in the Islamic tradition but really from every religious tradition.

For many reasons, which I will enumerate briefly, we live in a time in which the critical security threats we face come from religiously-motivated violence, which usually emanates from fundamentalist enclave cultures.

Juergensmeyer refers to Oklahoma City and the killing of Yitzhak Rabin. One might add that until 9/11, the murder of Rabin—which was just the assassination of one man—was probably the most strategic use of terrorist violence since the assassination of the Archduke in Sarajevo at the beginning of World War I. The assassination of Rabin was an act conceived of by a religious student who thought he had rabbinic authorization to end the life of someone who was giving holy land back to the Palestinians.

One can also add to this litany the effort to blow up the Temple Mount in the mid 1980s, which would have had absolutely cataclysmic impact.

There are a variety of reasons for this change, this shift to religiously-motivated violence.

Many of these enclave cultures, as we know from the scholarly analysis of fundamentalism, are plagued by a sense of encroachment by the forces of secularism, the technological society and globalization. There is a strong feeling that the state has failed to provide the social goods and the spiritual fulfillment that their peoples desire most. And, of course, the high road to religious revival—this is especially true of Islamization but it has contributed to the spread of Evangelical Christianity in parts of the world—has been through the supply of social services, whether the provider is *Hamas*, missionary churches, Hezbollah or any number of other religious organizations. Obviously, not all or even most of them support violence.

But, it is not only a sense of crisis that promotes this kind of fundamentalism. Historical events may do so as well. For example the Six Day War was a catalytic event in sparking a new religious fundamentalism in Israel.

It is interesting to note, that after the recent Israeli pullout from Gaza, one of the leading rabbis in the West Bank spoke of this being the moment to return to "normative messianism." This is a very interesting and unusual phrase.

In this case, it means returning to the viewpoint of Maimonides that the coming of the Messiah is a central article of faith but that Jews should not do anything to hasten it and don't expect this event to happen any time soon. Indeed, to do otherwise is to court a world of trouble.

Many of the different fundamentalisms that we face are animated by a messianism, and this is what often gives them a particularly lethal edge.

One of the curious things about radical Islamism and, particularly the form bin Laden espouses, is that is has an element of messianism which is quite uncommon in the mainstream Sunni tradition.

Perhaps one way to explain the emergence of this particularly virulent form of extremism is by looking at the ideological context and, specifically, the fact that every other ideology has failed the Muslim, and, particularly, the Arab world, whether it is Arab nationalism or Marxism. Compounding this is that we are in a period—and this is dividend of globalization—in which people are taking advantage of opportunities to shop for identities and return to old identities, which may be imaginary constructs but which they feel to be more authentic.

As a result, individuals are voicing their grievances in an idiom that seems to them more true and more justified than any other.

I believe the reason that religiously motivated violence challenges us so much more than the political terrorism that we have seen before is its different nature. Groups such as ETA or the IRA or even the urban terrorists of the 1970s and 1980s typically used limited violence to establish a bargaining position. They wanted to highlight their causes and wanted to try to attract adherents from a very broad segment of society. They were averse to committing atrocities, because that would essentially rule them out as partners in negotiations

By contrast, religiously-motivated terrorists seek unconstrained and often indiscriminate violence, whether by bringing down the Twin Towers or blowing up the Temple Mount. The violence is sacred and, therefore, the more the better. There is no thought of a negotiating process here. And what has made this so terrifying is the combination of deep religious belief and modern technologies of destruction. The violence associated with radical Islamism threatens us more than most other types.

The sense of a civilizational crisis in the Islamic world is heightened by a perception of decline *vis-à-vis* the West and a sense of imposition by the West. Moreover, a number of different developments suggest that we may be looking at the stirrings of a Muslim reformation. Now, this is something that people often say would be a great thing, because, after all, the problem with Islam, according to the newspapers, at least, is that there is no separation between religion and politics.

Let me suggest a few bits of evidence that we are on the cusp of such a development.

First of all, there has been an enormous rise of literacy and the use of print and other media in the Muslim world in the last century. We have seen the thread of religious tradition cut through the importation of modern Western-style education in the late 19th century and early 20th century as Muslim elites, impressed by the political and technological advances of Europe, decided to have their children educated in schools created on a European model. So the understanding of Islam that had traditionally been transferred from teacher to student across a table became an increasingly rare phenomenon.

As a result of European education, there was a new a sense of the empowerment of the individual. To paraphrase Martin Luther, it is one of the messages of radical Islam that every man is a priest, that every man is capable of having a direct and unmediated experience of the holy through the reading of scripture.

In part as a result of this, there is a crisis of authority in the Muslim world, both between clerics and believers and in the relationship between the governed and government. In large measure, this has to due with the prevalence of authoritarian regimes, but also because the *ulema*, the clergy, has been largely viewed as discredited because they tend to be in the pay of the government and, as a result, tend to be a force for stability and not for reform.

The distinguished scholar of Islam, Richard Bulliet, has summed this up by saying that at the street level there is no agreement on what Islam really means. If you look at some of Islamist websites or listen to some of the upstart preachers who are not the products of seminaries, but are largely self taught, you can see that this is true. Some of these people will find a rationale to justify anything under Islam. As one of the leading radicals in Britain said: All these years of writing—what has it done for the Muslim people? And with that, he wrote off hundreds of years of commentary and reflection.

Let me add one more parallel with the European Reformation, and that is that the radical Islamists have essentially proposed a reconfiguration of the sacraments, much as occurred in Protestant Europe in the 16th century. They have taken the traditional five pillars of Islam and effectively added *jihad* or even raised it to be the highest obligation. *jihad* is, of course, the military *jihad* and not the "Greater *jihad*" or the internal struggle for self-betterment. For them, *jihad* is, above all, to be understood as military action.

Now, when it comes to a reformation, we shouldn't be too excited, because it is one of those things where you have to be careful what you wish for!

The European Reformation went on for a century and a half and in its worse spasm—the Thirty Years War—cost at least one third of the population of Europe.

I confess that in a era in which there are weapons of mass destruction, this gives me pause. By the way, if you look back at the history of the early Reformation, the period was characterized by a number of very violent episodes in which antinomians, people who were convinced that they understood the truth of religion, took over cities such as Munster, or larger areas, such as the rebel Thomas Muenzer did in Germany. We may be seeing something not unlike that.

So, what is it that we are supposed to do in the face of this religious challenge?

Well, we are discussing religion and civilization. To be almost trite about it, the answer to a challenge from religion is more civilization.

Some things are obvious and many of these have been discussed in terms of fighting the war on terror, if we can use that problematic term. I should add that as a former Presidential speech writer there was never going to be another phrase regarding how the United States would confront its foes after 9/11 simply because war, although it means different things in different languages, signifies in English what you do when you are most serious.

It's an unfortunate choice of term, because it translates so poorly and plays into our enemies' hands, but nonetheless, it was an inevitability. I am sorry it hasn't disappeared by now, but there it is.

Anyway, the things that we need to do at the tactical level, are, I think, quite obvious. We need to protect our citizens and prepare our societies for attacks, because this is going to be with us for a while. Moreover, our efforts must involve not only the protection of our own societies. As has been noted many times, one of the problems of terrorism is a weakness in state capacity. Many states are not capable of dealing with these threats, especially in the developing world, and we need expansion of state capacity when it comes to police work, intelligence work, training of judges, prosecutors and education, and such areas as border controls.

It is also important, however, to go beyond the tactical. This is where we have failed thus far, and it seems to me that a key element of strategy is not to allow the generation of a countermovement in the West that will create a dynamo effect and result into further radicalization and an intensification of hostilities.

There are two forms that I worry about principally.

The first, believe it or not, has to do with events in secularized Europe. Florence Taubmann has expressed concerns about America and I will get to those. But it is not just an American problem.

Given the demographics and the nature of the Muslim community in much of Europe, the threat of inter-communal violence is growing. One only needs to look at the 20 or so arson attacks that occurred after the killing of Theo van Gogh in Holland, which is widely considered to be Europe's most tolerant state. If what demographers tell us is true—that Europe will probably be 20 percent Muslim in about 30 years or so—then tensions are likely to grow, given the nature of the community that settled in Europe and the fact that most Muslims came as guest workers and have not been integrated very well.

There is a view that Europe is targeted mainly because radicals want to peel it off from America. I disagree with that quite strongly. We are witnessing a phenomenon with the growth of Islamic radicalism in the cities of Europe, in which there is a kind of blurring or meshing of grievances, both global and local. In the document that Mohammed Bouyeri left behind pinned to the chest of his victim, Bouyeri makes it clear he was equally affronted by the war on Iraq *and* suggestions for changes in Dutch administrative law that would have required screening to see if job applicants were radical.

Local and global grievances are fed by the neo-umma that Farhad Khosrokhavar addresses in his chapter, and one sees the sense of grievance being propagated with extraordinary effectiveness by the Internet.

These tensions are unlikely to subside when very distinguished Europeans, such as the Queen of Denmark, say that it's time we stood up and took action, or that we have been lazy too long in allowing Islam to grow and it must be confronted. Or when Silvio Berlusconi says that Western civilization is clearly superior to Islam, and it is time that we reassert ourselves.

On the other side of the Atlantic there are also very large challenges. Florence Taubmann has touched on some, but let me put them even in higher relief.

Within the United States there are at least two different camps. One has more to say to Europeans about how we should deal with the problems before us. But another one is, very powerful and does not agree with this approach I've tried to sketch out of avoiding polarization.

There are roughly 15 to 20 million people who could be called Christian Zionists. These are evangelical Christians who are politically to the right of the Likud Party in Israel, and they feel very strongly that Israel should not give up an inch of territory, and that Israel's rights, when it comes to dealing with terrorists, should be entirely unlimited. They believe that ultimately Israel must experience an ingathering of exiles and a confrontation with its enemies, which will be the prelude to the tribulation and end of history.

Needless to say, this group of people is not inclined to be very helpful if you are trying to conduct Middle East peacemaking, but the fact is that this is a highly influential constituency. It has accounted for, according to reporting that we put forward in our book *The Next Attack*, the White House's change of mind on the issue of criticizing Israeli attacks on *Hamas* leaders. In other words, the White House actually changed its tone from one day to the next, and went from being critical to issuing an endorsement of Israel's right to defend itself.

Even more worrisome is the growth of Islamophobia more broadly in the evangelical world. It is very real and it is very worrisome. For many of these people, the Muslim world now fills the place that the Soviet Union and global communism once filled.

If we allow these different forces to influence our governments and our policy, then I fear that we are headed for more confrontation rather than less, at a time, when the best strategy, seems to me, is to embrace a civilizational approach rather than a purely religious one.

What might we do? Here are a few thoughts.

We need to be more active about reducing local grievances, especially the conflicts around the world that feed the global *jihad*, whether in Chechnya, Kashmir, Southern Thailand, Indonesia or Palestine. There was a moment after 9/11 when there seemed to be a chance for diplomacy to make a sort of new start and rise to this occasion. But that passed. It will be very difficult for us to regain that moment, but we need to try.

We need to work on integration of minorities, particularly in Europe.

We need to avoid alienating the well-integrated Muslim minority in the United States. I fear that our aggressive law enforcement practices may be doing exactly that. This is something that we in America need to worry a great deal about.

We need to recognize that our approach towards combatting terrorism has been grossly over-militarized.

We need to recognize that there are two narratives. One narrative is the Islamist one—bin Laden's—in which the United States is depicted as seeking to occupy Muslim countries and destroy Islam. Unfortunately, for many Muslims this view has unintentionaly been given credence by the U.S. invasion of Iraq.

If you ask most Americans what they think our narrative is, they would say that the West is a benign agent of modernization, and that we seek to integrate the Muslim world into a world—I would refer to Isaiah Berlin's term—of negative freedom. This is a world in which people can choose whatever religious obligations and creeds they want. This is not a world of positive freedom like *Sharia*, where there is a comprehensive obligation to behave in a certain way, but one where markets are free and people can improve their lives in ways they choose and have a better future for their children.

At the moment, I am afraid, we are not making that argument. Due to our presence in Iraq we are unfortunately stuck on the wrong side of this battle of ideas.

I believe it is around this framework of two narratives that we have to compose our strategy for the future.

Part III:
Media and Terrorism

Chapter 9
Media and Terrorism

Christine Ockrent

Since I am in the news business, let me begin with a news item. In the fall of 2005 the UN Special Prosecutor delivered his report on the assassination of former Lebanese Prime Minister Rafik Hariri. The report documents an entire chain of events underscoring the symbiotic use of the media not only by terrorists, but by all who want to use it as a disguise.

A few hours after the huge blast killed Hariri and another 17 people, Al-Jazeera broadcast a video featuring a bearded young man who claimed responsibility for Hariri's assassination in the name of a previously unknown terrorist organization.

Thanks to the UN's very energetic German prosecutor, however, we now know that this bearded young man was a fake. He was used by the Syrian Secret Services and probably their Lebanese friends to pose as a terrorist claiming responsibility for the assassination.

This episode epitomizes in my view the stage we have reached: a terrorist *mise en scène* used by traditional secret service people and broadcast immediately by Al-Jazeera.

The other phenomenon, of course, is that we in the West have lost the monopoly of information. This major turn of events happened at the end of the 20th century, when three news Arab networks, starting, of course, with Al-Jazeera in 1995, began broadcasting.

I would like to make three main points. My first point is obvious: the media are very much a tool of terrorism. My second point is that the media are also a sort of fuel for terrorism. My last point is that the media can be a weapon against terrorism.

Media as a tool used by terrorists has been amply demonstrated. Terrorism is theater, it is propaganda by deed, as the famous formula goes, dating back to the Russian anarchists of the 19th century.

Manipulation and exploitation of the media are, indeed, very much part of terrorism today. It's not new.

There is no Greek tragedy without a messenger. In the Middle Ages the Shia sect of assassins used word of mouth in the mosques to instill fear among the population.

Closer to us, the Italian Red Brigades always chose to perform their violent acts on Wednesdays and Saturdays, because they knew that the circulation of Italian newspapers would be higher the following day. And we all recall that in 1972, at the Munich Olympics, the members of Black September were well aware that about five hundred million viewers would witness their act.

The media are a tool, but a slippery one. Semantics play a role as well. What makes someone a "terrorist," an "insurgent," a "rebel," or a "freedom fighter?" Let us remember how we used to label the PLO in the days when they would hijack planes in the 1970s, then when Arafat showed up at the UN, when he won the Nobel Peace Prize. At least until the second *intifada*, for many he bore the label of statesman. Palestinians have succeeded, in a way, to change our vocabulary. They have grown from terrorists into a cause that has appealed to many people in our part of the world.

Look also at perceptions of the IRA in Northern Ireland. Years ago they were portrayed as fighting for their religion and their freedom. Over time, however, perceptions changed, and they slipped into the category of bloodthirsty terrorists, increasingly rejected by their own people.

The same change in media and public perception can be seen in the case of ETA in Spain.

In each of these cases it is interesting to check the vocabulary used by the media in that limited part of the world where the media are free. You will not find a French newspaper, a Scandinavian newspaper, an Italian newspaper or an Israeli newspaper using the same words to describe the same groups.

The media themselves have been undergoing tremendous techno-logical change, and terrorist organizations have been prompt in adjusting. One can find almost anything on the Internet, including various ways to make a bomb. Mobile phones, MP3—there are many ways to exchange data, even from the Afghan-Pakistan border, if you want to ignite human bombs here or there.

Another factor has to do with the evolution of the news business itself, mainly live 24- hour TV news. The moment that satellites covered the developed part of the world, live TV news became the unwitting partner of terrorism. Why? Because terrorism is news. Terrorism is a show. We have seen that over and over again with 9/11 in New York and Washington, 3/11 in Madrid, 7/7 in London.

Moreover, all the news networks are very competitive, and their treatment of news is more and more like that of tabloids. The news dwell upon emotion. We all are, in a way, accustomed to having our emotions stirred before anything else. Moreover, speed is of the essence. We are no longer bewildered to see an event on the screen before we know what has actually happened. The development of headlines news helps terrorism have an immediate impact upon a vast number of people.

Media are also a tool in the hands of terrorists inasmuch as journalists themselves have become targets. We maybe remember that, in the days of the endless Lebanese civil war, an AP reporter, Terri Andersen, was held hostage for 7 years. A few French journalists were also held. In Spain, ETA has killed or wounded several journalists. Daniel Pearl of *The Wall Street Journal* was killed in Pakistan. In Iraq, many journalists have been held hostages, sometimes killed or exchanged for ransom, such as Florence Aubenas of *Libération* or the Italian journalist, Giuliana Sgrena, who had been very sympathetic to the very people who kidnapped her. In Baghdad in October 2005 insurgents decided to blast the hotels where foreign media stayed.

Journalists can be targets, but journalists can be partners. There are many cases where journalists have been tempted, out of sympathy for a cause, or because they are being manipulated, to play an active part in a terrorist chain. The Syrian-born Spanish journalist Tahir Alumni, for instance, who was the only reporter in Kabul to cover the fall of the Taliban for Al-Jazeera, was condemned by the Spanish courts to 7 years in prison for his links with Al-Qaeda.

Media can also act to fuel terrorism. It is a dimension of the problem which we journalists, in our part of the world, find difficult to accept. But the display of our ways of life, more than our values, all over TV, our prosperity, our violence, our attitude towards sex or pornography, as they are being depicted and often caricatured in TV series or in advertising are very strong incentives to feed terrorist ideologies that rely on hatred.

It is remarkable that to some extent even we Europeans have joined into this new age of innocence best illustrated by the American media. Having worked for some of them I have great respect for most of them. A whole new generation has entered the media arena, convinced that live TV news can be a formidable instrument to advance democracy and propagate values, and thus help the world. In fact, however, it has proven much more difficult to conquer minds than to conquer markets. In a vain attempt to try and change Arab perceptions of America, Washington has even gone so far as to launch an all news TV channel called Al-Hurra to compete with Al-Jazeera, Al-Arabia and the other Arab TV channel. It is not really a success.

Karen Hughes, a long-time supporter and close adviser to President Bush, recently visited Saudi Arabia. As Undersecretary of State she is in charge of improving the image of the United States. In Jeddah, she talked to a group of women at the local university and said candidly: wouldn't it be wonderful to imagine the day when you will take off your veils and be able to decide for yourselves what to do with your lives!

Well, her speech turned out to be a terrible disaster! Not only because the audience probably was not quite as free as she expected it to be, but because somehow the speed of live TV news does not match the pace of cultural and social change.

Today, we use the code phrase "international terrorism" to speak exclusively about Islamist terrorism.

Al-Jazeera has just hired David Frost and has decided to launch an English speaking news service. This service is bound to be quite different from Al-Jazeera's programs in Arabic.

There is a preacher who appears only on the Arab speaking program of Al-Jazeera named Al Qaradawi. Al Qaradawi has become famous all over the Arab world because he preaches violence, anti-Semitism, anti-Israel, anti-West, anti-pornography, etc. He symbolizes the fuel that the media give terrorism, especially at a time and age when terrorism relies upon religion. Religion, of course, provides indoctrinated youth with a cause—in their view, probably, a just cause. In Islam, there is no clear hierarchy, no authoritative message coming from the top. Of course it is always a shock to us not to find Islamic clerics appearing on Arab media who would explain that violence and killing fellow Muslims and killing civilians is not necessarily the best way to reach heaven and get hold of all these virgins.

There is an additional phenomenon accounting for the important role played by the media as fuel to terrorism, and that is the intense competition and focus of the media on mass entertainment. Today, for all of us—and more often than we acknowledge it—the desire to be entertained takes over the need to know.

My last point has to do with the role that the media can play, and do play, as weapons against terror. For all the exploitation and manipulation to which the media is prone, it is very important to understand that publicity is not propaganda. Terrorists love publicity—that is why they try to use the media—but they hate information. The media give publicity, but they hardly ever deliver the propaganda message as terrorists would like them to do.

We all know the ghastly videos of hostages being humiliated, slogans and hoods over their heads. They usually come with some messages from the terrorists. It is interesting to notice that even Al-Jazeera has decided never to air them. They show the pictures, they relate the facts, but they do not broadcast the propaganda, even in the most heated hours of the Bin Laden track and the most heated and horrible episodes of hostages being taken and slaughtered in Iraq.

There is more to say about self-control and self-restraint from most media than is usually admitted. I remember being in my friend Dan Rather's office, who was still anchoring the evening news at CBS, at the time of the anthrax attacks, just after 9/11.

When Dan received an envelope full of white powder, there was instant control over the newsroom, immediate consultation, not only with internal experts but with the FBI. There was no mention of the incident on the air. I believe there would be a similar response in Europe. In France, for instance, it would never occur to me or to any of my colleagues that we should immediately relate to our viewers whatever threat messages we may receive from any activist group.

In the 1980s Prime Minister Thatcher decided that the BBC and other British media should not, in her famous phrase, "give oxygen to terrorists." The BBC was forbidden to broadcast the voices of Sinn Fein leaders. It proved very effective, because Sinn Fein could not use the major British television media to promote their cause. But the BBC, being very independent, decided that they would use actors and voice-over the pictures of these Irish leaders. Nevertheless, it was an attempt, in a democratic society, of government control over a major media.

After 9/11 American networks agreed to the Bush Administration's request not to broadcast any more video by Bin Laden for fear that it would contain coded messages to terrorists ready to blow up more planes and more buildings. But after that period of intense patriotic fervor, when all American media sacrificed to for reasons not very well understood in Europe, they went back to their tradition of independent reporting during Hurricane Katrina.

It is tricky to move from self-control to control, as former Spanish Prime Minister Aznar learned after the 3/11 blasts in Madrid. It was interesting to see how, in a democratic society, the Spanish government pressured Spanish public television; Aznar himself called the Editor of *El País*, to whom he had not spoken during all the years he was at *La Moncloa*, to convince journalists that ETA was responsible for these terrible terrorist acts. The move served neither Aznar nor his political party well; they lost the elections a few days later.

Another interesting example is that of Vladimir Putin in Chechnya. The media can help fight against terrorism in societies which are free—not in a system like Russia today where the government controls most of the media. When Chechen President Maskarov was murdered, he was labeled, of course, as a terrorist by the Russian media. We in the West hesitated: in the beginning, Chechens were labeled as freedom fighters in most of our media. Now they have become terrorists. Remember the school in Beslan—a terrible terrorist act by some Chechens, including women. The manner in which Putin tried to control his own media and the world media, for that matter, to hide all the damage and actual assassinations committed by his own elite troops trying to free the hostages in the school, was an interesting test case. At home, Putin has been largely successful at using his own controlled media to convince his public opinion that any attempt to contest his rule is a form of terrorism.

In order for the media to be effective weapons against terrorism, we have to take into account the structural changes we are witnessing in the media scene. Technology will get faster and become more globalized and more difficult to control. Even the Chinese communist regime, which is doing its best to exert such control, will not in the long run manage to control the Internet.

There are more and more satellites. There was a difficult moment in France a year ago when it was discovered that Hezbollah was using Eutelsat, the European satellite, to broadcast its own network, called Al-mana, with anti-Semitic propaganda and violent messages. The French Broadcasting Authority decided to ban that channel and Eutelsat dropped it, but it was immediately taken over by another satellite.

So, the technology is there, and it will be more and more difficult to control.

On the other hand, there will be more and more media, with or without journalists' contribution and control. Blogs contribute to the extraordinary proliferation of news or pseudo-news, even if the whole bubble, the whole gargle, of information is, indeed, a way for traditional media to try and maintain their brands and their utility. The "me generation" coincides with the era of technological convergence.

My conclusion has to do with the values and the functioning of our open society.

We all know that terrorists use what they condemn, which is our freedom of expression and communication. We have to find new ways to operate.

We need a more effective public information policy. There has to be a better link between the media and the government agencies in charge of security. Journalists are often much more ignorant than they pretend to be. There has to be an open data base that would provide more knowledge and more exposure to what we know about terrorist organizations, their methods and their disguise.

I have always been a journalist and I dream of no other activity, but I don't believe that freedom of information is an absolute freedom. In our free societies we all accept that freedom of information stops when racism steps in or when incitation to violence or killing or disrespect to any other human being is expressed. Core values of individual freedom and dignity, the rule of law—all these pillars of our systems have to be accepted by the media, respected by the media, protected by the media. It is up to our governments and to our media people to forge new ways of adjusting to the challenges and dangers facing our societies. Media are also here to build consensus, to help all of us to relate to one another, to help immigrants and their children to forge a sense of belonging and sharing of our values.

It is important that we, in Europe, remember that we belong to a part of the world where the media have been free for a very long time. For all their excesses, weaknesses and changes, they contribute to the very texture of our societies. We need more harmonization of our laws and regulations. Altogether I believe we all need more Europe to promote more cultural diversity. Freedom and diversity are the only long term answers that we, in the media, can contribute when it comes to fighting terrorism.

Chapter 10

Terrorism and Media in the Age of Global Communication

Brigitte L. Nacos

In the aftermath of the devastating 7/7 (July 7, 2005) bombings of London's transit system and a failed follow-up attempt two weeks later, shocked Britons and observers elsewhere wondered how home-grown young Muslims came to be infected by the terrorist ideology of Osama bin Laden and/or like-minded extremists. There was no mystery. In the age of global communication and international media the messengers of hate and terrorism are no longer impeded by national borders; they spread their powerful words and images around the globe, and they condition impressionable young men and women for recruitment into their violent causes.

To be sure, there are other factors as well, such as the influence of radical Islamist clergy and other fundamentalists in the Arab and Muslim diaspora in the West and the easy movement of terrorist propagandists from country to country and from continent to continent. Yet, the traditional media and advanced communication technology are exploited by international terrorists to achieve a host of important media-dependent objectives—most of all the dissemination of propaganda among friends and foes around the world. 9/11 (September 11, 2001) in New York and Washington, 3/11 (March 11, 2004) in Madrid, and 7/7 in London demonstrated once again how the architects of international terrorism exploit mass media and global communication—including the Internet—for their publicity needs. This paper, then, examines the role of global media in the communication and propaganda scheme of international terrorism.

Terrorists and their Need for Publicity

Each major act of terrorism (and, in fact, most minor terrorist deeds as well) results inevitably in news coverage. While I do not suggest that the news media favor this sort of political violence, it is nevertheless true that terrorist strikes provide what the contemporary media crave most—drama, shock, and tragedy suited to be packaged as human interest news. As a result, terrorists get precisely what they want: massive publicity and the opportunity to showcase their ability to strike against even the strongest nation states. And the media are rewarded as well in that they energize their competition for audience size and circulation—and thus for all-important advertising. In this respect, the two sides enjoy a symbiotic relationship—they feed off each other.

Terrorists at all times understood the need to advertise their existence and their causes by publicizing their deeds. For this reason, 19th century anarchists explained their violence as "propaganda of the deed." Whenever possible, terrorists have not relied solely on the traditional media (newspapers, newsmagazines, radio and television) but communicated their messages directly to their friends and foes. In the late 1960s, the Brazilian revolutionary Carlos Marighela wrote about this two-fold approach in the *Minimanual of the Urban Guerrilla*. He suggested that the modern mass media were important instruments of propaganda but that this opportunity should not prevent "freedom fighters" from utilizing their own presses and copying machines. In addition to their own printing presses and copying machines, terrorists have used on- and off-shore radio transmitters, satellite telephones, and, in the case of the Lebanese Hezbollah, their own television-network (Al Manar). Since terrorists always embraced the newest information and communication technologies, it was hardly surprising that they recognized the utility of the Internet early on and exploited it for their purposes. But while the Internet opened a new chapter in terrorist communication and information, the traditional media remain for the time being the most important sources of information and thus figure prominently into contemporary terrorists' publicity calculus.

To be sure, in order to understand terrorism and propaganda fully, we need to examine other carriers of terrorist messages—new media such as video tapes, audio cassettes, DVDs, and entertainment media, such as video games, popular music, and novels. Video tapes, audio cassettes and DVDs have been used by al-Qaeda and like-minded groups in the Middle East, Europe, and elsewhere to spread propaganda and condition teens and young adults for recruitment. Hamdi

Issac, who was one of the participants in the failed London bombing attacks on July 21, 2005 told Italian interrogators after he was arrested in Rome that he had been recruited by another would-be bomber, Said Ibrahim. According to Isaac,

> We met each other at a muscle-building class in Notting Hill and Muktar (Said Ibrahim) showed us some DVDs with images of the war in Iraq, especially women and children killed by American and British soldiers. During our meetings we analyzed the political situation and the fact that everywhere in the West Muslims are humiliated and that we must react.[1]

Video games, such as Umnah Defense I and Umnah Defense II are advertised and sold on the Internet. The description of the scenario for Umnah Defense I begins with the sentence, "It is the year 2114 and the Earth is finally united under the Banner of Islam." Some of these video games are made in U.S.A. There is also a lucrative international music scene that produces and distributes White supremacy songs advocating hate and violence against non-white Christians. While Islamic fundamentalists condemn as decadent Western popular culture, "radical Islamic groups have harnessed the influence of Hip Hop in American culture by producing their own [Hip Hop} bands" that try to indoctrinate young listeners.[2] According to Madeleine Gruen, "The most extreme militant Islamic Hip Hop is known as 'Terror Rap.' The video 'Dirty Kuffar' by the British Hip Hop group Soul Salah Crew features a masked 'Sheik Terra' dancing in front of the camera with the Quran in one hand and a gun in the other."[3] The lyrics leave no doubt that the message is in favor of terrorist violence, as the following verse attests:

---

[1] "Italy arrests another brother of London bomb suspect." Agence France Presse, July 31, 2005. Retrieved from Yahoo ! News, July 31, 2005, at http://news.yahoo.com/afp/20050731/wl-uk-afp/britainattacksitaly-050731153552&prin...

[2] Madeleine Gruen, "Innovative Recruitment and Indoctrination Tactics by Extremists: Video Games, Hip Hop, and the World Wide Web." In James Forest, ed. , *The Making of a Terrorist, Volume I* (Westport, CT: Praeger Publishers, 2005).

[3] Ibid.

Peace to Hamas and the Hizbollah
OBL [Ossama bin Laden] pulled me like a shiny star
Like the way we destroyed them two towers, ha-ha
The minister Tony Blair, there my dirty Kuffar
The one Mr. Bush, there my dirty Kuffar.
Throw them on the fire.

Finally, books—even when veiled as fiction—can serve as powerful propaganda tools and how-to-commit-terrorism guides. For example, using the pseudonym Andrew MacDonald, the founder of the neo-Nazi/White supremacy organization National Alliance, William Pierce, provided blue prints for big style terrorism in *The Turner Diaries* and Hunter. As he planned the Oklahoma City bombing of 1995, Timothy McVeigh followed the prescriptions in *The Turner Diaries*. A copy of *Hunter* was found in the possessions of McVeigh's accomplice, Terry Nichols. Headquartered in the United States, the National Alliance has followers in other countries as well.

While one needs to be aware of the importance of all kinds of media in the terrorist propaganda efforts, my focus here is nevertheless on the news media and the utility of the Internet.

The Triangles of Political Communication in the Terrorist Scheme

In liberal democracies and their mass societies, modern-day politics mostly comes down to mass-mediated communication, because personal encounters between citizens and elected and appointed government officials are the exception, not the rule. Thus, political communication occurs mostly within what I call the triangle of political communication in which the mass media, the public, and governmental decision-makers form the three corners. The media gate-keepers do not only control access to the news, but access to the general public and to government officials as well. Unless well funded and well connected, peaceful groups with extremist agendas rarely get access to the mainstream media. However, when extremists resort to political violence—terrorism in other words—, the media gates open for the "propaganda of the deed" and spread the terrorist messages to the general public and government officials.

Apart from working in the domestic setting, there is a global or international triangle of political communication that works along the lines of the domestic triangular links: Continents, countries, policies, movements, religions, and so on, that often get at best spotty international news coverage, will instantly receive a great deal of attention by the news media around the world, whenever terrorist stage a major act of political violence.

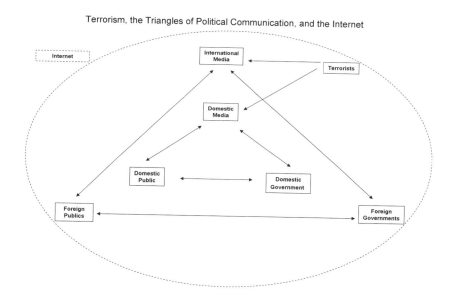

Terrorism, the Triangles of Political Communication, and the Internet

Finally, the Internet circumvents the gatekeepers of traditional media and allows groups and individuals—including terrorists and their targets, conventional media and governments, the general public and interest groups—to communicate with their neighbors and, more importantly, with people across the country and around the globe.

Terrorist Propaganda in the Changing Media Landscape

In addition to always utilizing the newest information and communication technologies, terrorists adapt their propaganda approaches to the changing media landscape as well. Al-Qaeda and bin Laden are an excellent example in this respect. During the 1990s, when western television and radio networks, wire services, and leading print outlets dominated the global media, bin Laden recognized that granting interviews to Western media was the surest means to get the attention of his enemies. Indeed, in the mid-1990s, bin Laden had an Arab student in the United Kingdom establish an office in London "as the media wing of al-Qaeda."[4] An equally important reason for using influential television networks for his publicity campaign was bin Laden's recognition that this sort of news showcased his extreme ideology for the benefit of followers and potential recruits. To this end, footage from bin Laden's TV interviews with Western reporters became an integral part of al-Qaeda propaganda used in Afghan training camps and in recruitment campaigns. Bin Laden's so-called *fatawa* or religious edicts that boiled down to a declaration of war against the United States, western crusaders, Israel and Zionists, were first publicized in the London-based newspaper Al Quds Al Arabia. But when Al-Jazeera emerged as major global television network at the outset of the war in Afghanistan against the Taliban and al-Qaeda, bin Laden and his associates sent audio or videotapes and granted interviews exclusively to this Arab news organization. When Al Arabiya emerged as another Arab television network and global player in the changing media landscape, al-Qaeda tried to exploit this network as well for its publicity needs.

Terrorists and their Media-Centered Objectives

Terrorists' ultimate objectives are political, even if promoted as religiously motivated. But terrorists know that publicity and propaganda are necessary means to their larger ends, such as national independence, regime change, the removal of foreigners from countries or regions, etc. Without making friends and foes aware of their existence, of their motivations, and their objectives, terrorists would not see a chance to further their political agenda.

Thus, when terrorists strike or threaten to commit violence, they have the following media-dependent objectives in mind:

- First, terrorists want the awareness of various audiences inside and outside their target societies and thereby condition their targets for intimidation.

---

[4] Rita Katz and Michael Kern, "Center of the Jihadist World." National Review Online, July 11, 2005. http://www.nationalreview.com , retrieved July 22, 2005.

- Second, terrorists want the recognition of their causes, they want people to ask, Why do they hate us? Why do they attack innocent civilians?

- Third, terrorists want the respectability and sympathy of those in whose interest they claim to act.

- Four, terrorists want a quasi-legitimate status and the same or similar media treatment that legitimate political actors receive.

In view of these objectives, one wonders whether and to what extent news coverage furthers one, several, or all of these terrorist imperatives.

The Awareness and Intimidation Goals

New York Times columnist Thomas Friedman has suggested that Osama bin Laden "is not a mere terrorist" but a "super-empowered" man with geopolitical aspirations who does not seek news coverage but wants to kill as many Americans as possible.[5] This idea—that in the age of catastrophic terrorism there is no longer the need for publicity on the part of terrorists—is shared by others who argue that the new "terrorism of expression" speaks for itself, and does not need to be explained, not even by claims of responsibility. I disagree with this assessment. Just think of al-Qaeda's media-savvy operations, which included an information and media arm and a video production team for propaganda purposes. Moreover, a training manual that was used in al-Qaeda's training camps in Afghanistan advised recruits to target "sentimental landmarks" such as the Statue of Liberty in New York, the Big Ben clock tower in London, and the Eiffel Tower in Paris, because their destruction would "generate intense publicity."[6]

In terms of getting the attention of friends and foes, the strikes of 9/11 in the United States, 3/11 in Spain, and 7/7 in the United Kingdom were more successful than any previous terrorist deed—including the brutal attack on Israeli athletes at the Munich Olympic Games in 1972 by "Black September" terrorists. In 1972, the

---

[5] Thomas L. Friedman, "No Mere Terrorist," *New York Times*, 24 March 2002, sect. 4, p. 15.

[6] Hamza Hendawi, 'Terror Manual Advises on Targets.' http://story.news.yahoo.com/news?tmpl=story&u+/ap/20.../afghan_spreading_terror_retrieved February 11, 2002.

Palestinian terrorists calculated correctly that they would get world-wide attention because they struck at a place where the international media had gathered to cover the premier sporting event. As for the attacks on the London's transit system, while certainly well planned in advance, the architects of the quadruple bombing picked a date that coincided with an important G-8 summit in Scotland. By striking at the outset of that meeting, the terrorists hijacked the news and swept the leaders of the eight most powerful countries off the television screens and front pages. Just take the *New York Times* the day after the London bombings as a typical example: The front page was mostly devoted to the 7/7 attack. The execution of the Egyptian ambassador to Iraq by a bunch of terrorists made page one as well, but the G-8 summit did not. What a publicity success for the perpetrators of terror! In the weeks thereafter, refueled by the failed follow-up attack in London, the terrorist threat continued to dominate the news as did counterterrorist measures in the U.K., U.S., and elsewhere. Moreover, in the United States there were alarming reports about expert warnings, how easily a number of identified sites could be attacked by terrorists. It is known that terrorists are well informed about a variety of targets, but is it necessary for the media to provide them with what adds up to laundry lists of vulnerable sites?

Closely tied to the terrorist goal of dominating (and even dictating) the content of breaking news is the desire to intimidate a targeted population, to spread fear, and undermine the declared values of the targeted political system by pushing a frightened society and government into overreaction. The propaganda of fear has proven to be quite successful. In the days and weeks after 9/11 public opinion polls revealed that many Americans were traumatized: they suffered from sleeplessness, felt depressed, and feared that they or their loved-ones could become the victims of future terrorism. While these feelings subsided, many people—especially in New York and Washington, as well as other places considered to be likely targets—retained a great deal of anxieties. Heavy news consumers were more plagued by fear of terrorism than those who did not follow the news very closely.[7]

[7] For example, see Andrew Kohut, "Washington 2002: Attitude Adjustment—The 9/11 Effect is Starting to Fade," *Columbia Journalism Review* no. 5 (September-October, 2002). Online at: http://www.cjr.org/issues/2002/5/wash-kohut.asp

This is precisely the reaction that terrorists desire. Certainly bin Laden and his associates aimed for such effects. Speaking about the impact of 9/11 on the American people, bin Laden remarked with obvious satisfaction, "There is America, full of fear from north to south, from west to east. Thank God for that."[8]

Given the magnitude of 9/11, the mere threat of new terrorism resulted in substantial news coverage and reawakened feelings of anxiety in the American public in the years following the attacks. It did not matter whether Osama bin Laden threatened Americans with new violence or whether administration officials in Washington raised the color-coded threat alerts, the effects were the same in every instance: the news media reported extensively, even excessively, and the public took notice. When the threat alerts were decreased, there was very little or no reporting.

Further, it does not require spectacular acts of deadly political violence to trigger massive news coverage that results in the attention that terrorists aim for. For example, consider the small group of self-proclaimed anarchists that dominated the news of a summit meeting of the 1999 World Trade Organization (WTO) in Seattle, Washington, after they used hammers, baseball bats, and spray paint to damage store fronts, and clashed with police. While the media all but ignored some 50,000 peaceful anti-globalization demonstrators and the summit proceedings, relatively minor acts of political violence took center stage in television and print news. Indeed, so carefully had the media-savvy anarchists prepared this stage media event that they referred reporters' requests for interviews to their own "publicist." After everything was said and done, the anarchist gang was utterly happy with the results of the media event they staged. Although chiding the "corporate media" for biased reporting, the anarchists recognized the value of nonstop media attention. "The WTO protests are a watershed," they proclaimed on one website and predicted that "after [what the media dubbed as] the Battle of Seattle, the anarchists will no longer be ignored."[9] If this seemed an overly optimistic assessment, it was not. The anarchists' publicity success in Seattle ignited a chain

---

[8] 'Text: Bin Laden statement.' http://www.guardian.co.uk./waronterror/story/0,1361,565069,00 html retrieved April 7, 2002.

[9] The statement was posted at http://www.chumba.com/_gospel.htm.

reaction, in that subsequent international meetings of the International Monetary Fund, the World Bank, and other international organizations attracted more (and a greater variety) of extremist groups and individuals, set on political violence for the sake of "selling" their propaganda via the media.

The Recognition Goal

For terrorists, winning the attention of the news media, the public, and government officials and intimidating their declared enemies is not enough. They typically want to publicize their political causes and depend on the mass media to explain and discuss their rationale for resorting to violence. This exercise in strategic communication or public diplomacy is designed to inform and educate both friends and foes about the motives for terrorist deeds. For this to happen the perpetrators of terrorism do not necessarily have to do the explaining themselves, the media do it for them.

On this count, too, bin Laden and his comrades in arms were quite successful. Before September 11, 2001 the American news media did not report a great deal about the growing anti-American sentiments among Arabs and Muslims in the Middle East and in other parts of the world. This changed after 9/11, in that the news media expanded their reporting from these regions. Instead of sticking to their typical episodic coverage of foreign news (e.g., events within the Israeli-Palestinian conflict), there was suddenly far more contextual reporting that provided viewers, listeners, and readers with a better understanding of the Middle East and its peoples.

Suddenly, there were many stories that pondered the question that President George W. Bush had posed shortly after the events of 9/11: Why do they hate us? The focus of this sort of reporting was not simply on the motives of the terrorists themselves, but, more importantly, on the many non-violent Arabs and Muslims who resented the United States as well. More than ever before, the American and western media carried stories on Islam, a religion most members of their audiences were not at all familiar with. One comprehensive content analysis of religious news in ten American daily newspapers, nine newsmagazines, and one wire service (the Associated Press) found that stories on Islam and Muslims dominated this coverage in the weeks following the events of 9/11. Indeed, 70 percent of the stories fully devoted to religion concerned Islam and Muslims, while the remaining 30 percent dealt with Christianity and Christians, multi-faith, Judaism and Jews, non-denominational, and Buddhism and Buddhists.[10]

As a result, people in the United States and the West became far more interested in (and knowledgeable of) the history of the Middle East and the tradition of Islam. Never before were so many people in North America and Europe interested in pertinent books and courses. This reaction in the West was not lost on bin Laden. In a videotaped conversation with associates, the al-Qaeda founder said:

> I heard someone on Islamic radio who owns a school in America say, "We don't have time to keep up with the demands of those who are asking about Islamic books to learn more about Islam." This event [9/11] made people think, which benefited Islam greatly.[11]

To be sure, frequent and contextual news coverage of countries and regions abroad is highly desirable. The problem with the described post 9/11 changes and improvements in the U.S. media was, of course, that they were the direct results of horrific acts of terrorism, and in an ironic way furthered the recognition goal of bin Laden and like-minded terrorists.

Or take the 7/7 bombings in London that resulted in an avalanche of reports on the sentiments and grievances of Muslims in the United Kingdom and elsewhere in Europe and on the role of the Iraq war in the recruitment of home-grown British subjects. The U.S. news media did carry stories on the radicalization of young Muslims in the European diaspora before 7/7, but this coverage paled in comparison to similar reporting in the wake of the successful and failed bombings on the London transit system. Once again, horrific acts of terrorism triggered news coverage that informed the public in the United

---

[10] "A Spiritual Awakening: Religion in the Media, Dec 2000-Nov. 2001." Study prepared by Douglas Gould & Co. for the Ford Foundation.

[11] The quote was taken from the translation of a videotape, presumably made in mid-November 2001 in Afghanistan. Available at http://www.washingtonpost.com/wp-srv/nation/specials/attacked/transcripts/binladentext_121301.html, retrieved April 7, 2002.

Kingdom and all over the globe about the most likely motives and jus-
tifications for this kind of political violence from the terrorists'
perspective.

The Respectability and Sympathy Goals

Osama Bin Laden and like-minded terrorists did not win the
respect of the American people by committing anti-American
terrorism on U.S. soil and abroad, nor did the Madrid and London
bombers endear themselves to the Spanish and British people. On the
contrary, for many Americans, Spaniards, and the British the architects and actual perpetrators of terrorist spectacular became the per-
sonification of evil with bin Laden seen as the villain-in-chief. This
reaction did not come as a surprise to bin Laden and his kind. After
all, when international terrorists strike abroad, they do not strive to be
loved by their target audiences; they want to be feared. But at the
same time, they hope for increased respectability and sympathy in
those people in certain societies on whose behalf they claim to act.
This is precisely what bin Laden, his closest aides, and the al-Qaeda
organization achieved in the aftermath of 9/11: He and his associates
won the respect and sympathy of many people in Arab and Muslim
countries and in the Western diaspora as reflected in transnational
public opinion surveys. In the spring of 2005, for example, the majority of Jordanians (60 percent) and Pakistanis (51 percent) had a lot or
some confidence in Osama bin Laden "to do the right thing in world
affairs," and this confidence was higher than two years earlier, when
55 percent of Jordanians and 45 percent of the Pakistani public had
such trust in the al-Qaeda leader. While the respect for bin Laden as
doing the right thing in world affairs declined during the same period
in Indonesia and Morocco to 35 percent and 26 percent respectively,
there was still significant support in both Indonesia (35 percent) and
Morocco (25 percent). In Turkey and Lebanon, the confidence in bin
Laden as a good figure on the stage of world politics was modest to
begin with in 2003 (15 percent in Turkey and 14 percent in Lebanon)

---

[12] Surveys were conducted for The Pew Global Attitudes Project of the Pew Research
Center for the People and the Press in 2003 and 2005. See, http://www.people-press.org,
retrieved August 2, 2005.

and declined by 2005 to 7 percent in Turkey and 2 percent in Lebanon. Still, although in hiding since the fall of 2001, nearly four years after 9/11 bin Laden had the respect of many million of admirers.[12]

The Quasi-Legitimate Status Goal

In April 2004, about five weeks after the train bombings in Madrid sent a shock wave through Western Europe, Osama bin Laden offered to halt terrorism in European countries that withdrew their military from Muslim lands. In an audio taped message that was first aired on the Arab television network Al Arabiya, bin Laden said, "The door to a truce is open for three months. The truce will begin when the last soldier leaves our countries."[13] Like all of his and his lieutenants' previous communications, this particular bin Laden message was prominently reported and commented on by the news media in the West. Within hours, high ranking officials in several western European countries went public with responses from their respective governments. Although all of these governments rejected the truce offer categorically, the immediate reaction to the uttering of the world's most notorious terrorist leader was a testament to bin Laden's quasi-legitimate status. In other words, high government officials of leading Western nations responded to bin Laden's much publicized communication as if he were a legitimate world leader. Government officials were probably prompted to respond immediate by the high degree of attention the media paid to bin Laden's tape, if only for the sake of assuring their respective publics that they were not giving in to terrorist demands. But as German TV commentator Elmar Thevessen noted:

> I think it would be better not to react to the tape in the way many governments did today. Of course, one [presumably the media] shouldn't keep quiet about it, but by talking about bin Laden's message all the time, we are upgrading him to a global player.[14]

If there were doubts that bin Laden himself longed for the status that is reserved for world-class leaders and statesmen, they were laid

---

[13] Richard Bernstein, "Tape, Probably Bin Laden's, Offers Truce to Europe," *New York Times*, April 16, 2004, p. 3.

[14] Ibid.

to rest when the al-Qaeda leader released a videotape five days before the 2004 U.S. presidential elections. Instead of wearing his familiar military attire, holding a weapon, and using threatening language, bin Laden was dressed in a softly flowing robe and spoke in the measured tone of a statesman. This change in style was not lost on experts who concluded that this particular speech was "carefully staged and worded to present him as a polished statesman and the voice of a broad movement, instead of a terrorism-obsessed religious fanatic."[15] While his seemingly new persona hardly attested to a change in bin Laden's attitude toward the United States, the West, and foes elsewhere, the news media nevertheless offered extraordinary air time and column inches to a "news" event that was staged by the al-Qaeda leader and his media-savvy staff. And again this media attention was not lost on political leaders. While the two major presidential candidates refused to comment on Laden's pre-election day message, sources in their respective camps span their takes on the al-Qaeda leader's rationale for addressing the American electorate.

In the summer of 2005, President George W. Bush responded to a videotaped message by al-Qaeda's Ayman al-Zawahri shortly after it was aired by Al Jazeera and reported by U.S. media organizations. The second in command in the al-Qaeda leadership, al-Zawahri threatened the United Kingdom and the United States with more terrorism. But the President would have been well advised to follow the example of Prime Minister Tony Blair who, this time around, refused to comment. Instead, the American President's widely reported response proved once again that when leading terrorists speak, the news media report, and even the most influential leaders listen—and respond.[16]

To be sure, bin Laden was not the first and last terrorist leader to use the news media to cultivate his status and the image of a quasi-legitimate political leader. Yassir Arafat exploited the media's obsession with terrorism to become an internationally recognized leader and eventually make the transition from terrorist to legitimate political leader in the eyes of many (although not everyone).

---

[15] Craig Whitlock, "From Bin Laden, Different Style, Same Message," *New York Times*, November 25, 2004, p. A20.

[16] Al-Zawahri's video message was aired and reported on July 4, 2005 and within hours President Bush responded during a meeting at his ranch at Crawford, Texas, with Colombian President Alvaro Uribe.

Wittingly or not, the news media bestow a certain status upon terrorist leaders. The mere practice of media representatives interviewing leading terrorists and treating them like legitimate political actors elevates the status of terrorists. For example, during the build-up phase to the first Persian Gulf War, Ted Koppel—of ABC-TV's "Nightline" program—interviewed Dr. George Habash of the Popular Front for the Liberation of Palestine (PFLP). Habash repeated and expanded on his threats of violence against Americans in case of military actions against Iraq and its occupation of Kuwait, and spoke about Arab grievances against the United States. Saudi Arabia's ambassador to the U.S. was a guest on the same program and topic.

More recently, Koppel devoted a full "Nightline" program to an interview with the Chechen "rebel leader" Shamil Basayev who claimed responsibility for two most deadly terrorist incidents in Russia: the take-over of a Moscow theater in the fall of 2002 and the Beslan school siege in September 2004 that resulted in the death of at least 330 persons, most of them children.[17] While the interview was conducted by a Russian reporter, Ted Koppel nevertheless provided a publicity stage to an unapologetic terrorist leader who used the opportunity to explain Chechen grievances against Russia. In this setting, the terrorist was treated like a legitimate political actor. While this did not justified a move by the Russian government to deny ABC News access to its Defense Ministry or other official sources, Russian officials were not the first to protest the glorification and legitimization of terrorists by offering them access to major media. Twenty years earlier, when appalled by American and western journalists' presence at a press conference held by the Lebanese hijackers of a TWA airliner who had killed an American passenger, then Secretary of State Alexander Haig warned that "when TV reporters interview kidnappers, it risks making international outlaws seem like responsible personalities. Television should avoid being used that way."[18] What Haig said, was right then and is right now. Of course, in liberal

---

[17] The Nightline program was aired on July 28, 2005. The Russian Foreign Ministry tried to convince ABC News not to broadcast the interview and protested against the program after it had been aired.

[18] Haig was quoted by Brigitte L. Nacos, *Terrorism and the Media* (New York: Columbia University Press, 1994), p. 67.

democracies these decisions must remain the domain of the media and not of governments.

All of this is not to say that the media are alone in unwittingly bestowing quasi- legitimate standing to terrorist leaders. Take the post-9/11 cross national surveys, commissioned by an organization in the United States, that asked respondents in several countries about their degree of confidence in world figures to do the right thing regarding world affairs. Bin Laden was included in the list that otherwise contained legitimate leaders, such as U.S. President Bush, British Prime Minister Blair, French President Chirac, United Nations Secretary General Annan, etc.[19]

Teaching Terror through Showcasing Violence in the Media

One consequence of the opportunity to showcase their "propaganda of the deed" on a global scale is undoubtedly that terrorists in different parts of the world learn about and embrace the most successful methods of mass-mediated terrorism. Thus, the 9/11 attacks by hijackers willing to die in order to kill innocent civilians highlighted the effectiveness (from the terrorist perspective) of suicide terrorism. Yes, there was suicide terrorism before—most of all perpetrated by the Tamil Tigers and Middle Eastern groups, such as Hizbollah, Hamas, and Islamic Jihad. But 9/11 provided a most attractive model and enhanced the attractiveness of this terrorist method. In the fall of 2002, when Chechen separatists seized a Moscow theater and threatened to kill themselves and hundreds of Russians, Anne Nivat—a reporter and expert on Chechnya—suggested that "there is definitely a 9/11 element in this new way of acting. They [the Chechen hostage holders] saw that it was really possible to have a huge impact by being ready to lose their lives."[20]

---

[19] "Views of a Changing World 2003," http://www.people-press.org/reports/ display.php3? ReportID=185 , retrieved August 2, 2005.

[20] Nivat is the author of a book titled *Chienne de Guerre: A Woman Reporter Behind the Lines of the War in Chechnya*. She was quoted in Serge Schmemann, "The Chechens' Holy War: How Global is it?" *New York Times*, 27 October 2002, Section 4, p. 3.

After terrorists in the Middle East beheaded a number of their kid-nap-victims in 2004, there were several copycat killings (or threats thereof) outside the Middle East. In Haiti, for example, the bodies of three headless policemen were found; they were victims of terrorists who explained their action as "Operation Baghdad"—a label that had no meaning in Haiti's civil strife, except for the cruel method of mur-der in Iraq.

And then there was the beheading of a Buddhist official in a village in Thailand which was described as an act of revenge for violence against Muslim rioters. After the shooting of Dutch filmmaker Theo van Gogh (his killer tried to cut his throat as well), self-proclaimed *jihadis* in the Netherlands threatened to decapitate other critics of Muslim extremists. All of these perpetrators had recognized the shock-value and media attractiveness of a news terrorist method.

Finding "significant evidence of a contagion effect wrought by [news] coverage," Gabriel Weimann and Conrad Winn observed:

The suggestiveness of mediated terrorism operates on the minds not merely of the maladjusted but also on the minds of the rela-tively normal. Sane people may see the terrorist model as a plausi-ble outlet for their sense of rational grievance. For suggestive normal people, mediated terrorism disseminates the precedence of violence and reinforces the sense of righteous anger.[21]

In essence, then, the uniquely public nature of mass-mediated ter-rorism allows individuals and groups worldwide to showcase and learn from what they deem effective terrorism tactics.

Terrorist Propaganda and the Contemporary Media

While the press has always been interested in reporting violence, the proliferation of television and radio channels and the emergence of mega-media organizations has resulted in greater competition and insatiable appetite for shocking, sensational infotainment that is believed to keep audiences captivated and boost ratings, circulation, and, most importantly, increase profits. Few, perhaps no other events

[21] Gabriel Weimann and Conrad Winn, *The Theater of Terror: Mass Media and International Terrorism* (New York: Longman, 1994), pp. 217, 277.

fulfill the requirements of gripping infotainment more than acts of terrorism and the plight of terrorist victims.

To be sure, the most fundamental function of the free press is its responsibility to fully inform the public. Thus, terrorism must be reported; the question is, how and how much to report on this sort of political violence.

Is it in the public interest to replay the shocking images of deadly attacks over and over again? Is it responsible journalism to show the victims of terrorism regardless of the horror of such images? Should the news media display visual images of victims regardless of his or her condition?

In the case of 9/11, the published images of people jumping to their death from highest floors of the World Trade Center's come to mind. Equally unsettling were the emotionally wrenching videotapes that depicted hostages begging for their lives in Iraq and Saudi Arabia. By displaying these sorts of images, the media provide terrorists with a platform for practicing their psychology of fear, addressed to the societies they terrorize. Even without publishing the visuals of actual beheadings, detailed textual accounts of the victim's predicament can cross the line of what is ethical. Consider, for example, the following description of an American civilian's decapitation by his terrorist kidnappers as published in a leading U.S. newspaper:

> As the insurgent speaks, the gray-bearded man identified as Mr. Armstrong appears to be sobbing, a white blindfold wrapped around his eyes. He is wearing an orange jumpsuit. The masked man then pulls a knife, grabs his head and begins slicing through the neck. The killer places the head atop the body before the video cuts to a shot of him holding up the head and a third, more grainy shot showed the body from a different angle.[22]

There is no need to provide such graphic details without violating the free media's responsibility to inform the public. Nor is there a need for critiquing the videotape scenes of hostage ordeals and executions as if they were parts of Hollywood movies. One such newspaper account first described a video released by a militant group in Iraq

[22] Neil MacFarquhar, "Acting on Threat, Saudi Group Kills Captive American." *New York Times*, 19 June 2004, p. 1.

that showed "insurgents slicing off the head of a man identified as Kenneth Bigley, the British engineer who was kidnapped here last month."[23] Then, mentioning an earlier video by the same group that showed the same hostage in distress, the reporter wrote:

> The captors have shown a cold cinematic flair. At the end of the 11-minute video, they showed a series of title cards in Arabic and English on a black screen in which they asked whether a British civilian was worth anything to Blair. The last screen read, "Do leaders really care about their people?"[24]

By referring to the "cold cinematic flair" of these terrorist productions, this description read more like the review of a well done motion picture than the report of a cold-blooded, real-life murder.

Domestic versus International Media

Not so long ago, the news media operated mostly within national borders, despite foreign correspondents, international wire services and broadcast networks that reached beyond the domestic spheres. The international media and communication nets of the past pale in comparison to today's global communication systems. Moreover, satellite television networks like Al Jazeera, Al Arabiya, or Al Manar challenge the international dominance of the American and western media. Add to this the reach of the Internet! In short, today's global communication and media networks overshadow the domain of national media. This point was driven home in the fall of 2002, when Chechen terrorists seized a theater crowded with Russians. As soon as the Chechens controlled the hostage situation, their comrades outside delivered to the Moscow bureau of Al Jazeera—not Russian TV—a pre-produced videotape on which the terrorists articulated their demands and their willingness to die for their cause. Within hours, the clip was aired by television networks around the world. It did not matter that the Russian government censored their own broadcast stations' reporting on the hostage situation, because interested Russians were able to get information on the video tape and the hostage drama

---

[23] Edward Wong, "Video Shows Beheading of Kidnapped British Engineer." *New York Times*, October 9, 2004, p. 6

[24] Ibid.

via CNN and other global TV networks. This case demonstrated the limits of domestic media censorship by governments—which is, of course, incompatible with the values of liberal democracies. But the incident illustrated also the limitations of sensible self-restraint on the part of domestic news media with respect to covering terrorism. Even if national media organizations would agree to follow a set of guidelines, this would not prevent the public from accessing foreign media without such self-imposed reporting limits.

But most of all, the Internet circumvents all other media—national and global—and allows terrorists to communicate with each other and with audiences around the world. Many contemporary terrorist groups have communication experts among their members and work with sophisticated computers and video recording and editing equipment; they also hire media experts. In October 2005, for example, the pan-Arab daily newspaper Asharq al-Awsat reported that al-Qaeda placed a "help wanted" ad on an Internet site that described job openings in the communication field. Al-Qaeda looked for a person to compile material on Iraq, including audio and video clips, and an editor with excellent English and Arabic grammar skills. Around the same time, the "Global Islamic Media Front," an al-Qaeda mouthpiece, inaugurated "The Voice of the Caliphate," a weekly television broadcast on the Internet. The first newscasts featured an anchor and propaganda reports from various countries and regions, among them Iraq, Afghanistan, Gaza and Sudan.

Today's terrorists perpetrate violence and, if they choose, report on their own deeds themselves. This was certainly practiced in Pakistan, Iraq, and Saudi Arabia, when terrorists beheaded their victims and posted video tapes of their murderous actions on Internet sites. Here the terrorists were the sources and the reporters of terrifying news. The traditional media was left to report on these news productions.

In sum, then, terrorists were always successful in exploiting the news media for their purposes and they always preferred to work around the professional media gatekeepers. But more recent developments, such as the proliferation of television channels , the growth of mega-media organizations, the reach of global television networks, and the emergence of the Internet, play into the hands of international terrorists—especially the world-wide network of al-Qaeda and like-minded groups.

Part IV:
Law and Terrorism

Chapter 11
Terrorism and Just War

Monique Canto-Sperber

The September 11 attacks started a new and critical age in international relations. Western countries, as well as moderate Muslim states, became aware that they could find themselves under a permanent threat of terrorist attacks. Our world has become a world of threat and restless violence. But, in the same time, it has become increasingly moral over the last four decades. The use of force is now more than ever under stringent moral constraints. Sovereign domination of states, conflicts of interest and competition for power which have long determined international relations, seem to have at least partially given way to cooperation between nations, concern for human rights, defense of liberty, and desire for justice.

One may wonder whether this moral evolution of our world is an illusion that hard times and international turmoil will rapidly dispel, or whether it is an irreversible movement. Whether temporary or definitive, these moral concerns made the question of morality of violence an unavoidable one. For more than 15 centuries many philosophers and theologians have exercised their minds over the issue of the legitimacy of the use of force, the limits imposed on violence and the definition of proper targets. They elaborated the very notion of just war, which can be traced back to Greek and Roman antiquity, and specifically to the 5th century AD and the time of Saint Augustine.

How do the criteria of just war deprive terrorism of any kind of moral justification? How can these very criteria be applied to the struggle against terrorism? Can the "war on terrorism" be a just war? As we wage war on terrorism, are we not running a crucial moral risk if we happen to lose sight of the moral limits which are to be imposed on any use of force? Such are the questions I will consider in this paper.

Just War in Today's World

Today's world is unstable and poses new threats. It is a world in which one very powerful country, the United States, coexists with powers such as China and India, which are undoubtedly destined to upset the balance of the world order; with countries of various development levels; with countries plunged in misery ; and, finally, with the prosperous and peaceful European Western democracies that seem to share the international organizations' respect for the *status quo*. It is a world in which the attacks of September 11 brought into light the reality of an Islamic terrorism fueled with hatred for the West. It is also a world that fears that the global proliferation of weapons of massive destruction (nuclear, chemical, biological) will be used to perpetrate future attacks. Lastly, it is a world that is gradually waking up to the fact that the way of life of the developed countries and global economic growth threaten irremediably to destroy the resources of the planet. Never has the feeling of vulnerability, especially in the Western camp, but also on a global scale, been so acutely felt.

Ethical judgments have never been entirely absent from the use of violence. Respect for moral principles, a concern for the good, willingness to avoid suffering, have historically been set up repeatedly against force and predatory interests. But in today's world faced with the threat of terrorism, with the significant power of one state also faced with the risk of conflicts between conquering powers and faced with a progressive deterioration of human life on Earth, is there any place for the idea of just use of violence?

The notion of just war traces back to antiquity. Thucydides testified to this, in the fifth century BC, in his recounting of the terrible war between Athens and Sparta. Reflections on the moral limits of the conduct of war continued to develop for several centuries within the Christian tradition. Closer to our time, Spanish theologian Vitoria at the beginning of the 16th century, philosopher Francisco Suarez a bit later on, and Hugo Grotius at the dawn of the Thirty Years' War that would tear Europe apart in the 17th century, have all formulated the foundations for an idea of just war that condemned the abuses of force and limited its exercise.

At the beginning of the 21st century we inherit a set of criteria related to the tradition of just war, with which we may assess the legitimacy of war. The tradition of just war, with roots deep in Christianity, has been liberating itself progressively from theological assumptions. Criteria of just war have now become a sort of moral givens. The just war theory presents itself as an autonomous political theory and brings us back to the fundamental issues of the ethics of violence. The theory of just war is indeed a very old one, but that does not imply that it is a dead one, as several recent books clearly demonstrate.[1]

The just war criteria are limiting criteria, i.e. they impose constraints and restrictions. Reflections on just war should not be limited to the Western world. They can be found, and in a very sophisticated manner, in the Muslim and Eastern traditions too. But below the apparent differences between these traditions in the very definition of war, the ideas of just war are all concerned with the same general question: how to limit violence and put constraints on its use. A just war is a war that can be justified and in which one can give reasons for the use of violence and for the means employed. In all traditions, these reasons are discriminating reasons, i.e. making distinctions, defining proper targets and adequate means, and imposing limits.

Criteria of a just war relate first of all to the reasons of war and constitute the *jus ad bellum*. They relate also to the conduct of war, *jus in bello*.

As to *jus ad bellum*, criteria of a just war define contraints posed on the agent of war (people who launch war have to represent legitimate authority), they pose limits on the reasons of war (the cause of war must be a just cause, and the set of intentions that lead to the war must be a righteous one while the reason of war must be a proportionate one). Finally, they relate to the modality of war (war has to be properly declared, it must involve a reasonable rate of success and it must be an ultimate recourse).

At the begininng of the 21st century, some of those criteria of *jus ad bellum* have lost their moral bearing (e.g., modern wars are no longer declared), others seem to be quite obscure (the righteousness of intentions, or the proportionnality of motives). But a few of those criteria

---

[1] Michael Walzer, *Just and Unjust Wars* (1977, 2000); Monique Canto-Sperber, *Le Bien, la guerre et la terreur*, Paris, Plon, 2005.

remain in place: mainly the criteria of a just cause (self-defense and a moral obligation to prevent significant evil from happening), of a real hope of success, of legitimate authority and the requirement to use war as an ultimate recourse.

As to *jus in bello*, two criteria are decisive: discrimination between combatants and non-combatants and proportionality of means. Those two criteria have kept all their force and play a crucial role for the moral assessment of terrorism.

New International Relations

Before entering the debate whether terrorism is a just war, one must ask the question of whether terrorism is a kind of war at all. War is traditionally characterized as a war between political authorities. September 11 revealed that the very matter of international relations had changed. This has been repeatedly emphasized.

A first obvious modification is that international relations are no longer conducted only between states since states are no longer the only actors on the international stage. International actors now include independent groups, organizations, associations and networks. Furthermore, international relations are no longer defined in terms of war and peace. They are no longer exclusively political, but also economic and cultural, owing to the internationalization of exchanges or life styles.

With the advent of terrorism, we met new actors with shifting identities and no direct territorial bases. One observes a proliferation of entities with which states must deal, willingly or not, peacefully or violently. One sees a multiplication of the sorts of relations in which states find themselves caught. In particular, considerations of comparability of forces and systems of alliances that were useful for predicting the outcome of conflicts between states lose their meaning when states stand up to terrorist networks or groups. In order to identify potential aggressors, a state must no longer merely look at those states more powerful than itself. Owing to links between certain states with terrorist organizations and the proliferation of weapons of mass destruction, the international stage became much more complex and risky. This new situation puts the states in a quandary once confronted with terrorism, mainly because the international strategy of states is conceived in terms of interaction between states and of measures of retaliation against aggressors that are located in well-defined zones. None of it is possible with terrorists groups.

There is an obvious asymmetry between al-Qaeda, an armed gang of a few thousand members, and the United States of America. States have the advantage in terms of power, but not in terms of their capacity to be identified. In fact, a network such as al-Qaeda is not, strictly speaking, a target with a territory against which it is possible to retaliate. If the international actor directly responsible for the September 11 attacks had been a state, its leading a terrorist attack against the United States would have been suicidal since, in exposing itself to reprisals, it would have signed its death warrant. It is clear that the numerous operations against al-Qaeda carried out by the United States have had little effect in dismantling the organization. The target has been almost impossible to locate.

The attack on Afghanistan by an American led coalition in December 2001 has certainly weakened al-Qaeda, whose capacities were thereby reduced. But since then al-Qaeda seems to have been changing form. Instead of organizing terrorist attacks, it inspired and subcontracted them. It has cut its ties with the Afghan territory and branched out into a multitude of local outposts. Three years after its deadly appearance on the world scene, it would seem to have accomplished a part of its mission. Americans will leave Saudi Arabia. They have lost their allies for fear of terrorist attacks (the attacks in Madrid in March 2004 were followed by a withdrawal of Spanish troops in Iraq). Thanks to the American intervention, Iraq itself has become the new arena for the *jihad*.

With the war in Iraq, concepts that served to analyze global interactions have shown themselves to be not only inappropriate but sometimes counter-productive. The war in Iraq was supposed to be part of the plan on fighting terrorism, but it has instead partly worsened it. The story went like this. There were no known links between the Iraqi state and al-Qaeda. The U.S. Administration feared that such links would develop. It took advantage of the fear that connections would be established between a rogue state, i.e. Iraq, suspected of possessing weapons of massive destruction, and terrorist groups. This was used to justify the war in Iraq. Interestingly, the links have indeed been created but in fact, they have been created as a very consequence of the operation that was meant to preclude them. The bloody terror-ist attacks in Iraq since Spring 2003 exhibit the existence of collusion between the former Sunni establishment and international terrorism. American intervention in Iraq helped to provide new arenas and new recruits for the groups that depend on al-Qaeda.

Another characteristic element of today's international scene is that the result of the competition between states and the new types of actors is an emergence of a new and violent mode of interaction put forward by terrorism: violence without warning, without any declared war goals. Different requirements are now at stake in international interactions. Identification of national vital interests capable of guiding rational behavior of the actors, including terrorist groups is an increasingly diffi-cult task. Unpredictability of strategies grows insofar as they no longer seem to be guided by a concern for preserving major interests. This also holds true for networks and, in some respect, for states too.

Afghanistan under the Taliban committed suicide by forming a close alliance with al-Qaeda, which had plans to attack the United States. When Saddam Hussein refused to take the American ultima-tum seriously, encouraging the belief that he could defend his own territory, he distorted the expectations of those who were going to attack him. On the other hand, al- Qaeda undermined the categories of traditional strategy. The organization widely broadcasted its objec-tives and "war goals"—to get Americans out of the Middle East and to establish Islamic fundamentalism from Morocco to Pakistan—while simultaneously declaring that it was going to destroy the Western world (ambition which cannot in any way be called a "war goal").

Faced with such enemies, ordinary solutions in international rela-tions are no longer available: neither peaceful exchanges, nor negotia-tion, nor even neutrality reached by compromise. The only option is a fight to death. Here we have an unprecedented condition on the world scene. With the emergence of terrorism, because of the power acquired by these new, non-state actors, states can no longer moderate international violence with the laws of reciprocity or dissuasion or retaliation. Interactions on the world stage are henceforth prone to limitlessness.

Faced with such a dark picture, we must conclude that the new set-ting of the international scene, in which states are confronted with non-state actors in asymmetrical relations, calls for an appropriate and effective strategy. The fact that we continue to speak of a "war on terrorism," when it is clear that the war is dependent on the existence of states and that the most insignificant terrorism today is transnational, underscores how inappropriate our current intellectual categories are. Such is the general framework in which the question of morality of terrorism must be assessed.

Terrorism and Just War

A characteristic feature of terrorism is the indiscriminate use of violence. This very feature confronts us with the threat of limitless violence. This absence of limits, in turn, requires that precepts of just war must play their discriminating role and implement restrictions and distinctions.

The contemporary world has seen a multiplication of terrorist attacks. The attack of September 11 allowed one to distinguish a certain number of common characteristics of such attacks.

Terrorism kills indiscriminately. While reflections on the legitimacy of violence attempted to define to what extent and under what circumstances violence may be employed, terrorist violence is characterized by the absence of discrimination. Limitlessness—once again a characteristic of terror—is to be found not only in the scale of terrorist violence but also in the forms it adopts: a rejection of moderation in the means employed, indifference to the identity of the persons harmed and indifference to the damages that are caused.

Let us first consider the lack of moderation in the means. Bombs manufactured by the comtemporary terrorists are filled with screws and nails. These bombs are equipped with mechanisms capable of ensuring that the explosion will be powerful. Their goal is to affect the greatest number of people and to mutilate them in the most atrocious way. The use of human bombs provides a radical method at the service of such an intent to do harm, because it transforms a person into a weapon capable of getting into the crowd in order to maximize destruction and death. The use of commercial airplanes by terrorists obeys the same wish to transform humans into weaponry capable of creating terror at the very heart of a given target. When the bombs become nuclear, terrorism will have achieved its ultimate capacity to strike without limits.

Limitlessness proper to terrorism is also manifest in the absence of discrimination among the people whom are targets of the strike. The fact that Muslim terrorists of al-Qaeda were convinced that in destroying the Twin Towers on Manhattan they would also kill children or Muslims did not stop them. Terrorism is indifferent to the identity of its victims. The fact that terrrorists annihilate themselves when killing is but one further degree of this indiscrimination.

Moreover, the distinction between civilians and combatants which lies at the center of moral reflections on the practice of war is systematically denied by terrorism. A major goal of terror is to wound civilians (including military personnel in civilian locations, e.g. the Pentagon). Among civilians, the victims are without qualities: men, women and children are all fair game, as are the infirm, the elderly and school children on their school buses. The targets of terror are arbitrarily chosen only because they happen to be in a given place at a given moment. In this regard, the attacks of September 11 removed the last taboo on a deliberate attack on civilians (followed by the hostage-taking of Beslan, attacks in Iraq and in Turkey). These attacks occurred outside any mutually recognized relationship of hostilities and were aimed at populations who thought they did not have any reason to worry.

Finally, terrorism strikes civilians in the very heart of social life, i.e. the city. Terrorist attacks take place in the middle of urban areas. This is not only done in order to produce as many victims as possible but also to destroy the way of life in which people can co-exist peacefully. Killing of civilians kills the city : it is an "urbacide," if I may coin such a term, that strikes at the city as almost a physical entity or, more specifically, as a cultural symbol.

One cannot overemphasize the fact that a systematic kilin of civilians beings us back to a cisutaion close to barbarian ways of behaving. Since antiquity philosophers and theologians have asked the question, "Whom should we protect from war ?" The use of violence and of retaliatory measures against civilians has been the object of repeated moral debate. The fate of the populations of besieged cities condemned to die of starvation or to be killed was discussed at length. Terrorism brings us to a world in which moral considerations of this kind, which have existed for almost two thousand years, disappears.

As to the criteria of *jus in bello*, the distinction between combatants and civilians and the requirement of proportionality in means, in which most of the idea of justice in a war is grounded, hold no moral bearing for terrorism. In that respect, terrorism denies any law of just war.

As to the criteria of *jus ad bellum*, debates are heated over this issue. Among the different criteria of just war I mentioned earlier, the criterion of just cause concentrates the moral bearing of the question. Is terrorism an act of war, morally excusable if operated for a just cause? It is beyond doubt that some terrorist acts could be inspired by a just cause, e.g. getting free from the oppressors in a dictatorship. The point with terrorism is that even if in some cases its causes might be just, the means it uses, which consist by definition of killing civilians, are intrinsicaly wrong. Righteousness of causes in the case of terrorism, if any, cannot be assessed independently from the way it fights its own causes. Terrorism, being by definition a killing of civilians, cannot be righteous, irrespective of the righteousness of its causes. Terrorism cannot be a just war given the means it uses. Even if terrorists are convinced that they perform a "moral" act, given the system of values in which they live, this "moral" act is indeed at the same time, without any doubt, a murder. And that very act is enough to assess the so-called morality of terrorism. The case of terrorism shows in a very striking manner how much the moral assessment of the use of violence cannot be dissociated from the moral assessment of the causes of war.

Neither Relativism nor Unilateralism

That is the reason why the debates over the morality of terrorism turn on the very understanding of morality. Sometimes morality looks like an empty shell to which any cause can lay claim. Everyone can claim to act on moral reasons. For instance, spreading one single faith all over the world cannot be seen as a moral act. But those kinds of "à la carte" definitions of morality can be sustained when confronted to what seem to be the very widely shared requirements of morality, that include the value of human life and a prohibition to kill innocent people. This widely shared morality is incarnated in basic human rights equally meaningful in all cultures, and above all in ones in which they are not enforced.

Morality does not consist of randomly labeling things and actions as "good" or "bad," nor are moral evaluations a projection of our preferences or interests. Rather, they consist in judging reality from the principle standpoint of accepted and justified values. The idea is that, when the world is viewed in the light of its values, we obtain better understanding of what the world is and what we should do about it. When described in moral terms, the world becomes clearer and more intelligible. This is why the moral condemnation of terrorism assumes a deep commitment to the value of human life and a rejection of relativism.

In excusing terrorism, a relativist proceeds as follows: since it is clear that there is no longer a universal morality in this world, given the plurality of civilizations, we must allow each culture to define its own norms and values. Some might consider that relativism is the best type of morality imaginable. I do not share this viewpoint. In my view, relativism is not a tenable position, either intellectually and morally. A belief in relativism results in moral passivity and laissez-faire policy. It denies the existence of values common to individuals and cultures.

A second danger is that of moral unilateralism, i.e. of an idea that there exists one particular morality, one particular definition of what is good that can be lawfully spread everywhere. But this will not work. It seems likely that a happy and voluntary universalization of the Western model is not going to happen. Attempts to impose this model by force will lead to an impasse. We must come up with a moral ideal, based on commom values, that is accessible to the whole world and thus eliminate this unilateralist option.

Given the state of the world as it is, an alternative in terms of moral conceptions does not consist of a laissez-faire relativism on the one hand, which abandons each country to its values—i.e., in most cases, to its horrors—and, on the other hand, an activism of goodness, most often conducted so as to impose the values of the superpower of the day. We must find something else in terms of morality.

We need a rational morality that proves capable of taking into account irrationality of some international actors, uncertainties of the world, irreversibility of our actions, and the weight of events and collective passions. We need an universal morality, composed of what is common to the moral values present in every culture. I would like to plead for an enriched and nuanced rationality.

In a world of standardizing market and mass societies where fear and awareness of threats tend to make us cast other cultures as enemies, morality ought increasingly to become the art of separation and of justified limits: it obliges us to distinguish between cases, to refuse imprecision, to admit that there are norms specific to human acts, to bear constantly in mind the distinction between explanation and justification. Without this rigorous work of discrimination, morality runs the risk of turning into triumphant relativism or a well-meaning preaching. The path is narrow, but it is impossible not to take it. This is the very idea at the heart of just war.

Just War Against Terrorism

Nevertheless, the phrase "World War IV has begun on terrorism," widely used at the time, is misleading. It is not war on terrorism, but a struggle against terrorists; and it cannot be so easily called a war.

Two rules have to be applied for this struggle to be just: keeping agreements between states and imposing limits on violence against terrorists.

I am not arguing for a return to a morality of international relations based exclusively on states. We must allow for new moral actors who, in the last fifty years, above and beyond the states, have emerged on the world stage (international organizations, NGOs, certain types of individuals). It is important to listen to these voices from which one hears more and more moral claims. But I would still argue that an association of states, founded on a modified practice of sovereignty, is the only way that ensures the preservation of liberty for peoples and for individuals, the only one that makes possible the exercise of collective responsibilities presently required by the world.

The second constraint is the limitation of violence. It is not true that all means can be used to fight terrorism. The moral predicament of struggle against terrorism is real too. This struggle is just and this gives a real legitimacy to the motives of self-defense and of the preservation of freedom, but it cannot be fought by any sort of means. Torture and retaliation against civilians are not among the available options; otherwise, the struggle against terrorism will run into a moral hazard, with wealthy and free societies turning barbaric, aping their enemies, denying the rules at the heart of their values. In those circumstances, it is more than ever necessary to moderate the use of violence, as the tradition of just war has been trying to achieve for many centuries.

Chapter 12

Terrorism as a Challenge for International Law

Stefan Oeter

Terrorism poses a very serious threat to international peace and security. It operates in international networks and threatens any country in the world. No person and no country—big or small, developed or undeveloped—can be isolated from its effects. As UN Secretary-General Kofi Annan expressed it: "Terrorism strikes at the very heart of everything the UN stands for. It represents a global threat to democracy, the rule of law, human rights and stability." Most world leaders share this assessment, as was made very clear in fall 2005 at the special summit of Heads of State and Government at New York to review the Millenium Development Goals and to focus UN reform.

Combating the threat of terrorism is a multi-faceted task that involves the police, the judiciary, the military, the financial sector, diplomacy and even civil society. In order to avoid any misunderstanding, one should add that any sensible political strategy against terrorism needs a two-pronged effort—a political effort intended to tackle the root causes of terrorist violence, the social problems, phenomena of injustice and repression that drive people into radicalisation and induce them to take recourse to forms of terrorist violence; and a decided effort by the police, the judiciary and the military to counter terrorist violence by policing the radicalized perpetrators of such boundless violence. The first effort—that of general politics to deal with root causes—is an issue of general international law, with its instruments to further peace, rule of law, human rights and economic and social development. The second effort—that of policing in a narrow sense—is the topic of a growing field of special instruments dedicated specifically to the combat against terrorism. The following paper will deal by and large with this narrow body of specific 'anti-terrorist' instruments developing in international law.

Unfortunately, the intellectual focus of this specialized sector of law has been a bit one-sided during the last few years. With the "war on terrorism," the military aspects have been very much in the forefront since 9/11. For a sustainable strategy, however, this risks setting the wrong priorities. Not that there are no situations where combating terrorism needs military operations. Failed or fragile states where terrorist movements can get a 'safe haven' are largely immune to classical forms of inter-state cooperation. This concerns only extraordinary situations, however, whereas the usual case of transfrontier counter-terrorist operations still will have to deal with traditional states enjoying more or less full control of their own territory. This state may have been violating international law by tolerating (or even assisting) terrorist activities. International law, however, prohibits brushing aside the state's sovereignty too easily and resorting immediately to military means. A sincere effort to push the responsible state into cooperation will be needed. Law should not be underestimated in this common type of situation as a resource in the struggle against terrorism.

Law fulfils a series of functions in the combat against terrorism. First, law defines what constitutes a crime of 'terrorism'—an act of illegal violence that should be prosecuted and punished as a criminal act. In defining the crime, law must distinguish terrorism from legitimate (and legally tolerated) forms of political violence, such as inter-state warfare, civil war, wars of national liberation. Law also structures the activities of the police apparatus and of the judicial system in combating terrorism. International law, in addition, must ensure the cooperation of states fighting against terrorism, must create a framework to coordinate police activities, must ensure that terrorists committing crimes against one state are also prosecuted in other states (and may be extradited). Law also sets limits to military strategies of fighting a "war on terrorism."[1]

In the following reflections, this paper deals with the role of international law in the combat against terrorism in four steps. First, it looks into the difficulties of finding a consensus on an agreed definition of what should be outlawed universally as constituting a crime of

---

[1] Compare Sionaidh Douglas-Scott, "The Rule of Law in the European Union—Putting the Security into the 'Area of Freedom, Security and Justice'", 29 *European Law Review* (2004), pp. 219 et seq.

'terrorism'. Second, it deals with terrorism as a fundamental challenge for law in general. In a third complex of reflections, it takes up the need of international cooperation in the combat against terrorism and the decisive obstacles inevitably met by all efforts to improve cooperation. Finally, it deals with the traps that might lead the 'war on terrorism' to a dead end, risking to lose the very essence of why we are fighting against terrorism.

The Struggle to Define Terrorism

The challenge of delimiting what kinds of violence constitute an internationalized crime of terrorism is a delicate task. Definitions are always laden with value judgments—and this is in particular true for all definitional attempts to clarify the legal nature of terrorism. There still does not exist a generally recognized formulation of what could be judged in general terms as being a terrorist activity. The international community for decades could not find a consensus on these issues, and had to limit itself to fragmented conventions on specific forms of terrorism.[2] For a long time, this seemed to offer a comfortable way out of the dilemma. One could single out the most heinous forms of terrorist violence and could build a consensus on the outrageous nature of such specific forms, thus circumventing the difficulties of finding a consensus on a general definition. The strategy had a price, however—the fragmented nature of the cluster of international agreements that resulted from this approach. Some of these conventions had overlapping scopes of application, whereas other forms of terrorist violence were covered by none of these agreements. The interlinkage between the various instruments was difficult to master and the implementation of these international agreements often was far from satisfactory, but due to the specialized nature of the issue it was difficult to organize the degree of concerted political pressure that would have been needed to improve the standards of implementation.

Only in recent years has a promising new effort in the direction of a comprehensive approach been made, and it seems that the community of states now might succeed in finding an agreement on the issue of

---

[2] Concerning the definitional problems see only Rosalyn Higgins, "The General International Law of Terrorism," in: Rosalyn Higgins / Maurice Flory (eds.), *Terrorism and International Law*, London and New York 1997, pp.13, 14 et seq.

terrorism in general. The definition contained in the UN Convention for the Suppression of the Financing of Terrorism of 1999[3] sets out the cornerstones of a definitional agreement on what characterises terrorism in general. The basic boundaries to be drawn to (legitimate) forms of warfare and armed resistance are set out in this convention as well as a sensible line how to deal with the issue of 'state terrorism'. Art. 2 para.1 of the Convention defines terrorist activities that are to be prevented as follows:

"Any person commits an offence within the meaning of this Convention if that person by any means, directly or indirectly, unlawfully and wilfully, provides or collects funds with the intention that they should be used or in the knowledge that they are to be used, in full or in part, in order to carry out

An act which constitutes an offence within the scope and as defined in one of the treaties listed in the annex; or

Any other act intended to cause death or serious bodily injury to a civilian, or any other person not taking an active part in the hostilities in a situation of armed conflict, when the purpose of such act, by its nature or context, is to intimidate a population, or to compel a government or an international organization to do or abstain from doing any act."

Proviso (a) refers to the inherited network of fragmented treaties on specific forms of terrorism, whereas proviso (b) attempts to set out a general definition of what might be regarded as 'terrorist' crimes that should never be encouraged, assisted or tolerated. The second part is the truly important innovation, since it is the first embodiment of a consensus on a 'nucleus' of a general definition of terrorism reached at all. Crucial are various segments of the definition. First, the two core elements of the definition, the "act intended to cause death or serious bodily injury to a civilian" and the required purpose, "to intimidate a population, or to compel a government or an international organization to do or to abstain from doing any act." Both core elements of the definition—the objective element of an assault on

---

[3] Published as an annex to UN-GA Res. 54/169 of 9 Dec. 1999; see also in detail the analysis of the text of the Convention by Roberto Lavalle, "The International Convention for the Suppression of the Financing of Terrorism," in 60 *Zeitschrift für ausländisches öffentliches Recht und Völkerrecht* (2000), pp.491-510.

the lives and/or physical integrity of civilians and the subjective element of political intimidation or compulsion—seem now to be beyond dispute.

This is not the case with the two other crucial elements in the 1999 definition. Difficulties arise first with the segment "or any other person not taking an active part in the hostilities in a situation of armed conflict," which excludes any kind of atrocities committed during armed conflicts against fighters of the other side from the concept of 'terrorism'. As justification for such a definitional exclusion one might point to the fact that atrocities committed by persons "taking an active part in the hostilities in a situation of armed conflict" by its nature constitute war crimes that lead to individual criminal liability under international law anyway, so that no new international legal instrument is required in that regard. Mixing up war crimes with terrorism might lead to conceptual confusion.

A second crucial element of the 1999 definition that is not without problems is the lack of any limitation towards private activities directed against a state, its organs or its civilian population—thus implicitly incorporating phenomena of so-called 'state terrorism'. This might to a certain degree contradict the first type of exclusion, since it means that 'crimes against humanity' committed by military and police officials as well as politicians outside situations of armed conflict may, under certain conditions, be covered by the definition of terrorism.[4] But one should take into consideration the different degree of legal codification of both legal concepts—the one, war crimes, being in detail dealt with in the Geneva Convention system that enshrines universal jurisdiction and a duty to prosecute such crimes, whereas the other, crimes of humanity, finding its basis only in customary law and general principles. Only recently some recognition has been granted to 'crimes of humanity' as concept of international criminal law by the statutes of the two ad hoc-Tribunals for Yugoslavia and Ruanda and by the Rome Statute founding the Permanent International Criminal Court. Accordingly, war crimes are a deeply

---

[4] Concerning the concept of 'Crimes against humanity' see only Matthew Lippman, "Crimes Against Humanity," in 17 *Boston College Third World Law Journal* (1997), pp.171-273, as well as Astrid Becker, *Der Tatbestand des Verbrechens gegen die Menschlichkeit*, Berlin 1996, and Cherif Bassiouni, *Crimes Against Humanity in International Criminal Law*, Dordrecht et al. 1992.

entrenched notion that goes along with a clear concept of universal criminal liability, whereas the legal consequences of 'crimes of humanity' are not that clear, beyond the fact that also such criminal acts fall under the jurisdiction of some ad hoc-Tribunals and the Permanent International Criminal Court.[5]

With the core elements of the definition, a kind of breakthrough was reached in 1999. Unfortunately the consensus enshrined in the Financing Convention could not be transferred to the discussions of the ad hoc-Committee of the UN-General Assembly working at the draft of a 'Comprehensive Convention on International Terrorism'. We will come in a later passage of the paper to the negotiations led in the UN on the draft of such a 'Comprehensive Convention'.

Terrorism as a Fundamental Challenge for Law

Before coming to the most recent attempts at coming to a consensus on issues of terrorism, we should risk a look to the more general issue of why terrorism constitutes a fundamental challenge to law in general and how legal orders react to this phenomenon. Terrorism, as was expressed so eloquently by UN Secretary General Kofi Annan in his remark cited in the introduction, must be perceived as a fundamental onslaught on basic values of humankind, as a frontal assault on human rights and the rule of law. Terrorist violence denies individuals their human dignity and physical integrity, since it sacrifices their lives to a greater political end. Whether the individuals becoming victims of terrorist violence are completely innocent, have any linkage to the authority against which terrorists declaredly fight, is completely irrelevant in the eyes of terrorists. What solely counts in their eyes is the purpose of intimidation or compulsion, the political end. Thus, terrorism is the extreme form of a political thinking that proceeds from the assumption that "political ends justify any means," a totalitarian thinking denying human dignity and human rights.

In a legal order based on the values of human rights, democracy and rule of law, the opposite should be self-evident: Certain means are never justifiable, they even threaten to delegitimize what would otherwise be legitimate political ends. The international fight against ter-

---

[5] See Antonio Cassese, *International Criminal Law*, Oxford 2003, pp. 125 et seq.

rorism is nourished by such a conceptual turn. This does not say that any use of violence denounced by state organs as being 'terrorist' should be judged as illegitimate and repressed. Unfortunately, the world knows a whole series of political regimes that tend to make use of terrorist means themselves. 'State terrorism' is a valid concept included implicitly in most current attempts at definition. Armed resistance against such 'terrorist' regimes may be a legitimate form of action, although the resistance movements should always take care not to fall into the trap of terrorist strategies themselves.[6]

States have not only a right to combat terrorist activities, but are legally obliged to do so, because otherwise they would not be capable to protect the rights (and the lives) of its citizens. The core arena of such (legally required) combat against terrorism still is the national level. States enact specific legislation against terrorist violence, maintain police forces and intelligence services that try to counter (and prevent) terrorist assaults and prosecutors and courts that will bring perpetrators of terrorist violence to trial. The policy mix that will develop in the combat against specific forms of terrorist violence threatening a particular society will show a huge degree of variation. Basic national legislation on terrorism already varies considerably, even in questions of fundamental definitions of what activities constitute terrorist crimes. Legislation varies even more concerning the powers and prerogatives which the legal order grants police forces and the judiciary. What may be done with suspects, under what conditions they may be held in police custody and then in pre-trial detention, the procedural rights before courts, the attribution of terrorist cases to specialized courts are issues that find rather different answers in various legal orders, although international instruments of human rights protection grant a certain common denominator in distinguishing between what means are allowed and what means are 'off limits' in the combat against terrorism.[7]

---

[6] See Antonio Cassese, "Terrorism is Also Disrupting Some Crucial Legal Categories of International Law," 12 *European Journal of International Law* (2001), p. 993, at pp. 998 et seq.; Judith G. Gardam, "A Role for Proportionality in the War on Terror," 74 *Nordic Journal of International Law* (2005), pp. 3 et seq.

[7] See Stefanie Schmahl, "Specific Methods of Prosecuting Terrorists in National Law, as well as various country reports," in: Christian Walter / Silja Völker / Volker Röben / Frank Schorkopf (Eds.), *Terrorism as a Challenge for National and International Law: Security versus Liberty*, Berlin / Heidelberg 2003.

After the events of 9/11, the majority of states in the world, even in Europe, tried to harden their anti-terrorist legislation. If this was done in the immediate aftermath of the dramatic events, legislative responses often tended to be too harsh and disproportionate. As was already mentioned, there exist severe limits to an increasing extension of executive powers—limits that reside in constitutional guarantees of fundamental rights and in international instruments of human rights protection. The issue of the Guantánamo detainees is one of the best known examples for these tendencies of over-reaction, and accordingly has attracted a lot of criticism. There are indications that Guantánamo constitutes only the tip of an iceberg, with even more problematic patterns of so-called 'remission' of suspect terrorists to torture-prone 'rogue-regimes' and with secret retention centers where torture is claimed to be routine procedure. U.S. federal courts in the meantime have started to correct at least some aspects of the over-extension of executive powers that tends to brush aside traditional civil rights and liberties, although this corrective move unfortunately seems to be limited to the issue of treatment of U.S. citizens. International organs such as the American Commission on Human Rights have voiced severe criticism towards U.S. measures obviously going beyond the established legal limits, however without much practical results in recent years.[8] But other states also deserve criticism in their efforts to counter terrorist violence. One should not fall victim to the temptation of blaming the United States for all the bad in the world. Other states have also overstepped legal boundaries, as demonstrated by the internment of suspect Islamist foreigners in the UK, a practice found by the House of Lords to be in contradiction of the European Convention on Human Rights.[9]

States such as the United Kingdom might hypothetically invoke the emergency clauses contained in international human rights treaties. Great Britain has tried to do so. It is difficult to argue, however, that the threat raised by terrorist activities really reaches the threshold of a whole-scale emergency. Even if one could argue such a case, the question of proportionality still remains—and proportionality tends to be overstepped soon if states attempt to show harsh reactions for symbol-

---

[8] See only Johan Steyn, "Guantanamo Bay: The Legal Black Hole," 54 *International and Comparative Law Quarterly* (2004), pp. 1 et seq.

[9] UKHL 56 (2004), 16.12.2004, concerning the Anti-Terrorism, Crime and Security Act 2001.

ical reasons. Internal security organs should remain aware that they have to protect the rule of law against an onslaught of lawless criminals, that they act on a different level which is not simply that of an armed organization fighting against an 'enemy' but that of a 'law enforcement' agency, the ultimate objective of which is the preservation of the rule of law. Sacrificing the rule of law in the process of combating terrorism would mean placing the state on the same level as terrorist bands—a confusion of roles that should never happen. Such a confusion of roles would blur the decisive difference between state organs and terrorist movements—a distinction reminiscent of the ancient Augustinian question what distinguishes a ruler and its officials from a band of armed robbers. The dignity of the state as an organization of government "from the people, by the people and for the people" is inseparably linked to the rule of law. The tragedy of the world order—and of international efforts to combat terrorism—is the fact that too many states forget this distinction and tend to make it very hard in practice to distinguish categorically both forms of institutionalized violence—state and organized crime.

International Cooperation in Combating Terrorism and its Obstacles

The temptation of state organs to forget about the basic foundations of legitimate authority—human rights and rule of law—creates enormous difficulties for all attempts at international cooperation. International cooperation, however, is desperately needed if the international community is to have a sincere chance to cope with international terrorism. Due to the international nature of modern terrorism, states are not capable of combating terrorist activities effectively without international cooperation. In order to cover up the structures of terrorist organizations, secure evidence for trials and arrest terrorist criminals, states need the assistance of other states. This is also true for the business of preventing terrorist activities and obtaining intelligence information. As long as states do not cooperate to the necessary degree, even purely national forms of terrorism are difficult to combat insofar as terrorists find 'safe havens'. A network of intelligence, police and judicial cooperation needs to be in place all over the world to prevent terrorists from finding a refuge and a place where they may create a support base.

Unfortunately, the decades of 'cold war' saw a standing practice of secret services instrumentalizing terrorist movements as a device used to harness the enemy, or even of engaging themselves directly in terrorist activities. As long as such practices persist—and in some parts of the world they still belong to political routine, as the recent 'Mehlis Report' on the assassination of the former Lebanese Prime Minister Hariri recently demonstrated—it is nearly impossible to unite states in the fight against all forms of terrorist violence. States themselves engaged in such forms of violence can never be trusted to cooperate sincerely, and will always be under suspicion of using international cooperation as a mere camouflage. But ideological sympathy for movements involved in terrorist activities might also hamper international cooperation, as demonstrated by the long-standing dispute on terrorism and wars of national liberation. As long as states shield liberation movements pursuing political objectives with which they have sympathies, irrespective whether these movements engage in terrorist violence or not, deep distrust and disappointment will remain. Other states suffering from their terrorist violence will doubt the sincerity of their motives and will not be ready to any form of cooperation.[10]

Only when there is complete agreement on condemning any kind of terrorist violence, whether exercised by states or by clandestine organizations, will states be ready to cooperate without reservation. Such agreement should be expressed in a definitional consensus delimiting comprehensively which forms of politically motivated violence constitute 'terrorist' violence, a consensus that could enable international cooperation to work efficiently. The existing network of anti-terrorist conventions still is deficient and needs to be developed further. Of particular importance in this regard is the project of a 'Comprehensive Convention on International Terrorism' that was tabled as a draft by India in 1996.[11] Such a 'Comprehensive Convention' could fill the lacunae left by the series of special multilateral conventions against specific forms of terrorist activities, like the hijacking of airplanes and ships, terrorist bombings and acts of nuclear terrorism. If such a convention could be concluded, this would give the quest for legal cooperation in cases of terrorist violence a new impulse.

Unfortunately, the negotiations on the project of the 'Comprehensive Convention' have gotten stuck. This is mainly due to the still sub-

---

[10] See Gilbert Guillaume, "Terrorism and International Law," 53 *International and Comparative Law Quarterly* (2004), pp. 537 et seq.

[11] See the annex to UN-Doc. A/C.6/51/6 of 11 Nov. 1996.

sisting dissent on how to define terrorist acts covered by the convention. Although the topic of definition (of terrorism) might sound largely academic, it is an issue of an extremely high practical importance. Without a consented definition, states will not be willing to promise whole-scale cooperation against all forms of terrorism. The core elements of a definition seem to be largely agreed, in the sense of the definition contained in the Financing Convention of 1999. Two stumbling blocks, however, still lie in the way—the issue whether a categorical distinction should be made between activities of national liberation movements and terrorist acts, and the debated question whether the activities of armed forces during an armed conflict (and the activities of armed forces of a state in the exercise of their official duties) should be exempted from the scope of the convention. The debate currently has to deal with two competing texts, reflecting the positions of two polarized groups in the Ad hoc-Committee of the General Assembly working on the issue. The one group, consisting mainly of the United States and the members of the European Union (so-called Western Group), insists on exempting the activities of armed forces during an armed conflict and the activities of the military forces of a state in the exercise of their official duties from the definition of terrorism. The other group, formed around the member states of the Organization of the Islamic Conference, but including also most African states, maintains that terrorism should not be confused with a people's legitimate struggle for self-determination, and as a result insists that the activities of movements of national liberation as parties to an armed conflict, including in situations of foreign occupation, should not be governed by the new convention. At the same time, this group is not prepared to exempt armed forces of states from the scope of the convention if such armed forces do not act under the standards of international humanitarian law, whereas the Western Group rejects any exemption of national liberation movements.

Both issues are linked in an unfortunate way. There would be good arguments for including both cases, but one might also present valid reasons supporting both quests for exemption. In particular the rationale behind exempting state armed forces is striking, since the regular military is covered already by other rules of international law, mainly humanitarian law. Mixing up both sets of standards would confuse the relationship between humanitarian law and anti-terrorism conventions. Bearing in mind the decided efforts of all U.S. administrations to shield its military against any form of individual criminal responsibility under international law, one cannot escape the conclusion that a draft convention including activities of the regular military would alienate the United States from any future convention. But the European states are also reluctant, in particular because they have in fresh memory the various attempts to instrumentalize international legal standards in political campaigns led against military operations like the Kosovo intervention in 1999.

Nonetheless, it is difficult to argue that the regular armed forces of states should be exempted while the activities of national liberation movements should be included categorically. Both issues have a close linkage. If the argument is valid that regular armed forces are covered anyway by international legal standards (of humanitarian law), the same argument would be valid for national liberation movements as far as they are covered by international humanitarian law as well. This opens the way for a sensible reinterpretation of both issues, at least in theory. As far as wars of national liberation are covered by the standards of international humanitarian law, there would not occur any legal lacunae, like there can be no gap for military operations of regular armed forces in situations of armed conflict. A reference to Art.1 para.4 of Additional Protocol I to the Geneva Conventions might illustrate the point. Art.1 para.4 AP I explicitly includes wars of national liberation in the scope of application of Additional Protocol I. The relevant liberation movement must only express its willingness to be bound by the Geneva Conventions with a declaration according to common Art.2 para.3 of the Geneva Conventions.

This might open a sensible path of compromise, by exempting—together with regular armed forces—the activities of national liberation movements bound to international humanitarian law (IHL) according to Art1 para.4 AP I, common Art.2 para.3 of the Geneva Conventions. Unfortunately, however, the inclusion of wars of national liberation in the scope of application of AP I as such is heatedly disputed.[12] In particular the US administration heavily contested

---

[12] See only Elizabeth Chadwick, *Self-Determination, Terrorism and the International Humanitarian Law of Armed Conflict*, The Hague et al. 1996, pp. 207 et seq., as well as Stefan Oeter, "Terrorism and „Wars of National Liberation" from a Law of War Perspective," in: 49 *Zeitschrift für ausländisches öffentliches Recht und Völkerrecht* (1989), p.445, at pp. 479 et seq.

this move and took the inclusion clause of Art.1 para.4 AP I as one of its main arguments to reject the ratification of Additional Protocol I. Accordingly, it will not be easy—if possible at all—to build a compromise upon this equation of wars of national liberation with traditional inter-state armed conflicts. As soon, however, as one accepts the inclusion of wars of national liberation in the scope of application of IHL—and there exist good arguments for such a step—one has a perfect line of compromise, because (under the condition of being bound to the standards of IHL in general) national liberation movements are obliged to distinguish between military objectives and civilian goods and persons, are obliged to direct military force only against military objectives and become criminally liable for war crimes if they indiscriminately target civilians—which by definition converts into a war crime any terrorist act. Such line of compromise seems sensible since it requires national liberation movements to subject themselves to the standards of Additional Protocol I and reminds them to spare the civilian population from the effects of hostilities as far as possible. Movements resorting to forms of terrorism accordingly would not be liable for 'terrorism' in a strict sense any more, but would be covered by the concept of 'war crimes' and thus could not evade individual criminal responsibility for their misdeeds.

If both sides resist any move towards normative consensus-building, and be it by striking a compromise on exempting both activities of armed forces and national liberation movements, they risk falling victim to the logic of the 'partisan', as the famous (but disputed) German author Carl Schmitt described it in one of his last writings.[13] There exists a temptation for the week side in 'asymmetrical warfare' to hide in the civilian population and to take civilians as a kind of hostage, to instrumentalize them as an asset in the combat against an overwhelming enemy. For regular armed forces operating against a hostile or at least skeptical population there exists a corresponding temptation—a temptation to assimilate their strategies to the patterns of its enemy by deliberately terrorizing the civilian population as well. In doing so—and overlooking this was the error of Carl Schmitt—the military falls victim to the logic of the 'partisan' and begins playing its game, by blurring the qualitative differences between a state and a

---

[13] See Carl Schmitt, *Theorie des Partisanen. Zwischenbemerkung zum Begriff des Politischen,* 1963, in particular at pp. 95-96.

band of political criminals. In the eyes of the target population, the regular military becomes thus indistinguishable from 'terrorist' criminals and loses all its dignity—the crucial mistake according to the strategic lessons of counter-insurgency. With other words: Such logic of the 'partisan' is a trap in which armed forces should never end up. Combating terrorism is not an armed conflict, a 'war' fought against an equal enemy, but is a combat against organized crime, although crime with a political motive. The state should always remember that it acts on a completely different normative level in such a struggle, often with bounded arms in order to preserve one's normative dignity, but at the same time with a completely different basis of legitimacy. It is not the difference in resources and the size of men in arms which constitutes the decisive difference, but it is the different role that gives a state a decisive comparative advantage. The tragedy of the struggle against terrorism is that states in the world too often forget about this difference, either because there is no real distinction or because the armed forces and the police are driven away by the logic of armed conflict against 'partisans'.

Traps Lying Ahead: The 'War on Terrorism'

The lesson should be clear: in essence, combating terrorism is mainly a task of police forces and of the judiciary, since terrorism is mainly a form of organized crime. Thus the overall importance of treaties of cooperation in police and judicial matters. The use of military force plays only a supplementary role. There exist situations where international cooperation reaches its limits, because either the relevant state is not willing to combat terrorist movements acting in its territory, or because the state is so weak and fragile that it simply cannot do anything against armed terrorist movements acting from its soil. Here military operations may be necessary under certain conditions. Such operations should be kept within the limits of international law, however, in particular as far as the principle of distinction is concerned.[14] Military force should only be exercised against military objectives—such as the base camp of a terrorist organization, its support bases or its deployment area. Civilians should be spared of the

---

[14] See Michael N. Schmitt, "Targeting and Humanitarian law: Current Issues," 34 *Israel Yearbook on Human Rights* (2004), pp. 59-104, at pp. 81-89.

effects of military force—a condition which is not easy to meet, since terrorist offenders tend to act covertly under the guise of being members of the civilian population. Nevertheless the state and its organs should do its best in order to limit its military operations to uses of force strictly limited against the terrorist organization as such.

Captured terrorists might constitute protected civilians in the sense of Art.4 para.1 of the IVth Geneva Convention, at least if they are captured in occupied territory, and should be treated according to the standards set out in detail in the IVth Geneva Convention. In certain cases, when captured while being members of the armed forces of a belligerent power, terrorists might even constitute prisoners of war. The judicial guarantees provided for both call for a regular court procedure if one of them should be brought to trail. Such court procedure might be operated by (regular) military courts if these courts would be competent for analogous crimes of armed forces members of the detaining power. But excluded are proceedings conducted by ad hoc-organs like the military commissions instituted by the Pentagon in the aftermath of 9/11 in combination with the Guantánamo precedent. Even for an observer sympathetic to U.S. policy and accustomed to the logic of military law, it is difficult to understand the rationale underlying such a strange construction. IHL, including Geneva Conventions III and IV, are flexible enough to integrate considerations of practical utility and to cope with all legitimate concerns of an occupying power that has to deal with phenomena of wide-spread terrorism. The Guantánamo arrangement, with its reliance on the ad hoc-category of 'illegal combatants', and the linked scheme of proceedings by military commissions, in comparison, grant only very small and marginal tactical short-term advantages in dealing with suspect terrorists while these precedents threaten to erode the overall edifice of IHL. This neglect for the civilizational progress embodied by the Geneva Conventions leads back to the underlying theme running through this paper—the question of how to preserve and use the difference in legitimacy that characterises a civilized state possessing all the attributes of rule of law and democracy. Forgetting the fundamental Augustinian question in the combat against terrorism would result in a Pyrrhic victory—the state might still be able to overwhelm its enemies by sheer force, but it might lose its spirit of being different, the very essence of why we want to defend the state's public order against terrorism.

Chapter 13

Recent Developments in Anti-Terrorism Law: How to Fill Normative Gaps

Sergio Marchisio

This chapter addresses a very broad topic, namely on-going developments in anti-terrorism law at large. Therefore, I will limit myself to underlining some features which, in my opinion, characterize these developments. As a European lawyer, I will evidently stress developments mainly of interest to European legal systems. I do not claim to make comments of universal scope.

Permit me to make two preliminary points. First, I would like to recall, quoting from Latin wisdom, that law more often than not follows reality (*ubi societas ibi ius*). Second, I fully share the view that terrorism is a mutating and global phenomenon. Faced with the global character of terrorism, we lack a global system of law to deal with it. The world is still divided into more than one hundred and ninety legal systems. Law is fragmented and presents many gaps, exploited by terrorists to realize their objectives. On the one hand, we have to rely on international law, including its regional expressions. On the other hand, we have to rely on national law. I will not cover European law, which is addressed elsewhere in this volume.

International Anti-Terrorism Law

Regarding international law, in recent decades various international obligations have been imposed upon states to make them prevent, detect, prosecute and punish terrorist offenses. Apart from the treaties already in force, such as the United Nations Conventions of 1973 (crimes against internationally protected persons), 1979 (on hostage taking), 1997 (on the suppression of terrorist bombing), 1999 (on the financing of terrorism) and the Conventions on offenses against civil aviation (Tokyo 1963, The Hague 1970, Montreal 1971 and 1988) and maritime navigation (Rome 1988), a new Convention for the Suppression of Acts of Nuclear Terrorism was opened to signature in New York on April 13, 2005. Moreover, various regional conventions on terrorism are already in force at European, African and other levels. These international treaties provide the legal framework for the suppression of terrorist acts and the pursuit of perpetrators of terrorism, and set out ways to limit illicit access to the tools of terrorism.

Since September 11, 2001, state commitment to these treaties has increased dramatically. According to the Secretary General of the United Nations, ratification of the key anti-terrorism conventions has risen by 15 per cent since 2001. Fourteen countries have now ratified all the core treaties, and the 1999 Convention on the Suppression of the Financing of Terrorism has entered into force in record time.

At the same time, since September 11 terrorism has been constantly on the Security Council's agenda, and this has led to the adoption of binding decisions aimed both at limiting the space in which terrorists act and minimizing their ability to garner support. Its achievements since then range from the broad—such as resolution 1373 of 2001, which obliges states to criminalize the provision of funds to terrorists, freeze the financial assets of people who commit terrorist acts and prohibit the provision of services to those who participate in terrorism—to the specific—such as Resolution 1390 of January 2002 which extended and strengthened sanctions against Osama bin Laden that the Council had imposed in 1999.

In these resolutions, the Security Council recalled the principle of general international law under which states are obliged to refrain from organizing, financing, encouraging, providing training for or otherwise supporting terrorist activities and to take appropriate measures to ensure that their territories are not used for such activities.

More recently, the World Summit outcome, adopted by heads of state and government gathered at the United Nations from September 14-16, 2005, summarized the general principles applicable in the fight against terrorism. One is the condemnation of terrorism in all its forms and manifestations, committed by whomever, wherever and for whatever purposes, as it constitutes one of the most serious threats to international peace and security. Another is the necessity that international cooperation to fight terrorism be conducted in conformity with international law, including the Charter of the United Nations, relevant international conventions and protocols, in particular human rights law, refugee law and international humanitarian law. Finally, the summit stressed the importance of assisting victims of terrorism and of providing them and their families with support in coping with their loss and grief. International law has indeed established a clear set of obligations incumbent on all states to prevent, detect, prosecute and punish terrorist offenses and to ensure that they are punishable by penalties which take into account their grave nature.

Therefore, states should take necessary measures to ensure that acts of terrorism are defined as offenses under national law and are punishable by effective, proportionate and dissuasive criminal penalties. They should also take necessary measures to ensure that physical persons who are perpetrators, instigators or accessories in acts of terrorism can be held liable under criminal law.

Domestic Emergency Legislation

Within this international legal framework, states have adopted domestic legislation, including emergency provisions, which address issues ranging from the introduction and punishment of new terrorist offenses and the financing of terrorism to immigration laws.

Legislators have tried to understand the real scope of the threat, in order to develop proportional responses through adjustment of legislation or other instruments in their counter-terrorist toolbox. Some states have argued that existing legal provisions are adequate in dealing with terrorism and thus have refrained from invoking emergency legislation; other states have argued, on the contrary, that the effectiveness of national responses without such legislation is gravely undermined as a result.

The UK Anti-Terrorism Crime and Security Act (ATCSA) of 2001 allows the Secretary of State to order indefinite detention without charge on suspicion of terrorism. Detainees are not given access to the evidence against them on the grounds that to do so would threaten national security. To pass the Act, the UK had to withdraw from part of the European Convention on Human Rights (ECHR), through a special derogation order. In fact, the Convention itself provides for the right to derogate under two conditions: in times of war or public emergency threatening the life of the nation, but only to the extent strictly required by the exigencies of the situation. Any measures taken must not be inconsistent with the contracting party's obligations under international law. In the *Belmarsh* case of 2004, the House of Lords concluded that the UK Government had not acted fully within the constraints of the derogation right. While they did not dispute that the public emergency criterion was fulfilled, they ruled that because the Act only applied to immigrants its was not consistent with the second of the two requirements, i.e. it was not proportionate to the situation and it was discriminatory. This is an example of how national legal systems can be placed under stress by anti-terrorist legislation. In fact, terrorism is a continuously changing phenomenon and despite the preparedness of many states, terrorists often go unnoticed. The London bombings show the asymmetric threat of terrorism, which is likely to be enduring in nature and, potentially, deeply divisive within our democratic societies.

New Emerging Trends

If we look more carefully at recent trends in international treaties and national legislation, it seems that the main purpose of anti-terrorism law is now to strengthen efforts to prevent terrorism. Accordingly, states try to cover the main *lacunae*, addressing important and controversial issues and introducing new criminal offenses, particularly sanctioning certain actions which, though not terrorist acts *per se*, may lead to the commission of terrorist offenses.

A new trend in this direction is emerging both at the regional and universal level. I would like to mention in this respect the new Convention of the Council of Europe on the prevention of terrorism opened to signature on 16 May 2005 in Warsaw, and Resolution 1624 (2005), adopted by the Security Council on 14 September 2005. In fact, they are based on the same rationale.

We begin with the Council of Europe. This Organization concluded in 2003 that a legal instrument dealing with the prevention of terrorism and covering existing *lacunae* in international law, would bring added value to its actions. In particular, it appeared that a majority of member states did not recognise the "*apologie du terrorisme*" and "incitement to terrorism" as criminal offenses in their national legislation.

Accordingly, a new Convention was negotiated with the purpose of strengthening the efforts of parties in preventing terrorism with its negative effects on the full enjoyment of human rights and most particularly the right to life. The convention, which was finalized in Warsaw in May 2005, purports to achieve this objective on the one hand by establishing as criminal offenses certain acts that may lead to the commission of terrorist offences, and on the other by reinforcing cooperation on prevention both internally and internationally. It does this by supplementing and modifying existing extradition and mutual assistance arrangements and by providing for spontaneous information, together with obligations relating to law enforcement, such as the duty to investigate, obligations relating to sanctions and measures, the liability of legal entities in addition to that of individuals, and the obligation to prosecute where extradition is refused.

The UN Security Council moved in the same direction by adopting on September 14 2005 Resolution 1624 (2005), which clearly confirms that a new generation of legal texts is integrating previously existing international instruments dealing with counter-terrorism.

In fact, this Resolution makes express reference to incitement of terrorist acts and attempts at the justification or glorification (*apologie*) of terrorist acts which may incite further terrorist acts, condemning such behavior. It also states that incitement of terrorist acts motivated by extremism and intolerance poses a serious and growing danger to the enjoyment of human rights, threatens the social and economic development of all states, undermines global stability and prosperity, and must be addressed urgently and proactively by the United Nations and all states. Furthermore, it emphasizes the necessity to take all necessary and appropriate measures in accordance with international law at the national and international level to protect the right to life.

Accordingly, the Security Council requested that all states adopt measures to: (a) prohibit by law incitement to commit a terrorist act; (b) prevent such conduct; (c) deny safe haven to any persons with respect to whom there is credible and relevant information giving serious reasons for considering that they have been guilty of such conduct; (e) cooperate to strengthen the security of their international borders, including by combating fraudulent travel documents and by enhancing terrorist screening and passenger security procedures with a view to preventing those guilty of the forbidden conduct from entering their territory.

In other words, anti-terrorist law must counter incitement of terrorist acts motivated by extremism and intolerance and prevent the subversion of educational, cultural, and religious institutions by terrorists and their supporters.

In sum, both the Council of Europe's Convention and the Security Council's Resolution refer to new criminalization provisions to be provided for in national anti-terrorism legislation.

New Criminal Offenses: Public Provocation

In the first place, these provisions establish criminal offenses concerning three categories of behaviour, namely *"public provocation to commit terrorist offenses," "recruitment for terrorism"* and *"training for terrorism,"* coupled with a series of accessory crimes. These offenses are considered terrorist offenses of a serious nature related to terrorist offenses as they could lead to the commission of terrorist acts. However, they do not require that a terrorist offense within the scope and as defined in one of the international treaties against terrorism be committed. Second, these offenses must be committed unlawfully and intentionally.

I would like to add a few words about public provocation. Public provocation to commit a terrorist offense includes the instigation of ethnic and religious tensions which may provide a basis for terrorism; the dissemination of "hate speech" and the promotion of ideologies favorable to terrorism. It implies the distribution, or otherwise making available, of a message to the public, with intent to incite the commission of a terrorist offense, where such conduct, whether or not directly advocating terrorist offenses, causes a danger that one or more such offences may be committed.

It is evident, to my mind, that when we talk about distribution, this term refers to the active dissemination of a message advocating terrorism and making it available in a way that is easily accessible to the public, for instance, by placing it on the internet or by creating or compiling hyperlinks in order to facilitate access to it.

It is been discussed whether this offense is consistent with the freedom of expression, one of the essential foundations of a democratic society, which applies not only to ideas and information that are favorably received or regarded as inoffensive but also to those that "offend, shock or disturb." I do not want to deny that the question where the boundary lies between indirect incitement to commit terrorist offences and the legitimate voicing of criticism is a difficult one. We are just on the borderline. However, I will note that, in contrast to certain fundamental rights which admit no restrictions, interference with freedom of expression may be allowed in highly specific circumstances. For instance, the ECHR lays down the conditions under which restrictions on the exercise of freedom of expression are admissible,[1] while it provides for possible derogations in time of emergency.[2] The European Court has already held that certain restrictions on messages that might constitute an indirect incitement to violent terrorist offenses are in keeping with the Convention.

As far as recruitment of possible future terrorists is concerned, this crime is to be understood as solicitation to carry out terrorist offences whether individually or collectively, and whether directly committing, participating in or contributing to the commission of such offenses. For the crime to be committed, it is necessary that the recruiter successfully approach the addressee. It is known that active recruitment occurs across Europe principally in certain radical environments, such as prisons, mainly in France and Italy, and in cyberspace used as a tool for disseminating terrorist ideology.

Another key development regards criminalization of training for terrorism, namely the supplying of know-how for the purpose of carrying out or contributing to the commission of a terrorist offense. This means providing instruction in methods or techniques that are suitable for terrorist purposes, including the making or use of explosives, firearms and noxious or hazardous substances. For such conduct to be criminally liable, it is necessary that the trainer knows that the skills provided are intended to be used in the commission of or to contribute to committing a terrorist offense.

---

[1] See Article 10, para. 2.
[2] See Article 15.

Furthermore, we must consider ancillary offenses related to attempts at or complicity in the commission of the other crimes, such as participation as an accomplice in the commission of any crimes related to terrorism. Liability for such complicity arises where the person who commits a crime is aided by another person who also intends that the crime be committed.

A further point which should be stressed within recent trends in anti-terrorism law is the recognition of the liability of legal entities, in line with the United Nations Convention on Transnational Organized Crime, opened to signature in Palermo in December 2000. This is intended to impose liability on corporations, associations and similar legal persons for the criminal actions undertaken to the benefit of that legal person. Liability may be criminal, civil or administrative, each state having flexibility to choose to provide for any or all of these forms of liability, in accordance with its legal principles. In any case, the sanction, whether criminal or not, should be effective, proportionate and dissuasive and should include monetary sanctions.

Investment in Intelligence

Another field registering new developments in anti-terrorist law concerns the new preventive measures which call on states to support each other through exchange of information, best practice, training and formation of joint teams for analysis and investigation. It is commonly understood that investment in intelligence is the first-line of defence against terrorism. Towards this end there is further scope for states to improve intelligence-gathering, analysis and intelligence-sharing.

Under the terms of this cooperation, states are committed to investigate information provided to them that a person who has committed or who is alleged to have committed a terrorist crime may be present in their territories. Of course, it is up to national legislation to define the conditions that the information must have to satisfy their terms of reliability in the context of legal proceedings or for the purposes of law enforcement. It is also up to national legislation to determine which measures the state in whose territory the offender or alleged offender is present can take to guarantee that person's presence for the purposes of prosecution or extradition.

Judicial Cooperation

Concerning judicial cooperation, recent trends are illustrated by the introduction of the European arrest warrant, which came into effect in 2004 and noticeably streamlined traditional extradition procedures. It is known that the European warrant procedure has recently been applied between Italy and the United Kingdom for the surrender of one of the alleged offenders in planning new terrorist activities in London (case of *Hamdi Isaac*). I would like to emphasize the most positive aspect of this procedure. According to the traditional extradition system, the Italian judicial authority (*Corte d'appello*), which would have been asked to rule on the legality of the surrender, could have postponed the British request arguing the priority of Italian jurisdiction over the crime of conspiracy for international terrorism committed by the requested person under Italian legislation.

I must also mention that, more generally, the new treaties on international judicial cooperation amend or modify existing extradition treaties in order to take into account the exigencies of the fight against terrorism. I am thinking of the Protocol amending the European Convention on the Suppression of Terrorism, the Second Additional Protocol to the European Convention on Mutual Assistance in Criminal Matters, the United Nations Convention against Transnational Organized Crime and the Council of Europe Warsaw Convention. Where extradition and mutual assistance are concerned, these treaties modify previous extradition treaties making the offenses set forth by them extraditable, and imposing on contracting parties an obligation to provide mutual legal assistance respecting them.

Once again, it is true that safeguards must be provided with regard to extradition and mutual legal assistance which make clear that these conventions cannot derogate from important traditional grounds to refuse cooperation under applicable treaties and laws as for example, refusal of extradition where the person will be subjected to torture or to inhuman or degrading treatment or punishment, or to the death penalty, or refusal of either extradition or mutual legal assistance where the person will be prosecuted for impermissible purposes. Where the person is not extradited for these or other reasons, the state in which he or she is found has the obligation to submit the case for domestic prosecution.

Of course, the exclusion of the political exception clause also aims at facilitating international cooperation. In fact, law must exclude any justification of terrorist offenses, while recalling that all measures taken in the fight against terrorism must respect the rule of law and democratic values, human rights and fundamental freedoms as well as other provisions of international law, including, where applicable, international humanitarian law.

The exclusion of the political exception clause is recognized by several treaties. It aims at facilitating international cooperation by excluding the political character of the offences for the purposes of extradition or mutual legal assistance. Accordingly, a request for extradition or for mutual legal assistance based on such an offense may not be refused on the sole grounds that it concerns a political offense or an offense connected with a political offense or an offense inspired by political motives. Of course, this opens the way for the application of reservations. The application of the principle *aut dedere aut judicare* must be balanced with a degree of flexibility which reflects the necessity for full co-operation between concerned parties for the successful prosecution of such crimes.

Terrorism and Human Rights

Another prominent feature is that anti-terrorist law is beginning to recognize in a more complete way the relationship between terrorism and basic human rights. There is a growing focus on the rights to life and security. The right to life is the supreme right of the human being. It is basic to all human rights and without it all other rights are meaningless.

In this respect there are two growing concerns: some lawyers stress that there has been, until now, a greater emphasis on national security rather than on individual security as a human right, and that it is the duty of the State to protect human life against terrorist violence by making effective provisions in criminal law to deter the commission of acts of terrorism, and the establishment of law enforcement machinery for the prevention, suppression, investigation and penalisation of acts of terrorism. They mention the ICCPR, which states that everyone has the right to liberty and security of person,[3] while requiring, at

---

[3] Article 9(1).

the same time, the prohibition of incitement to hostility or violence on the basis of national, racial or religious hatred.[4]

In the same vein, we may note that recent international and national instruments emphasize that the human rights that must be respected are not only the rights of those accused or convicted of terrorist offences, but also the rights of the victims, or potential victims of those offences. In this perspective, a number of provisions regarding the protection, compensation and support of victims of terrorism are consistent with recent developments in international law, reflected, for example, in the European Convention on Compensation of Victims of Violent Crimes, the Council of Europe Guidelines on Human Rights and the Fight against Terrorism and the additional Guidelines on the Protection of Victims of Terrorism, the New Warsaw European Convention for the Prevention of Terrorism and several United Nations Security Council resolutions, including Resolutions 1566 of 8 October 2004 and 1642 of September 14, 2005.

The protection afforded to victims might also include many other aspects, such as emergency and long-term assistance, psychological support, effective access to the law and the courts (in particular access to criminal procedures), access to information and the protection of victims' private and family lives, dignity and security, particularly when they cooperate with the courts.[5]

Yet, another issue of major concern regards the new emerging legislation and practice on asylum-seekers, including expulsions and removal of the immigration risk offshore. The case of expulsion of those suspected of terrorism to their countries of origin, assurances that their human rights would be respected notwithstanding, could pose risks to the personal safety and lives of the persons expelled.

There is in fact a tendency in the national legislation of some countries at least, to increase the number of aliens who may be removed. This is the case under new Italian legislation passed in July 2005 (Law n. 144 on Urgent Measures to Counter International Terrorism), according to which the Minister of the Interior can expel an alien in derogation to the normal procedures provided for by immigration

[4] Article 20.
[5] See Italian Law n. 206 of August 3, 2004.

laws, if there is reason to believe that their permanence within the Italian territory might help support terrorist activity.

In the end, we can pose the question whether an effective fight against terrorism which fully respects human rights is possible. It depends, of course, on what we mean by "fully respects." There is no doubt that a certain degree of restriction is inevitable, not only for the rights of suspect terrorists but of everyone. Now, it is my conviction that certain rights may not be derogated from under any circumstances. They include the right to life, the freedom of thought, conscience and religion, freedom from torture or cruel, inhuman or degrading treatment, the principle of precision and non retroactivity of criminal law except where a later law imposes a higher penalty.

From this point of view, I cannot accept the suppression of the right of terrorist suspects to an open trial, detention without criminal charge, and the doctrine of the preemptive strike or even the use of targeted assassinations of terrorist subjects.

As regards other rights, a derogation must be permitted in the special circumstances defined in international human rights law. It must be of exceptional character and legally weighted, and any such measures must be strictly limited in time and substance by the exigencies of the situation. Finally, they must be subject to regular judicial review.

Since many legal democratic systems are under pressure, it should be ensured that the balance is constantly readjusted as circumstances change, in accordance with law.

Defining Terrorism

Before concluding, I would like to add just a few words about a comprehensive convention on international terrorism which would define it and declare it a crime against humanity. I firmly believe that such a Convention can help fill normative gaps at the national and international level, occasioned in part by the less than comprehensive ratification of the separate, existing treaties. Judges have often thrown out terrorist charges, finding insufficient evidence to link suspects with nebulous Islamic militant networks, and thus sentencing those suspects to lesser offenses such as forging documents. In early 2005, a judge in Milan set off a storm of controversy by ruling that some

Islamic militant activists were not terrorists but supporters of insurgents in Iraq and for this reason could not be found guilty of the crime of international terrorism provided for by Article 270 bis of the Italian Criminal Code. The first time prosecutors managed to secure convictions using tough international terrorism legislation introduced by Italy in the wake of September 11, was later in 2005 in the Tribunal of Brescia. The suspected terrorists were in fact convicted because they were part of a cell that had planned to attack a subway station in Milan.

Currently, legal texts do not define terrorist offenses in addition to those included in the existing international conventions against terrorism, but usually refer to the treaties in force. Many are international conventions relating to various aspects of the problem of international terrorism which condemn certain specifically defined criminal offenses as *acts of terrorism*. These are all the acts, methods and practices, criminal and unjustifiable, wherever and by whoever committed and or supported, directly or indirectly (including by states), which endanger or take innocent lives, jeopardize fundamental freedoms and seriously impair the dignity of human beings, including those which aim at the undermining of human rights, fundamental freedoms and the democratic basis of society.

There is a case, accordingly, for saying that key rules should be gathered together under a new umbrella convention, which does clearly and unequivocally articulate the basic norms which should drive all law and policy. It is known that such a universal convention already exists in draft form in the United Nations and the essential obstacle that prevents its adoption is the problem of definition.

Different views were expressed with respect to how a definition should be formulated. The working group recognized in this respect the significant progress made in identifying the key elements of a definition of terrorism in Security Council resolution 1566 (2004) and paragraph 164 of the report of the UN High-Level Panel on Threats, Challenges and Change, which would facilitate international consensus on the issue. Against this background, they decided not to propose a definition of their own or to endorse any existing proposal. However, the members of the group agreed that, irrespective of how a definition is formulated in legal technical terms, it should be clear that terrorist acts can never be justifiable by considerations of a political, philosophical, ideological, racial, ethnic, religious or similar nature. In essence, this means that acts specifically targeting civilians or non-combatants, whatever the context and whatever the motive, must be outlawed.

A clear-cut and universally endorsed definition of terrorism that would trigger remedial measures by States and international organisations would further the process of de-legitimizing terrorism in part by detailing those acts deemed to be 'terrorist'.

However, the common sense definition of terrorism is not enough to forge a universally accepted legal definition. There are those who argue that the definition of terrorism should be narrower, in the sense of excluding so-called freedom fighters, or wider, in the sense of including those who are targeted in some uniformed or official capacity. Therefore, it is critical to articulate the central core of the prohibition on which there should be no disagreement. Even though they do not define the crime of terrorism, the most recent treaties and anti-terrorism legislation recognize that terrorist offenses are characterized by so-called terrorist motivation, which is not, however, a substantial element. In fact, acts of terrorism have the purpose, by their nature or context, of seriously intimidating a population or unduly compelling a government or an international organisation to perform or abstain from performing any act, or of seriously destabilising or destroying the fundamental political, constitutional, economic or social structures of a country or an international organization.

In this vein, it seems to me that the specific aim of a comprehensive convention should be to sanction once and for all those acts specifically motivated by their terrorist purpose and targeted against civilians or non-combatants. Nor should these terrorist acts ever be justifiable by considerations of a political, philosophical, ideological, racial, ethnic, religious or similar nature.

Part V:
Responding to Terrorism

Chapter 14

Responding to Terrorism: A Global Stocktake

Gareth Evans

As I write this, it is four years since 9/11 and—with the invasion of Afghanistan—the commencement of the "War on Terrorism." But it is only eighteen months since Madrid, three months since London's 7/7, only a month since the latest Bali bombing, and just hours since the latest outrage in Iraq. Unhappily, it seems just as possible to repeat now the comment I made two years earlier at Davos: "the most visible product of the war on terrorism so far has been more war and more terrorism."

But is that judgment too superficial? Where *do* we stand in the global response to terrorism? How much have we learned about the menace we are confronting and how effective have we been in confronting it? What can we now conclude about what the elements of an effective strategy should be?

What have we learned?

Bearing in mind that none of us, least of all governments, know nearly as much as we would like to know, or sometimes say we know, let me sketch out what I think we *do* now know on the core questions of who are the terrorists, what are their motives, what causes them to act as they do, what capacity do they now have to cause harm, and how effective the so-called war on terrorism has actually been.

Who are the terrorists?

The terrorism causing most contemporary international concern is a very complex phenomenon, involving quite different levels of organization and group identity. If this is a war, we certainly don't know as much as we should about who the enemy actually is, and where he is to be found.

The immediate focus after 9/11 was, understandably enough, on the organizational masterminds of international terrorism. Though finding them was something else, al- Qaeda and Osama bin Laden could easily, and accurately, be identified: they were at least notionally findable, targetable and destroyable. Concerns still rightly exist about activity around the Afghanistan-Pakistan border, but there is little doubt that the combination of military, intelligence and policing measures that have been deployed against al-Qaeda have been successful in dramatically diminishing their direct organizational effectiveness. Claims that periodically emerge, usually through videotapes surfacing on al-Jazeera, of direct al-Qaeda responsibility for this or that new bombing outrage, should no longer be taken at face value.

There is a second level at which, however, the influence of al-Qaeda continues to be strongly felt, even if this is now much more inspirational than organizational. In a number of countries groups exist that identify with its stated objectives and methods, often on the basis of personal links forged in Afghanistan training camps or in certain notable religious schools in Pakistan and Indonesia in particular; it has to also now be increasingly assumed that the 1000 or so foreign jihadist fighters participating in the Iraq insurgency will sooner or later become dangerously influential elsewhere, like the Afghanistan fighters before them. (One of my International Crisis Group Middle East analysts has described Iraq in this respect as being 'like Afghanistan on steroids'). There are also some documented instances of itinerant al-Qaeda operatives and bomb-makers acting as middlemen, giving strategic and technical advice to local cells of Islamist extremists who otherwise lacked the knowledge to launch sophisticated attacks.

But overall what is involved here is an at best amorphous network of loose affiliates and franchisees and imitators, whose component groups are constantly dissolving and reforming, often with highly localized factors being more important than anything else (as Crisis Group has meticulously documented, for example, in the case of Jemaah Islamiyah, or JI, and its multiple splinter groups in Indonesia). These groups might be notionally identifiable and targetable, but in practice they are extremely hard to pin down, not least because there are no control lines which can be readily cut: it cannot be assumed any longer, if it ever could, that any group with an extreme jihadist ideology must be directed by al-Qaeda, or by one of its regional offshoots.

The third category of terrorists of contemporary concern is the most difficult of all to identify and pin down because they involve small groups of self-starting, self-motivated individuals with no discernible organizational links with anyone else at all, getting whatever technical advice they need from the internet, and whatever bomb-making materials they need from readily publicly-available sources: the London bombers are the clearest and most disconcerting example, and the fear is that there are many more such individuals scattered through other European and Western countries.

What motivates terrorists?

For what might be described as 'traditional' terrorist organizations—like the Stern Gang, the Basques' ETA, the IRA, and the Palestinian groups that have embraced terrorism—there are relatively clear and straightforward political grievance motives, that are at least notionally capable of being redressed. We can reasonably assume that if these grievances are addressed, so too would their terrorist activity cease.

But for the brand of terrorism that is causing overwhelmingly most contemporary concern—that perpetrated by certain Islamists—the answer as to what motivates them is much more complicated. It is critical, for a start, to appreciate that those Muslims engaged in terrorist activity are only a tiny proportion of those who can be described as Islamists (or Islamic activists), and that Islamists in turn are only a very small proportion in turn of those who practice the religion of Islam. It would be a grotesque travesty to regard Islam and terrorism as somehow indistinguishable, and would be few policymakers anywhere in the world who would these days think so crudely. But there is still an extraordinary disposition to identify Islamic activism, or Islamism, with terrorism, and a failure to recognize that there are, within the majority Sunni brand of such activism alone, very clear distinctions.

As described in the recent Crisis Group report, *Understanding Islamism*, the critical distinctions are between, first, those whose motives are entirely non-political and missionary in character, focused on preserving Muslim identity and Islamic faith; secondly, those who have Islamic political motives or objectives—the adoption of sharia law and so on—but who have completely renounced violence as a means of achieving them (Egypt's Muslim Brotherhood being the best known example); and thirdly, those with political objectives who have *not* renounced violence as a means of achieving them.

This last group, of violence-inclined salafi jihadis, itself exists in three main variants: internal (combating nominally Muslim regimes considered impious); irredentist (fighting to redeem land ruled by non-Muslims or under occupation); and global (combating the West). For the first two of these, the political grievances in question—whether they involve the perceived apostasy of various governments in the Arab/Islamic world, foreign support for those apostate governments, the presence of foreign infidels on holy soil, or the perceived occupations of Palestine, Iraq and Afghanistan—are at least notionally able to be addressed and accommodated.

These categories of jihadis are handful enough, but the most trouble of all comes from those really extreme anti-Western jihadis—for whom all non-Muslims are kafir (infidels) and therefore by definition enemies of Islam, for whom Muslims allied or associated with the West in any way are themselves kafir, and for whom the killing of innocent Muslims in order to attain victory over the kafir is acceptable collateral damage. This is not the kind of world-view susceptible to any kind of grievance-remedying strategy.

What causes terrorist behavior?

When it comes to identifying the causes of terrorist behavior—what leads people to develop the motives and objectives just described, and which then in turn to engaging in terrorist behavior, we again don't know as much as we need to know, although an impressive body of case-study research is beginning to emerge.

For traditional terrorist groups, and perhaps for what I've described as the internal and irredentist streams of violent salafi jihadism, cause and motive are perhaps almost indistinguishable: one does not need to look much further than the objective grievance to explain the behavior. That said, there will always be room for exploring the factors—psychological and otherwise—that will lead some to take up arms to resolve a grievance while others feeling the grievance just as strongly will remain committed to peaceful means.

Clearly education and training and the role of religious mentors are significant factors, but as the work of Crisis Group in Indonesia has shown, that's not the whole story: in West Java the young people that go into jihadist organizations are disproportionately from families with ties back to earlier rebellions or one particular local puritanical Islamic association; in Sulawesi the most radical are those who lost family members in earlier violence. It's as much a cultural and historical and family legacy as an issue of ideology or religious belief.

While it is very hard to establish any direct connection of a statistically significant kind between poverty and terrorist behavior—whether in the case of individuals, groups or whole societies—it is hard to shake off the impression that any environment in which a sense of deprivation, relative or absolute, despair, humiliation or general hopelessness about one's future prevails is one in which terrorism will potentially flourish. And it is hard no to believe, in particular, that in that kind of environment young men and women will become increasingly vulnerable to recruitment by those who play upon that insecurity, fire up a more focused sense of grievance, and critically, offer a religious justification for making holy war.

Since the London bombings there has of course sprung to center stage the notion of a sense of hopelessness or alienation, combined with the impact of particular religious mentors or role-models, as a significant cause of terrorist commitment among young, second generation immigrants who have not succeeded in their new world but who feel they are losing, or have lost, the cultural moorings of their old. The phenomenon is real, and its extent almost by definition is unknown. It has certainly created a whole new set of headaches for those trying to identify an appropriate policy response.

What capacity for harm do terrorists now have?

One possible response to the contemporary problem of terrorism is to say 'don't overestimate its significance'. Even the numbers for 9/11 and Iraq, for all their horror, don't look so big by comparison, for example, with the 30 000 still dying every month in the Congo, and the 5,000 dying each month in Darfur, from continuing violence and war-related disease and starvation.

That said, there is a significant capacity for terrorists to do harm, and on a very large scale, and it should never be underestimated. Commuter transport systems remain immensely vulnerable in every major city in the world; highly destructive conventional bombs can be made from the cheapest and most freely available materials by those without professional technical skills; and while chemical and biological weapons are much more difficult to deploy, the fear that even small such attacks induce can be more paralyzing for large cities than bigger conventional attacks.

But the risk that really keeps policymakers awake at night around the world is that of the 'big one'—an attack bringing together the sophistication and ruthlessness of the attack on the twin towers with the use of nuclear weapons, perhaps delivered by something as simple as a large delivery van driving down a city street, with an accompanying loss of not just thousands, but hundreds of thousands, of lives. We know very well how limited our capacity is, and always will be, to deny access by terrorist groups to chemical, and especially biological, weapons, given their nature. But the same is also true of nuclear weapons. We are not doing any better than we were in keeping under control the stockpiles of fissile nuclear material that litter the landscape of the former Soviet Russia, and after the exposure in Pakistan we know far more than we did about the global market for nuclear technology, materials and expertise—and all of it is alarming.

The level of technical sophistication required to make a nuclear explosive device is certainly above the backyard level, but it is not beyond competent professionals. And there is enough already fabricated such uranium and plutonium lying around now to make some *240,000* such weapons. Much of it—particularly in Russia—is not just poorly, but appallingly, guarded. And when it comes to transporting the finished product, and it is worth remembering that only a tiny proportion of the millions of cargo containers arriving each year in the world's ports will ever be opened for inspection.

The reality of any threat, or risk, is a function not just of capacity, but intention, and here again we simply don't know enough to make confident judgments. What we do know about contemporary terrorism is that it has been a constantly mutating phenomenon, with a continuing capacity to surprise and shock us—in terms of who has been targeted, when and how and on what scale. Terrorists simply don't always do what others expect them to do.

How effective has the war on terrorism so far been?

If the war on terrorism as it has so far been conducted has been an overall success, that's a well kept secret. Terrorist attacks classified by the U.S. government as 'significant' more than tripled worldwide to 650 last year from 175 in 2003, and this was the highest annual number since Washington began to collect such statistics two decades ago. Nearly a third of those attacks—198 of them, nine times the number of the year before—took place in Iraq, meant to be the central front of the war on terror. More than 4,000 Iraqis have been killed by terrorists in Baghdad alone since April: while the terrorist connection was the least plausible of all the reasons for going to war in Iraq, terrorist violence has now become the most harrowing of all its consequences.

Of course there have been some apparent successes, like the capturing or killing of some two-thirds of al-Qaeda's leadership, but while this has undoubtedly diminished its organizational capacity, it hasn't done anything to diminish its global following.

What are the elements of an effective global response?

Recognizing, as we must, the huge complexity and difficulty of the issues with which we are now dealing, and how far we have come but how far we yet need to go, how can we pull the threads together and define the elements of an effective global response?

Two points need to be made at the outset. The first is that talking about 'war on terrorism' encourages thinking only about defense and attack, what we have to do, as in any other war, to rid ourselves of our enemies. But the language of war here contributes no more to clear operational thinking than talking about waging 'war on evil'. Terrorism is not in and of itself a self-driving concept, or in and of itself an "enemy." It is not even an ideology, as anarchism was in the 19th century. Rather it is a technique or means, a tool or tactic—for the pursuit of political or ideological or even personal ends. And its manifestations are as many and various as its motivations.

Mercifully, some senior policymakers in the U.S. are at last starting to get this message: the preferred terminology, at least in the State Department, is no longer 'Global War On Terrorism' (GWOT), but 'Global Struggle Against Violent Extremism' (GSAVE). This epic linguistic shift—from GWOT to GSAVE—hasn't quite captured the attention and emulation its proponents no doubt hoped, but at least it's a move in the right direction.

The other preliminary point, following from everything I have said so far, is that contemporary terrorism is not something that remotely lends itself to one-track or two-track quick fixes. That much was agreed—although not much else—at last month's World Summit, when the world's assembled heads of state and government urged the General Assembly to develop a comprehensive strategy document, going beyond intelligence and policing.

The question remains how to characterize and articulate the necessary multi-dimensional response in a way that one sees the overall forest, and doesn't get lost in a jungle of detail. Kofi Annan in Madrid in March sketched out what was needed in terms of 'five Ds':

> *dissuade* disaffected groups from choosing terrorism as a tactic to achieve their goals, *deny* terrorists the means to carry out their attacks, *deter* states from supporting terrorists, *develop* state capacity to prevent terrorism, and *defend* human rights in the struggle against terrorism.

That list of objectives remains extremely helpful in capturing the flavor of what is required. But I would prefer to put the elements of the required strategy in slightly more operational terms, in terms of 'five P's': a *protection* strategy, a *policing* strategy, a *political* strategy, a *peacebuilding* strategy and a *psychological* strategy.

Protection Strategy. This speaks for itself so far as airline travel, border protection and all the rest of the familiar homeland security measures are concerned: these measures may only make a difference at the margin, and it is important to go on weighing the costs against benefits of each of them, but their relevance cannot be denied. An important addition to the repertoire would be to a much better job at denying potential access by terrorists to fissile material, at home and especially abroad—and abroad, as I have earlier said, especially in Russia.

Policing Strategy. Good police work, supporting intelligence work, and ultimately (in occasional extreme situations) military operations, are all an indispensable part of the counter-terrorist repertoire, whatever else is needed as well. Enhancing the analytical capability and operational effectiveness of police and intelligence services remains a high priority

The most controversial and difficult issue that arises with policing, in all its dimensions, is, of course, just how many intrusions on traditional civil liberties can be justified in the name of counter-terrorism. The basic principle must be that the risks have to be very great and very immediate to justify putting under strain core values about individual freedom and dignity that are at the heart of making our societies what they are, not what terrorists want them to be.

I don't think the point has ever been better or more clearly made than by Israel's Chief Justice Aharon Barak in his judgment last year on the West Bank Security Wall, in the course of which he quoted his own earlier judgment prohibiting the use of torture against Palestinian detainees:

> We are aware that in the short term, this judgment will not make the state's struggle against those rising up against it any easier…This is the destiny of a democracy: she does not see all means as acceptable, and the ways of her enemies are not always open before her. A democracy must sometimes fight with one arm tied behind her back. Even so, democracy has the upper hand. The rule of law and individual liberties constitute an important aspect of her security stance. At the end of the day, they strengthen her spirit, and this strength allows her to overcome her difficulties.

I just wish that governments in rather more countries—in Europe and North America, in Israel itself, and in my own country Australia not least—would take these principles a little more to heart.

Political Strategy. A variety of familiar political grievances—the occupation of Palestine and Iraq pre-eminent among them, along with foreign support for so-called apostate governments and so on—are a significant part of the motivations of at least some categories of terrorists, and in this context it is important that Western governments be seen to be willing to somehow address them, however difficult that may be.

But the main point I want to make about addressing, and being seen to seriously address, political grievances, is that this is not just a strategy designed to appeal to violent extremists themselves, many of whom we know all too well will not be in the slightest moved by advances of this kind. It is above all, a strategy designed to change the atmospherics in the communities in which terrorists swim, to deny them some of the oxygen they breathe when there is support for their presumed objectives, if not always their most violent behavior. And, in the case of governments in countries where there is strong street sentiment in favor of the political objectives in question, it is a strategy designed to improve the *will* and *capacity* of those governments to cooperate effectively internationally, and to crack down effectively domestically.

Political problems that are seen as such throughout the Arab/Islamic world, and which are unresolved, unaddressed, incompetently or counter-productively addressed, or deliberately left to fester until they become so acute they explode, are not the stuff of which willing local governments, capable of acting effectively, are made.

Peacebuilding Strategy. 'Peacebuilding' is perhaps an unusual word to use here: we usually think of it in the context of conflict within and between states, and the measures of reconstruction, economic development, human rights protection and overall governance that are necessary to ensure that conflict does not start, or re-start. But I use it deliberately to make the point that the kind of security threats we face in the 21st century are highly interdependent, and that some of the standard elements in the peacebuilding repertoire are highly relevant to the struggle against terrorism, or violent extremism.

The general point of peacebuilding in this context is to help states develop the capacity to prevent and deal with terrorism more effectively themselves. More particularly, one of the central preoccupations of peacebuilding is to avoid the emergence or continuation of failed states—in Afghanistan, Somalia, Sierra Leone or wherever—and we are all acutely now conscious, after the Taliban in Afghanistan, of the role that such states are capable of playing in harboring and nurturing terrorist groups capable of causing real damage elsewhere.

Other relevant elements are economic strategies designed to ensure that there is less of a pool of those without hope of any decent earthly future for terrorist recruiters and jihadists generally to be able to draw upon; and human rights and democracy strategies that will open up multiple channels for the expression of concerns and grievances. It is when the door of the mosque is the only one open that grievance does sometimes take more of an Islamist character than might otherwise be the case: one of Crisis Group's most consistent messages to Central Asian governments, for example, is that those who are most anxious about Islamist extremism do most to promote it by cracking down relentlessly on free expression and association elsewhere.

Psychological Strategy. The final element in what I would describe as an effective global strategy is straightforwardly psychological in character, designed to change the way people think and feel about terrorism, and to remove any vestige of a comfort zone around it either for the individuals engaged in terrorism, or for the countries and communities that to a greater or lesser extent support them.

At the global level what is needed above all, once and for all, is agreement on what actually constitutes terrorism, viz. a definition that makes attacks on civilians, whatever the context—resistance to foreign occupation or anything else—as absolutely and comprehensively prohibited, and as absolutely indefensible, in the 21st century as slavery and piracy became in the 19th. The UN, which remains hugely important as a global norm-setter on issues like this, has been enormously reluctant to go down this path, with a handful of resisting states ensuring at the September World Summit that there was, yet again, no agreement on this issue, although the leaders there gathered did go so far as to condemn terrorism 'in all its forms and manifestations, committed by whomever, wherever and for whatever purposes'. This is a start. But so long as anyone anywhere nurtures the belief the that it is not always wrong to kill civilians—that maybe that's not even terrorism, but rather an act of liberation or whatever—then a basic precondition for ridding the world of terrorism will not be there. The struggle against violent extremism starts with the battle of ideas.

At the individual and group level, among those who are or would be terrorists, the psychological task is very specific—to make them understand the wrongness, the indefensibility of their acts, and in the case of Muslims to make them appreciate that such acts, and the suicides so often involved in their perpetration, are absolutely not sanctioned by anything in the Koran. The absence of any kind of accepted institutional hierarchy of authority in Islam on a state or global as distinct from local level, like that which prevails in most other religions, makes very difficult the emergence of authoritative pronouncements in this respect. But efforts have increasingly been made to bring senior clerics and scholars together in Europe and North America and elsewhere to agree upon and pronounce appropriate *fatwas*, and those efforts should continue. Anything that spreads the belief that nothing can justify terrorism, that nothing can be an alibi for murder, cannot be anything but helpful.

We should not nurture too many illusions, however, about the likely effect of this on some of the individuals we worry about most. In Indonesia, for example, it is Crisis Group's judgment that the kind of individuals who I referred to earlier as going into jihadist organizations in West Java and Sulawesi, are not the kind of constituencies that are likely to respond positively to exhortations from moderate Muslim leaders to eschew violence, let alone to the product of interfaith dialogues. It may be possible to turn away present members and potential recruits from using violence, but that can probably only be done through individuals who have legitimacy within the salafi jihadi network. And I suspect that what is true of Indonesia is true in most other parts of the world as well.

Conclusion

As much as I would like to be able to offer in conclusion a clear single prescription for how the global response to terrorism should be conducted, there simply isn't one. We are dealing with a complex, multi-dimensional phenomenon, which demands a complex, multi-layered response. Good policy sometimes requires not simplification but complexification.

With nearly all the international and national debate we have had on this subject, there has been an over-supply of rhetoric and an undersupply of thoughtful analysis. The struggle against violent extremism can be won, but it is going to be neither quick nor easy, and it is going to require a lot more thought and application and persistence, a lot more balanced approach, and a lot more attention to underlying causes and currents as distinct from surface manifestations, than comes easily to most of the world's policy makers. Hopefully this publication will play its part in sensitizing them.

Chapter 15

The Threat from the Al-Qaeda Hydra: The Liberal State Response

Paul Wilkinson

Is Al-Qaeda Still an Organization?

Al-Qaeda is a transnational movement of 'ism' rather than a traditional highly centralized and tightly controlled terrorist organization. Its worldwide network of networks is bound together with a shared ideology, strategic goals, modus operandi and fanatical hatred of the U.S. and other Western countries, Israel, and the government of the regimes of Muslim countries which al-Qaeda's leaders accuse of being 'apostates' on the grounds that they 'betray' the 'true Islam' as defined by bin Laden.

This network of networks consisting of affiliated groups, operational cells and support networks in over 60 countries gives the al-Qaeda movement a greater global reach than any previous international terrorist network. It also provides al-Qaeda with the flexibility and resilience to adapt and sustain its global jihad in spite of the many severe blows the movement has suffered. Al-Qaeda's core leadership, communication and training capabilities suffered major disruption and damage when the Taliban regime in Afghanistan, which had provided al-Qaeda with safe haven, was overthrown in autumn 2001. Since 9/11, 15 leading al-Qaeda militants have been captured or killed, and over 3,000 suspected al-Qaeda followers have been arrested or detained. Moreover, millions of pounds of al-Qaeda assets have been frozen in the banking system. Yet despite all these setbacks the movement has continued to recruit and raise more funds worldwide and to commit atrocities such as the bomb attacks in Madrid and London, massive suicide bombings in Iraq and the beheading of hostages.

It is a dangerous illusion to assume that because al-Qaeda's core leadership does not carry out the detailed planning, organization and implementation of all the attacks carried out in its name, the movement no longer exists or has a purely marginal role. Bin Laden and Ayman Zawahiri provide the crucial ideological leadership and strategic direction of the movement. It is they who inspire new recruits to join the global jihad and to be ready to sacrifice their lives as suicide bombers for the cause. Al-Qaeda videotapes and websites demonstrate the great importance they attach to propaganda. Recently they have expanded into broadcasting their own news program called *Voice of the Caliphate*, which attempts to use world events to put over their movements' perverted doctrines. Al-Qaeda's leaders are well aware that they cannot rely on the mosques as the sole channel for spreading their ideas. Clear evidence that they continue to win the hearts and minds of those who are attracted to joining al-Qaeda affiliated and cells around the world is the way the websites of these affiliated groups swiftly claim the al-Qaeda connection in their claims of responsibility for attacks, and the al-Qaeda core leadership are so quick to claim 'ownership' for successful attacks. However, there are some clear risks involved in this decentralized network of networks structure. What happens if there is a schism over strategy and tactics between leadership and one of the affiliated? And what happens if a splinter group challenges the leadership by defying its decrees? From what we know of al-Qaeda's core leadership we can assume that they simply do not have the manpower and weapons to suppress of overrule the breakaway group. Another possible implication of the loose structure of the al-Qaeda network is that they may no longer be able to plan and execute complex coordinated spectacular attacks on the lines of 9/11, through some experts dispute this.

Aims, Capabilities and Plans

The main aims of the al-Qaeda movement are:

- to eject the U.S. and its allies from the Middle East and all Muslim lands;

- to overthrow existing Muslim governments/regimes, on the grounds that they are 'Apostate' regimes which betray the cause of the true Islam, as defined by bin Laden and Zawahiri; and

- ultimately to establish a pan-Islamist Caliphate to bring all Muslims under the rule of an Islamist super-state.

Al-Qaeda believes that the use of the weapon of mass casualty terrorism and the belief that Allah is 'on their side' will ensure that they win ultimate victory. The aim of killing as many of their 'enemy' including civilians, wherever and whenever the opportunity arises was spelt out in bin Laden's notorious Fatwa of February 1998. It is al-Qaeda's explicit commitment to mass killing, so horrifically demonstrated in its 9/11 attacks, that make it by far the most dangerous terrorist network in the modern world.

What do we know of al-Qaeda's capabilities? The key resource for any terrorist organization is its membership and their level of commitment, training, expertise and experience. In attack after attack al-Qaeda's network of networks has proved its ability to deploy large numbers of operatives and to recruit more than sufficient new members to replace those lost by capture and death in suicide bombing or in armed confrontations with security forces. We should remember that it only takes relatively small numbers to carry out attacks which can kill thousands and inflict severe economic damage and disruption. The 9/11 attacks were carried out by 19 suicide hijackers and a support network of a handful of people. There is no evidence that the movement is unable to obtain the funds and explosives it needs to carry out major coordinated mass-killing suicide bombing attacks. There is overwhelming evidence from a whole series of police investigations into al-Qaeda movement activities that the local networks are not only carrying out the planning and execution of operations: they are in most cases raising the cash to fund such operations and obtaining the explosives and other materials and vehicles or other equipment through thefts, corruption and organized crime in their own areas. However, although small scale terrorist bombing is a very low cost activity for the local networks the cost of mounting a coordinated mass-casualty attack may well be beyond the resources of a local network, and hence shortage of funds *may* act as a significant barrier to mounting more spectacular attacks. It has been estimated that the 9/11 attacks cost al-Qaeda around $500,000. At that time this was well within the financial capabilities of al-Qaeda's core leadership. It is unlikely that they would find it so easy to fund such a massively lethal and destructive series of attacks today. The freezing of al-Qaeda assets in the banking system has not been extensive enough though to deprive the al-Qaeda of all its resources, but it has compelled the terrorist leadership to rely more than ever on local networks for the resources to carry out local attacks.

By far the more important capability for carrying out local attacks is the availability of expertise, especially in bomb making, operational planning and tactics. The al-Qaeda network's supply of well-trained and experienced terrorist operatives has been enormously increased as a result of the field experience provided in the Iraq conflict. Foreign terrorists who have been involved with the al-Qaeda Jihad in Mesopotamia led by the Jordanian Abu Musab al-Zarqawi, are now able to return to their countries of origin, including the EU member states, battle hardened and with skills acquired and honed in Iraq. It is also noteworthy that in recent weeks we have seen tactics methods copied from the terrorist campaign in Iraq being used in Afghanistan by Taliban and al-Qaeda-linked groups and their Afghan warlord allies to attack. For example the terrorists have rammed a vehicle carrying British personnel with a vehicle packed with explosives. In another close parallel with Iraq the terrorists have also started to mount attacks on recruits to the newly-established Afghan army.

It is possible to obtain a clear idea of the al-Qaeda leadership's long-term strategy from their writings. Zawahiri's *Knights Under the Prophet's Banner*, for example, stresses the importance they attach to the dual strategy of seeking to establish control over a base area within the heart of the Muslim world while at the same time carrying the struggle to the homelands of the US and its allies. The U.S. military has just announced that they have recently intercepted a letter from Zawahiri to Abu Musab al-Zarqawi, Head of al-Qaeda in Iraq. Zawahiri is confident that al-Qaeda will gain a victory in Iraq, and sees this as the first step, the setting up of a Caliphate initially in Iraq, but followed by waging Jihad in Syria, Lebanon, Egypt, finally leading on to the destruction of Israel. The U.S. Department of Defense is convinced that his document is genuine, and, if so, it provides an interesting glimpse of al-Qaeda's strategic plans. The letter also reveals evidence of divisions within the global al-Qaeda network. Zawahiri warns that Zarqawi's particularly cruel measures such as the mass killing of Shia Muslims and the beheading of hostages may alienate public opinion in the Muslim world. If this letter is genuine, as the American government believes, it confirms that the core leadership is unable to control all activities carried out in the name of al-Qaeda. It also confirms the point made earlier regarding schisms: such a major split on questions of tactics suggests the possible development of deeper and more lasting splits in the movement.

As for plans for specific operations, alas we do not have adequate human intelligence on the precise intentions of the operational planners, cell leaders and support networks. However, we can learn from the investigations carried out by police and judicial bodies into previous attacks successful and failed, in order to learn more about their modus operandi. We know enough from the case history to understand the care and sophistication al-Qaeda network groups use to plan attacks. A vivid example was the information found on an al-Qaeda laptop computer captured in Pakistan which showed that the operations planners were closely examining not only the details of the security provided for key financial targets they planned to attack in the U.S., but also the precise structure of the buildings in order to decide on the type and strength of explosives to use. It is typical of the al-Qaeda network to engage in detailed reconnaissance and intelligence gathering in preparation for any major operation.

How the Iraq Factor has been Exploited by the Al-Qaeda Movement

One of the most significant developments in the evolution of al-Qaeda since 2003 has been the way the movement has exploited the allied invasion and occupation of Iraq. Whatever view one may take on the decision to invade Iraq it is simply ignoring reality to deny that the invasion and occupation have been a big boost for al-Qaeda and a setback for the coalition against terrorism. The invasion was a propaganda gift to al-Qaeda because they could portray it as an unprovoked imperialistic attack on a Muslim land. Al- Qaeda poses as the defender of Muslim lands and people everywhere. They used this as a recruiting sergeant and as an opportunity for fund raising for their global jihad. Moreover the conflict provided a rich concentration of U.S. and other western military and civilian targets in a country which the militants could enter all too easily across virtually uncontrolled borders. As this fragile experiment in establishing a democratic government moved forward in Iraq, al-Qaeda has a growing incentive to attack because the last thing they wish to see in Iraq, or anywhere else in the Muslim world, is the successful establishment of a democratic political system. Having failed to prevent the free elections in January 2005 they are now desperate to disrupt the efforts to secure and agreed democratic constitution for Iraq and to provoke an all out civil war between the

Sunnis and the Shiite majority. This is what the brutal al-Qaeda bomb attacks on Shiite civilians and clerics are designed to achieve.

It is absurd to suggest that recognizing the way al-Qaeda has exploited the war in Iraq to its own considerable advantage in some way 'excuses' al-Qaeda's terrorism. In my view there can never be an excuse for the use of terrorism, whoever the perpetrators. Terrorism involves the deliberate mass murder and injury of civilians and is a crime against international law and humanity. However, understanding more about the *motivation* of terrorists and how they are attracted into extremist groups and groomed to be suicide bombers, is a vital subject for research. 'Know thine enemy' has always been a key maxim of successful strategists. How are we to unravel al-Qaeda if we do not understand what makes them tick? Nor should we overlook unforeseen consequences of foreign policy decision-making, especially when the key decision are taken by a more powerful ally which may also have failed to anticipate and plan for the implications of their policy for the struggle against international terrorism.

International Efforts to Combat Al-Qaeda Terrorism

In spite of the setbacks in the struggle against al-Qaeda described above there have been some very positive developments in the international response which need to be taken into account if we are to get a more balanced assessment:

- In spite of deep divisions among members of the coalition against terrorism over the invasion of Iraq international intelligence cooperation in counter-terrorism especially at the bilateral level, has continued to improve. For example, Spain, France and Germany have continued to cooperation closely with the United States in sharing intelligence on the al-Qaeda network despite their opposition to Washington's policy in Iraq.

- EU member states (especially Spain, Germany, France and the UK) have shown considerable success in using their criminal justice systems to try persons suspected of involvement in al-Qaeda linked terrorism. The U.S. government's apparent determination to circumvent their own highly-respected Federal Criminal Court system and to resort to detention without trial for terrorist suspects is baffling and deeply damaging to America's reputation as a champion of democracy and the rule of law.

- One of the most encouraging developments in international response has been the un-dramatic but vital work of capacity building in the developing countries, for example the assistance program of the UK Foreign and Commonwealth Office in disseminating expertise in anti-terrorism law, policing and intelligence work and the work of the international agencies such as ICAO, IATA and ACI in enhancing aviation security and of IMO in maritime security.

- The valuable progress in counter-terrorism made by the EU following the Madrid and London bombings for example through the Europe Arrest Warrant mechanism, and the enhanced intelligence sharing and judicial cooperation procedures through EUROPOL, SITCEN, and EUROJUST. This cooperation provides a useful model for other regional IGO's and it is particularly encouraging that the UK has take a very useful role during the British Presidency of the EU to further enhance EU cooperation in this key field.

Major Weaknesses in the International Response to Terrorism

If asked to pinpoint major weaknesses in the international response to terrorism I would stress four massive problems.

First, in view of al-Qaeda's serious efforts to acquire CBRN weapons much more intensive efforts are required to tighten and police the international arms control and counter-proliferation regimes to enable them to encompass prevention of proliferation to non-state groups. Far more than changes in international treaties is required. We urgently need powerful international agencies to *police* such regimes. The IAEA is an encouraging, though far from perfect model. We need to build similar mechanisms to deal with chemical and biological weapons.

Second, many governments still show a lack of political will and courage to take an unambiguous stand against terrorism whoever the perpetrators and whatever their self-professed cause. There are no good terrorists. Terrorism is a brutal attack on the most basic human right of all, the right to life. It should be outlawed and suppressed wherever it occurs. Until this happens we will continue to see more atrocities like the 9/11 attacks, the Beslan school massacre, the Bali bombings, the Madrid and London bombings and hundreds of other acts of mass murder.

Third, there has been a tragic failure to wage the battle of ideas against the extremists who preach hatred and incite people to commit terrorism. All democratic governments, including our own have a special responsibility to actively promote democratic values, the role of law and human rights. Moreover this cannot simply be accomplished by radio and TV programs and political speeches. Action counts far more than words in the difficult world of upholding democratic values and human rights. If the behavior of democratic states flatly contradicts our stated values we lose our credibility in the battle of ideas worldwide.

Fourth, the struggle to uphold basic human rights is closely interwoven with the battle of ideas against the promoters and preachers of terrorism. While it is true that some extreme human rights campaigners elevate human rights into a totally impractical and irresponsible rejection of all collective moral and political obligations that make the enjoyment of human rights possible, most citizens of democracies and many who are working to democratize their countries would be shocked if we were told that some of our most cherished civil liberties (e.g. habeas corpus, the right to a fair trial, freedom of speech, freedom of religion, freedom of movement, freedom of assembly, freedom of expression), were to be suspended in the name of state security. If we throw away our basic liberties in the name of dealing with the terrorism threat we will have done the terrorists' work for them.

Conclusion

As Joseph S. Nye, Yukio Satoh and I recommended in our Trilateral Commission report *Addressing the New International Terrorism* (May 2003):

"Dialogues about the protection of civil liberties in the face of security threats should be a regular feature of the meetings of the home security officials and should be reinforced by meetings of judicial officials and parliamentarians. Assistance programs must include attention of human right issues. Not only are such values central to the definition of the civilization that we seek to protect, but overreactions to insecurity that infringe civil liberties undercut the sort of attractive power that is essential to maintain the support of moderate opinion and to deprive terrorists from recruiting new converts."

Chapter 16
Costs and Benefits of
Anti-Terrorism Policies

Bruno S. Frey and Simon Leuchinger

Over the last few years, terrorism has become a major concern in all societies. The terrorist attacks in New York, Madrid and London have had a large and lasting impact on both citizens and politicians alike.

Despite the vastly increasing importance of terrorism, the way terrorism is measured has not changed: it still only takes into account the number of incidents and the number of fatalities. These measures neglect the much larger consequences of terrorism on society, be they economic, social or political. This chapter presents a totally new approach to measuring terrorism, based on recently emerging Happiness Research. It shows that it is possible to measure the effect of terrorist activities on people's well-being. It includes all possible consequences on economic, social and political spheres, to the extent that they are considered to be relevant by the individuals. An application to terrorism in the United Kingdom and the Republic of Ireland shows indeed that people are really concerned about terrorism and that terrorist acts reduce their life satisfaction considerably.

Even more importantly, the recent surge in terrorism has led to large-scale anti-terrorist policies based on deterrence. The object is to severely punish actual and prospective terrorists in order to dissuade them from engaging in such activities. Experience has shown, however, that deterrence policy has not been effective; it may even have led to counterproductive effects. But what is the alternative? This paper suggests three specific anti-terrorist policies, based on a positive, rather than a negative, approach. A comparative analysis suggests that these policies are superior to deterrence policy and should be seriously considered.

The following section discusses the consequences of terrorism and presents the new measurement based on life satisfaction data. The third section suggests three anti-terrorist policies based on a positive, rather than on a deterrence approach. Section four concludes.

Consequences of Terrorism

In recent years, economic scholars analyzed the effects of terrorism on various aspects of the economy.[1] In the following, we present two studies that measure the costs of terrorism for the economy and the society as a whole. The first study measures the economic consequences of the Basque conflict,[2] whilst the second study measures the overall consequences of the Northern Ireland conflict.[3]

Economic consequences

Estimating the overall effect of terrorism on the economy is faced with the problem of how the economy would have developed without terrorism. To construct a counterfactual for the development of the Basque country, Abadie and Gardeazabal[4] use a weighted combination of other Spanish regions. This 'synthetic' control region resembles relevant economic characteristics of the Basque Country before the outset of Basque terrorism. The economic evolution of this 'counterfactual' Basque Country without terrorism is then compared to the actual experience of the Basque Country. Until 1975, the actual and synthetic Basque Countries behave similarly. After 1975, when ETA's terrorist activity becomes a large-scale phenomenon, per capita GDP in these two regions diverge. The Basque Country takes values up to around 12 percent below those of the synt control region. Overall, the result of this study suggests a 10 percent loss in per capita GDP due to terrorism in the 1980's and 1990's.

However, this study does not capture the total costs of terrorism. The fear of individuals and the grief of the victims and the bereaved

---

[1] For a review of the literature, see Bruno S. Frey, Simon Luechinger and Alois Stutzer, *Calculating Tragedy: Assessing the Costs of Terrorism.* (Munich: CESifo Working Paper No. 1341, 2004).

[2] Alberto Abadie and Javier Gardeazabal, "The Economic Costs of Conflict: A Case Study of the Basque Country," *American Economic Review* 93(1): 113-132 (2003).

[3] Bruno S. Frey, Simon Luechinger and Alois Stutzer, *Valuing Public Goods: The Life Satisfaction Approach.* (Munich: CESifo Working Paper No. 1158, 2004)

[4] See fn 2.

are disregarded. It follows that the damage caused by terrorism may be considerably underestimated. In the following, we present a study that tries to measure these overall consequences of terrorism.

Overall consequences

The analysis is based on data on self-reported life satisfaction collected in surveys. Self-reported life satisfaction expresses the extent to which respondents judge their lives in a favorable way. It is influenced by various factors, such as respondents' health and financial situation, but also by political stability or terrorism. These survey data are combined with indicators of terrorist activity. Using multivariate regression analysis, the effect of terrorism on life satisfaction and the effect of income on life satisfaction can then be estimated. With these two estimates, it is possible to monetize the overall consequences of terrorism. Frey, Luechinger and Stutzer[5] use this approach to assess the costs of terrorism in France, the United Kingdom and the Republic of Ireland. By way of illustration, an analysis of the Northern Ireland conflict is presented here.

Life satisfaction data are taken from the Euro-Barometer Survey Series (1970-1999); the variable is the categorical response to the following question: "On the whole, are you very satisfied [4], fairly satisfied [3], not very satisfied [2], or not at all satisfied [1] with the life you lead?" As an indicator for the salience and intensity of terrorist activity, the number of deaths resulting from the conflict in Northern Ireland is used, as compiled by Sutton.[6] This indicator is not restricted to terrorism in particular, but includes political violence in general. In order to identify the effect of terrorism on individuals' life satisfaction, the authors use a combined time-series (for the period 1975 to 1998) and cross-section analysis (with Northern Ireland, the Republic of Ireland and Great Britain). Specifically, a micro-econometric happiness function is specified, whereby the life satisfaction of an individual living in a particular region at a particular time is explained by differences in the level of terrorism across the three regions and over time,

---

[5] See fn 3.

[6] Malcolm Sutton, *Bear in Mind These Dead .... An Index of Deaths from the Conflict in Ireland 1969-1993* (Belfast: Beyond the Pale Publications, 1994). An updated index is provided by the Conflict Archive on the Internet (www.cain.ulst.ac.uk).

the individual's household income, other personal and socio-demo-graphic characteristics, as well as region and time fixed effects.

The estimation results suggest that the number of terrorist fatalities has a statistically significant negative effect on reported life satisfaction. For an increase of one standard deviation in the number of recorded fatalities, i.e. an increase of 53.7 fatalities, life satisfaction is lowered by 0.041 on the four-point scale. This effect is about a tenth of the effect of being unemployed rather than employed. Thus, the indicator for terrorism is correlated with people's subjective well-being in a sizeable way.

The estimated coefficients for terrorism and individual income can be used to calculate the hypothetical willingness-to-pay for a discrete change in the level of terrorism. Frey, Luechinger and Stutzer[7] calculate a hypothetical willingness-to-pay of a resident of Northern Ireland for a reduction in the number of fatalities to the average level of Great Britain and the Republic of Ireland. Accordingly, a resident of Northern Ireland (with average household income) would be willing to pay around 41% of his income for a reduction in terrorist activity to the level that prevails in the more peaceful parts of the country or its sister republic. This estimate is surprisingly high. However, it might to some extent reflect the ferocity of the conflict. After all, Northern Ireland was on the brink of all-out civil war. This result indicates that overall consequences may far outweigh purely economic consequences.

Alternative Anti-Terrorism Policies

In the following, we present alternative anti-terrorism policies to the widespread deterrence policy. These policies are favorable with regard to their effectiveness, but also because they are not expensive in terms of economic costs or infringements on civil liberties. The three policies proposed are the polycentricity strategy, the strategy of diffusing media attention and the strategy of positive incentives.

The policentricity strategy

Terrorists seek to destabilize the polity and damage the economy. One way to immunize a country against terrorist attack, and therewith

---

[7] See fn 3.

provide disincentives for terrorists, is to decentralize various aspects of the society.[8]

A system with many different centers is more stable than a more centralized one. When one part of the system is negatively affected, one or several other parts can take over. The more centers of power there are in a country, the less damage is caused in case of an attack. The terrorists anticipate that less damage will be caused in a decentralized society and have, for that reason, a lower incentive to attack in the first place. In contrast, in a centralized system, most decision-making power, with respect to the economy, polity and society, takes place in one location. This central power is an ideal target for terrorists, and therefore runs a greater risk of being attacked.

In the following, polycentricity in the economy, polity, and other parts of society are discussed.

Market Polycentricity. A market economy is based on an extreme form of decentralization of decision-making and implementation. Under competitive conditions, the suppliers are able to completely substitute for one another. If one of them is eradicated due to a terrorist attack, the other suppliers are able to fill the void. They are prepared, and have an incentive, to step in. No special governmental plans have to be set up for such substitution. The more an economy functions according to market principles, the less vulnerable it is to terrorist attacks.

The resilience of a market economy may be illustrated by the 9/11 attack. Though this was the gravest terrorist attack so far, the economic system as a whole was hardly affected. Due to its decentralized market economy, the United States' economy was only very marginally hit; the many other centers of economic activity were not directly affected at all. Even in Manhattan, the recovery was remarkably quick. This does not, of course, mean that there were no human or material losses. But the point is that even this dreadful blow was not able to seriously damage a decentralized economy like the American economy. Many of the high costs were the result of the political response to the attack, and not the result of the attack itself. Viewed from this

---

[8] See more fully Bruno S. Frey and Simon Luechinger, "Decentralization as a Disincentive for Terror," *European Journal of Political Economy* 20(2): 509-515 (2004).

perspective, the attack was far from being a victory to the terrorists, but rather demonstrated the strength of a decentralized economic system.

Political Decentralization. Political polyarchy may take two forms: horizontal decentralization or separation of powers, and vertical decentralization or federalism.

Separation of Powers: Political authority is distributed over a number of different political actors. Most important is the classical separation of power between government, legislature and courts.

Federalism: Political power can also be spatially decentralized and be divided over various levels of government.

Spatial decentralization and a polycentric society: The high population density typical for large urban areas makes them ideal targets for terrorists and other attackers. The spatial decentralization of the population is of particular importance in cases where terrorists use biological and chemical weapons. In areas of very dense population, viruses (such as smallpox) introduced by terrorists spread quickly, leading to many casualties in a short period of time.

The danger of physical centralization has been demonstrated by the two terrorist attacks on New York's twin towers. The first attack in 1993, when a bomb exploded in the basement garage of the World Trade Center, destroyed a central command post of the emergency services. Nevertheless, the Mayor of New York, Rudolph Giuliani, ordered the establishment of a new central Office of Emergency Management in a building next to the World Trade Center. On September 11, 2001, this Office, which was intended to coordinate all police and support units in the event of a catastrophe, including terrorist attacks, was again destroyed and proved to be useless.

When faced with terrorism, most countries have an overwhelming urge to centralize decision-making powers. One such example is the United States. The mega-merger of various bodies into the new Department of Homeland Security is a move in the wrong direction, and increases the vulnerability of these authorities. Any terrorist group able to attack this Department, e.g. by interfering with its electronic system, can inflict considerable damage.

More constitutionally, the separation of powers switched in favor of the executive branch.[9] The ability of the public, the press, and even Congress to gain access to information necessary in order to hold the executive accountable for their actions has been restricted.[10] But such reactions can also be observed in many other countries. According to a study of six countries—Canada, France, Germany, India, Israel and the United Kingdom—a common structural approach in the fight against terrorism is the centralization of decision-making.[11]

Why does such a centralizing policy reaction occur, despite the fact that it may be counter-productive? Two reasons may be adduced. First, deterrence and a "strong central command" visibly demonstrate the determination of politicians to fight terrorism. Second, government politicians and public bureaucrats exploit the unique situation created by terrorist threats to extend their own competencies. It is, therefore, all the more important to safeguard political and economic decentralization at the constitutional level.

The strategy of diffusing media attention

In this section, another anti-terrorism policy, based on reducing the marginal benefits of terrorism to terrorists, is discussed. The policy aims at reducing the amount of publicity terrorists can get from committing violent acts.[12]

Dramatic terrorist actions receive huge media coverage. Terrorists have become very skilled at using the media to achieve maximum publicity. Moreover, the media share a common interest with the terrorists: the desire to make news and to ensure the longevity of the

---

[9] David Cole and James X. Dempsey, *Terrorism and the Constitution. Sacrificing Civil Liberties in the Name of National Security* (New York: The New Press, 2002).

[10] Nancy Chang, *Silencing Political Dissent. How Post-September 11 Anti-Terrorism Measures Threaten Our Civil Liberties* (New York: Seven Stories Press, 2002).

[11] Raphael Perl, "Terrorism: Threat Assessment in a Changing Global Environment," Paper prepared for Statement before the House Committee on Government Reform, Subcommittee on National Security, Veterans Affairs, and International Relations, Washington D.C., July 16, 2000.

[12] Bruno S. Frey, "Fighting Political Terrorism by Refusing Recognition," *Journal of Public Policy* 7: 179-188 (1988); and Bruno S. Frey, *Dealing with Terrorism—Stick or Carrot?* (Cheltenham, U.K., and Northampton, MA: Edward Elgar, 2004).

"story."[13] The journalists are pressurized to enlarge upon incidents of potential interest to the viewers. This multiplies the effects of a particular terrorist act.

Terrorists can be prevented from committing violent acts if they benefit less from them. A specific way to ensure that terrorists derive lower benefits from terrorism consists of the government ascertaining that a particular terrorist act is not attributed to a particular terrorist group. This prevents terrorists receiving credit for the act, and thereby gaining full public recognition for having committed it. The government must see to it that no particular terrorist group is able to monopolize media attention. Therefore, several scholars advocate media censorship, statutory regulations or voluntary self-restraint.[14] All information as to who committed a particular terrorist act would then be suppressed. But in an open and free society, it is impossible to withhold the type of information which the public is only too eager to know. Further, such intervention does not bind the foreign press and news media. Any news about the occurrence of a terrorist act and the likely perpetrators is therefore very likely to leak out. Terrorists seeking publicity can easily inform foreign news agencies. This first strategy must therefore be rejected as being ineffective and incompatible with democracy, as the freedom of the press is seriously restricted.

We propose an alternative way of diffusing media attention without infringing on the freedom of the press. Media attention can be dispersed by supplying more information to the public than would be wished by the perpetrators of a particular violent act. This can be done by making it known that several terrorist groups could be responsible for a particular terrorist act. The authorities have to reveal that they never know with absolute certainty which terrorist group may have committed a violent act. Even when it seems obvious which terrorist group is involved, the authorities can never be sure. They have to refrain from attributing a terrorist act with any degree of certainty to a particular group, as long as the truth of the matter has not been established. In a lawful country, based on the separation of

[13] Brigitte L. Nacos, *Terrorism and the Media. From the Iran Hostage Crisis to the Oklahoma City Bombing* (New York: Columbia University Press, 1994).

[14] Paul Wilkinson, *Terrorism Versus Democracy: The Liberal State Response* (London and Portland, OR: Frank Cass, 2000).

power, this is the privilege of the courts, but not of the executive branch.

In the case of many spectacular terrorist events, no credible claims by the perpetrators have ever been made. Examples are the sarin nerve-gas attack in Tokyo (1995) or the bombing of the Federal Office Building in Oklahoma City (1995). Although the perpetrators were later identified and are known today, such knowledge did not exist when the events occurred. At that time, many different terrorist groups might have been credible attackers.

In many cases, however, several groups claim to have committed a particular terrorist act. For example, in the terrorist attack on the discotheque "La Belle" in Berlin in 1986, the Anti-American Arab Liberation Front, the RAF, and an offshoot of the RAF, the Holger Meins Commando, all claimed responsibility for the blast.

The government has to emphasize that any one of the groups claiming responsibility could be the one responsible. As a consequence, the media disperses public attention to many different, and possibly conflicting, political groups and goals. When only one group claims to have committed the terrorist act, the authorities responsible have to point out that such a claim is not necessarily substantiated.

The information strategy of refusing to attribute a terrorist attack to one particular group has systematic effects on the behavior of terrorists. The benefits derived from having committed a terrorist act decrease for the group having undertaken it. The group does not reap the public attention it hoped to get. This reduction in publicity renders the terrorist act (to a certain extent) pointless. The terrorists become frustrated and will either desist from further activities, or increasingly expose themselves to ordinary counter-terrorist methods by the police. The amount of terrorism will decrease; the dissatisfaction with existing political and social conditions will be expressed in different, less violent ways.

The strategy of positive incentives

Positive sanctions can consist of providing people with previously nonexistent or unattainable opportunities to increase their utility. Similarly, they can consist of offering non-violent alternatives to address terrorists' political goals. In economic terminology, the opportunity costs of being a terrorist are raised. We advance concrete anti-terrorist policies, based on opening up alternatives, namely reintegrating terrorists by providing them with access to the political process and welcoming repentants.[15]

In the following, two specific policies for reintegrating potential and actual terrorists are discussed.

Reintegrating Terrorists and Granting Access to the Political Process. One of the most fundamental human motivations is the need to belong. This also applies to terrorists. In most cases, former connections are completely severed when joining a terrorist group. The isolation from other social entities strengthens the terrorist group, because it becomes the only place where the sense of belonging is nurtured.

An effective way of overcoming terrorism is to break up this isolation. Interaction between groups tends to reduce extremist views. Stopping the vicious circle of segregation and extremism can be expected to lower terrorists' inclination to participate in violent activities. The terrorists need to experience that there are other social bodies able to give them a sense of belonging which, if that can be achieved, reduces the power of the terrorist leaders.

Further, terrorists can be granted access to the normal political process. This lowers the costs of pursuing the political goal by legal means and hence raises the opportunity costs of terrorism. There are various ways to motivate terrorists to interact more closely with other members of society and to pursue their political goals by legal means:

- The terrorists, and in particular their supporters and sympathizers, can be involved in the institutionalized political process. As will be discussed later, this approach was effective in the case of the Northern Ireland conflict.

- The terrorists can be involved in a discussion process, which takes their goals and grievances seriously and which tries to see whether compromises are feasible. There is strong evidence from experimental research in game theory that communication and personal contacts between players increases cooperation.

[15] See also Frey and Luechinger, 2003, op.cit.; Frey, 2004, op. cit.

Welcoming Repentants. Persons engaged in terrorist movements can be offered incentives, most importantly reduced punishment and a secure future, if they are prepared to leave the organization they are involved with and are ready to talk about the organization and its objectives. The prospect of being supported raises a member's opportunity costs of remaining a terrorist. Such an approach has indeed been put into practice with great success. In Italy, a law introduced in 1982, the *legge sui pentiti* (law on repentants), left it up to the discretion of the courts to reduce sentences quite substantially, on the condition that convicted terrorists provide tangible information leading to the arrest and conviction of fellow-terrorists. The implementation of this principal witness program turned out to be an overwhelming success.[16] It provided the police with detailed information, which helped to crack open the Brigate Rosse cells and columns.

A policy of providing positive incentives is far from ideal, but it has some important advantages compared to a deterrence policy. The interaction between terrorists and government is transformed into a positive sum game: both sides benefit. The proposals break the organizational and mental dependence of persons on the terrorist organizations. In contrast, deterrence policy locks prospective and actual terrorists into their organization and provides them with no alternatives but to stay on. The strategy proposed here undermines the cohesiveness of the terrorist organization. The incentive to leave is an ever-present threat to the organization. With good outside offers available to the members of a terrorist group, its leaders tend to lose control. The terrorist organization's effectiveness is thereby reduced. Although positive incentives may be insufficient to affect the hard core of the terrorist organization, they may still be effective in dissuading the sympathizers and supporters from supporting the terrorists.

Conclusion

This chapter aims at contributing to the debate on terrorism. First, we present a new and inclusive measurement of the extent of terrorism based on human well-being. This life satisfaction approach takes all consequences of terrorist acts into account, insofar as they affect individuals. We are able to show, in the case of France and the United

---

[16] Wilkinson, op. cit.

Kingdom, that individuals living in regions greatly affected by terrorist acts suffer a considerable reduction in their well-being.

Second, we present anti-terrorist policies based on a positive approach. We suggest that polycentricity, diffusing media attention and offering positive incentives to desist from terrorism are alternative policies. We argue that these approaches are, in many respects, more effective than deterrence policy and, in particular, do not violate the cherished values of democratic societies.

Chapter 17

Responses to Terrorism:
Some Political and Legal Perspectives

Yonah Alexander

The vulnerability of modern society and its infrastructure, coupled with the opportunities for the utilization of sophisticated high-level conventional and mass-destruction weaponry, requires nations, both unilaterally and in concert, to develop credible response strategies and capabilities to minimize the future threats. The stunning success of terrorist bombings, kidnappings, hijackings, facility attacks, and assassinations often result in a popular awareness of the important counter-terrorist measures that states apply. After all, states possess enormous legal, economic, police, and military resources that terrorists cannot match. Governments have taken domestic and international measures to deal with conventional acts of terrorism, and they have taken special precautions to deal with mass destruction threats.

And yet, an analysis of various governmental and inter-governmental as well as academic views on the subject indicates that there is no consensus of what terrorism is. On the other hand, there seems to be an agreement related to its several components, such as the nature of the act (e.g., unlawful); perpetrators (e.g., individuals, groups, states); objectives (e.g., political); intended outcomes and motivations (e.g., fear and frustration); targets (e.g., victims); and methods (e.g., hostage taking).

On the basis of these elements, it is reasonable to adopt the following working definition for the purpose of this discussion: terrorism is defined as the calculated employment or the threat of violence by individuals, subnational groups, and state actors to attain political, social, and economic objectives in the violation of the law, intended to create an overwhelming fear in a target area larger than the victims attacked or threatened.

To be sure, there are clear distinctions in international law and practice between terrorism and other forms of violence, such as "insurgency" and "guerrilla" operations. The following clarifications are relevant, particularly in light of the current security challenges facing the international community in Afghanistan and Iraq.

Insurgency is a condition of armed revolt against a recognized government that does not reach the proportions of organizing a revolutionary government or being recognized as a military belligerent. Its targets are usually military forces or installations, and it follows international rules of armed conflict. It actively seeks a basis of popular support for the goals it espouses and, if successful, would eventually conduct guerrilla military operations and organize a revolutionary regime.

The resort to terrorist methods by an insurgent group is a great temptation, particularly if a foreign state offers assistance in such tactics. These methods cannot be condoned, however, no matter how theoretically noble the objective may be. Insurgents using terrorist methods become outlaws in human society, just as the nation state does that supports acts of terrorism.

Insurgency without terrorist acts is merely the first phase of a legitimate attempt at revolution in which military violence is used for specific political and military gains rather than for the purpose of spreading fear. It may succeed or fail. It may either adopt or eschew terrorist methods. Outside support for insurgency will normally depend on whether the goals are politically compatible with the values of the nation concerned.

Guerrilla warfare, literally "a little war," is one of the oldest forms of conflict. With the rise of Leninist and Maoist models of communism, and particularly in view of Soviet direct or indirect support of guerrilla armies in various non-communist countries in the post-World War II period, the meaning of the term has been increasingly associated with terrorism. This may be partly because of the popularization of the term "urban guerrilla," which indeed means a terrorist acting in the anonymity of the big city. Classical guerrilla operations may or may not employ terrorist tactics and methods.

These distinctions suggest that guerrilla military operations are part of a campaign of combat against state authorities and armies that is progressing toward a full-scale revolution but has too few fighting forces and has them too dispersed to move into a formal political showdown battle. Guerrilla military operations may move on to this revolutionary attempt at seizure of power, or they may drop back to the sporadic, harassing operations best defined as insurgency. If the guerrillas confront oppressive dictatorships, if they avoid the temptation to win by spreading terror, and especially if they refuse help from another nation using terrorist methods, then their operations are a legitimate form of conflict.

Despite the foregoing distinctions, every state reserves for itself the political and legal authority to define terrorism in the context of domestic and foreign affairs. The United States is a case in point.

In the American federal system, each state determines what constitutes an offense under its criminal or penal code. States have therefore defined terrorism generically as a crime, thus ending the true need for the use of specific statues covering other selected criminal acts that are identified as terrorism. In general, state laws concerning terrorism appear under nine separate headings, including civil defense (interstate compacts and state emergency management plans), antiterrorism provisions, destructive devices, terrorist threats, enhanced criminal penalties, victim compensation, street terrorism, ecological terrorism, and taxes.

On the federal level, U.S. Department of State adopted a definition, which is contained in Title 22 of the United States Code, Section 2656f(d), stating that "the term 'terrorism' means premeditated, politically motivated violence perpetrated against noncombatant targets by subnational groups or clandestine agents, usually intended to influence an audience."

The term "noncombatant," according to the Department of State, is interpreted to mean, "in addition to civilians, military personnel (whether or not on duty) who are not deployed in a war zone or warlike setting." Moreover, "the term 'international terrorism' means terrorism involving citizens of the territory of more than one country," and "the term 'terrorist group' means any group practicing, or that has significant subgroups that practice, international terrorism."

The U.S. Congress, on the other hand, has tended to define terrorism mainly in terms of specific criminal offenses with an international aspect. The congressional acts include Crimes Against Internationally

Protected Persons, Crimes Against Aviation, and Crimes Against Taking of Hostages.

In general, the evolution of American perceptions has gradually emerged from traditional views that terrorism constitutes a "crime" to a new disposition that "terrorism" is a new unprecedented form of warfare. What particularly influenced this transition was the September 11, 2001 attacks by al-Qaeda, the international terrorist network, aiming at America's most visible symbols of prowess in New York and Washington, D.C. Indeed, 9/11 provided the U.S. government, particularly the President, exclusive wartime authority to protect the American people

Two particular legal steps undertaken by the executive branch of the United States are noteworthy. First, on October 26, 2001, President Bush signed into law the USA Patriot Act. At that time, he underscored the importance of the legislation in that it "will give intelligence and law enforcement officials important new tools to fight a present danger." He remarked at that time, "Countering and investigating terrorist activity is the number one priority for both law enforcement and intelligence agencies."

The USA Patriot Act enables the U.S. government to be better equipped to identify, investigate, follow, detain, prosecute, and punish suspected terrorists. As today's terrorist increasingly uses sophisticated tools—advanced technology and international money transfers—the government's capabilities must be formidable as well. In essence, the USA Patriot Act aimed to significantly improve the surveillance of terrorists and increase the rapidity of tracking down and intercepting terrorists.

A second measure was undertaken on November 13 of that year. President Bush stated that "an extraordinary emergency exists for national defense purposes" caused him to issue a military order which related to the detention, treatment, and trial of noncitizens suspected of being members of al-Qaeda, "engaged in, aided or abetted, or conspired to commit, acts of international terrorism," or harboring them. More specifically, the order allows for the secretary of defense to detain, either in the United States or abroad, such individuals and initiate charges against them in a military tribunal. The military tribunals are mandated to reach decisions following a two-thirds majority vote of the military commission members. The decisions are nonappealable, although they are reviewable by the secretary of defense or president at the latter's designation.

According to White House Counsel Alberto Gonzalez, the military tribunals would provide another avenue, disparate from civilian courts, by which to prosecute alleged terrorists. Critics of the presidential order proffer, inter alia, that the tribunal should include more procedural and substantive safeguards to suspects. It has been suggested that the U.S. action could prompt some foreign countries to charge U.S. citizens abroad with various crimes and prosecute them in their own military tribunals.

What appears mostly problematic is in the initiation of the Bush preemptive doctrine, unveiled on September 20, 2002, in the aftermath of 9/11 and before the invasion of Iraq. This policy, which shifted American strategy from its traditional deterrence and containment approach toward a more proactive and aggressive disposition, allows the United States to act alone and preemptively, if necessary, to exercise the right of self-defense in confronting global terrorism and threats from hostile states seeking weapons of mass destruction. Despite the continuing U.S.-led multilateral coalition efforts to prosecute the war against terrorism in both the "frontlines" of Afghanistan and Iraq, the likelihood of a military victory in the short term is doubtful, particularly in the current insurgency environments.

Nevertheless, the Bush administration reaffirmed the 2002 preemptive doctrine in the release of a new "National Security Strategy of the United States," dated March 15, 2006. In this White House document, the most controversial element, namely the elevation of preemptive strikes to a central component of American strategy is still followed. But beyond the need to project military power in order to prevent terrorist attacks before they occur and to deny the terrorists opportunities to control nations from which they could launch operations, there is a recognition that there is a long-term need to focus on "the war of ideas" and to expand human rights and democratic infrastructures

Now, almost four years after the "National Security Strategy" was initiated and recently updated, the key question is whether the United States is as safe as it needs to be in light of the conventional and unconventional challenges to homeland security. The defense gaps, ranging from adequately protecting the nation's critical infrastructure to first responders' preparedness, call once again for learning the lessons of the past and focusing more realistically than ever before on the structures, resources, and implementation of the counterterrorism recommendations offered by the various commissions over the past three decades.

It is obvious, of course, that despite the fact that the United States, thus far at least, is the only superpower, it must conduct the global counterterrorism campaign in close partnership with members of the international community. One example of international cooperation relates to the U.S. Measures Implementing the 2004 June U.S.-EU Declaration on Combating Terrorism. According to a statement by the State Department on June 20, 2005, this Declaration renewed the Transatlantic commitment to cooperate closely and continue to work together to develop measures to maximize capacities to detect, investigate, and prosecute terrorists and prevent terrorists attacks, prevent access by terrorists to financial and other economic resources, enhance information sharing and cooperation among law enforcement agencies, and improve the effectiveness of their broader information systems. The following statement is keyed to the points of the Declaration:

1. We will work together to deepen the international consensus and enhance international efforts to combat terrorism.
2. We reaffirm our total commitment to prevent access by terrorists to financial and other economics resources.
3. We commit to working together to develop measures to maximize our capacities to detect, investigate, and prosecute terrorists and prevent terrorist attacks.
4. We will seek to further protect the security of international transport and ensure effective systems of border control.
5. We will work together to develop further our capabilities to deal with the consequences of a terrorist attack.
6. We will work in close cooperation to diminish the underlying conditions that terrorists can seize to recruit and exploit to their advantage. By promoting democracy, development, good governance, justice, increased trade, and freedom, we can help end dictatorship and extremism that bring millions of people to misery and bring danger to our own people.

7. We will target our external relations actions toward priority Third Countries where counter-terrorist capacity or commitment to combating terrorism needs to be enhanced.

These strategic commitments to combat terrorism globally, while protecting human rights, underscore the world's disposition that comprehensive and proportionate responses to the criminal threats will make contemporary societies more secure in the post-9/11 era.

---

* This is a revised version of the Lisbon presentation based on research conducted on "Counter-Terrorism Strategies in the 21st Century." Some of the material was published previously in articles and books written by the author.

Chapter 18
The U.S. War on Terror

Richard Falkenrath

This chapter focuses on the United States and its approach to the war on terror from the perspective of someone who worked at the White House for the first term of the Bush Administration and experienced 9/11 there.

There were really three phases in the U.S. response to 9/11 and the war on terror: from 9/11 until the invasion of Iraq; from the invasion of Iraq until the 2004 elections; and from the election until today. Each represent quite different periods in U.S. foreign policy and our experience with the war on terror.

Phase I: From 9/11 to the Invasion of Iraq

It is hard to imagine from afar the impact that the 911 attacks had on the American psyche and on American politics. The United States had never been attacked in that way before, and unlike European countries had no experience with devastation, at home, in modern times. Unlike European countries and many other countries around the world, it really had no significant experience with Islamic terrorism directly inside the United States. These events, therefore, had a profound psychological impact on the American people and American leaders and, in particular, on President Bush, who had been in office only 8 months and really had not yet found his footing—he had not yet figured out what the purpose of his Administration was going to be. Suddenly, the attacks of 9/11 gave him a purpose that he didn't have before. 9/11 has been by far the single most important formative experience for the Bush Presidency.

It also was also important for domestic politics. It provided a rallying call for the country around the Republican Party and provided the President with a story for the American people about why his party should achieve majority status in both Houses of Congress and why he should be re-elected.

Moreover, in substantive terms, 9/11 precipitated a transformation in federal governance in the United States:

- Dozens of new laws were passed;
- The bureaucracy of the U.S. Government was reorganized—a difficult task;
- A war was launched to eliminate a sanctuary that had existed for half a decade in Afghanistan;
- The wall that had existed between domestic law enforcement and foreign intelligence was torn down;
- The rules by which U.S. domestic agencies could collect information, tap phones, and tap email were changed;
- U.S. efforts to secure its borders were totally transformed;
- Transportation security was dramatically enhanced;
- The U.S. budget for homeland security and defense against weapons of mass destruction was quintupled;
- The U.S. defense budget was increased by about 30% per year—a massive increase.

The list goes on and on. All the things that were done in that first year after 9/11 were done very quickly and, I must say, without careful consideration of the costs and benefits. For the United States, the year right after 9/11 was not a period of thinking twice. It was a period of acting quickly and decisively. If there was a strategy behind what the President was doing and what his Administration was doing. I would say it was one of relentless offensive action against the threats we face.

The single highest priority for President Bush and his Administration was not homeland security or transportation security *per se*; it was to prevent subsequent attacks against the United States or U.S. interests by identifying the threats that existed in the world and eliminating them in one way or another. That determination sprang from the experience of 9/11. This had never happened to us before and suddenly this terrible thing happened on a beautiful fall day. And when we thought about it we realized that these attacks had been developing for a very long time—that the threat that manifested itself on 9/11 had origins back in the 1990s. Fundamentally, however, our failure was perceived to be the failure to act preventively against the al-Qaeda threat as it was maturing in the hills of Afghanistan. This was the big lesson that the President and his principal officers took from the events of 9/11.

A lot may be said about the year following 9/11. It was a very interesting year, by far the most active year of my professional life. But things really changed in the fall of 2002.

Phase II: The Invasion of Iraq

In the fall of 2002 the President decided it was time to remove Saddam Hussein from power. The decision to invade Iraq and to remove Saddam Hussein from power would not have been possible without 9/11. Also it would have not been possible if the U.S. intelligence community and the U.S. policy community had not believed that Saddam Hussein had stockpiles of chemical and biological weapons. But we did believe it. At the time I was someone regarded as a critical consumer of classified intelligence, and I believed it as well. It turned out to be false. But I know of no person who was cleared to receive all the classified information who did not actually believe there were chemical and biological weapons in Iraq—Republican or Democrat, British, even French.

Now, in order to "sell" the invasion of Iraq to the American people the President elected to define it in terms of a war on terror. In fact he called it "the central front on the war on terror." This was a good, short term communication strategy. It was a compelling explanation for the American people and for the Congress, which authorized the use of force by a wide margin. But it was a very problematic decision on his part, one which has had very difficult long term consequences.

Today, the issue of the wisdom of invading Iraq and removing Saddam Hussein from power is tearing the Republican Party apart, and it is profoundly divisive in the United States. While Europe and most of the international community seem to have made up its mind, there is still a vicious debate in the United States. If one had to declare a winner or a loser today, one would have to say that the President is losing. He is losing the debate about the wisdom of removing Saddam Hussein from power. And the key reason for that—which gets to the question of the cost of the measures undertaken in the name of war on terror—is the issue whether we are making America and the world less safe by removing Saddam Hussein from power and by unleashing all the very complex forces that currently resulting in so much violence in Iraq.

I am very worried about that possibility. I am very worried that Iraq will, in fact, become a breeding ground for terrorists and contribute to the radicalization and sophistication of Islamic militancy worldwide.

At the moment, however, that idea is mainly a plausible hypothesis. It is not really proven yet. I am not aware of any terrorist who has gone to Iraq, become radicalized by those events, learned how to fight there, learned how to build a bomb and improvise nuclear device and then left Iraq and carried out an attack some place else. That might happen, it very well might. But, to my knowledge, until today it has not yet happened. In fact, many of the individuals who went to Iraq are dying there, whether through suicide bombs or other actions being taken against them. Evidence will accumulate over time, and it is entirely possible that with more evidence we will know, for certain, one way or another, the true impact of Iraq. But, at the moment, the notion that U.S. intervention has aggravated the threat is a plausible hypothesis.

The other point about Iraq is one of policy. When one is in government and has a position of responsibility for a policy, one really doesn't have the luxury of looking back and asking: did I make a mistake? Was it wrong? How badly did I plan and prepare? One needs to decide what to do that day and the next day. And from that perspective—the relatively narrow un-academic perspective of policy makers and former policy makers, such as myself—there is no real alternative to the present course of action in Iraq. We are there, the situation is as we find it, and we need to see it through. That kind of disciplining effect should temper some of the criticism that one reads in other chapters of this book and hears in various parts of the world, including Europe.

I am the first to admit that many mistakes were made in the run up to Iraq. But the fact is that we are there now, there is a coalition there, there is a terrible violent process under way, there is a flawed constitutional process moving forward, but there is really no alternative to try and see the job through. The President and his policy makers do not have the luxury of academics and editorial writers of simply criticizing something and walking away.

Phase III: The 2004 Elections and Their Aftermath

The 2004 election in the United States was important, because the President's opponent John Kerry presented no viable alternative. He didn't decisively oppose Iraq. Not only did he vote for the resolution of use of force he said he would have voted for it even if he had known there were no weapons of mass destruction. He failed to present any alternative in the American political process.

Since the election, however, President Bush has changed course, in subtle but important ways. There have been significant personnel changes in the U.S. Government. There is a certain new breeze coming out of Washington now that Colin Powell has departed and Condoleezza Rice has become Secretary of State and reigned in the Defense Department. There is a very clear understanding among the highest levels of the Bush Administration that the political aspects of global counterterrorism operations need to be re-emphasized, and that more time and effort need to be spent on public diplomacy and on the promotion of democracy, than on narrow military, intelligence or law enforcement operations. There is not a sense that the United States should stop pushing the harder edges of the war on terror, but there is a new consensus on the need for a better balance with the "softer" elements of the campaign.

This new consensus is tied to President Bush's call to advance democracy around the world. This is very important. He may be wrong, but the fact is that he really believes it. It deserves to be considered seriously. His new formulation places the global war on terror within a broader context, within a more complex struggle against Islamic militancy. The heart of the notion is that the way to get ahead of that problem, the way to really turn it around, over a period that could take decades, is to promote better governance in the Muslim and particularly in the Arab world. By better governance President Bush really means democratic government.

For 50 years, since the end of World War II, it has been very expedient for the United States and all Western powers to support governments in the Arab and Muslim world who were relatively compliant with our policy wishes in their external behavior, but were simply dreadful in their internal behavior. They failed to meet the fundamental needs of their people. This is completely documented in the Arab Development Report Commission conducted by the United Nations. It is really remarkable how badly governed this part of the world has been in terms of its economic models, its social liberalization, or its democratic processes.

In light of these developments, when the President says better government, he is taking a stand in favor of democracy. This can be a very dangerous thing to do, because the previous model, for all its other faults, did have certain aspects of stability. Nonetheless, he thinks it's the right thing to do. He is pushing it in a way that no President ever really has before. This is controversial. This theme has emerged only since the election, and is his attempt to tackle this terrible cancer of Islamic radicalism that has manifested itself as catastrophic terrorism, on 9/11 in the U.S. and repeatedly since in other cities in other countries.

U.S.-European Cooperation Against Global Terrorism

I want to conclude with a few words about U.S.-European cooperation in the struggle against global terrorism. I personally believe that Europe is a far more dangerous place than the United States. There have been no attacks in the United States since 9/11. There have been in Europe. There have been very serious operational cells arrested and taken down in Europe. This hasn't happened in the United States; the cells that have been arrested are mostly facilitators. There is simply a much higher degree of terrorist activity in Europe. The European Muslim population is far larger than the U.S. Muslim population, and appears to be a far more fertile recruiting ground for terrorists who seek to create new cells and identify new operatives to carry out new operations.

In short, Europe is a more dangerous place, right now, than the United States. I think that European leaders and the European public, by and large, agree with this assessment and are moving out very smartly in certain respects.

Transatlantic cooperation on counterterrorism is very good on a tactical bilateral basis. Whenever there is a specific case, a specific individual, or a specific operation, the U.S. government and whichever European government is involved often work together very well. I remember a case involving France during the absolutely worst period in U.S.-France relations, when the French government was actively leading a campaign against the President's Iraq policy. But just at this point a real situation developed, and at the professional level the cooperation was seamless and totally unaffected by the political temperature.

At the strategic policy level, however, U.S.-EU cooperation leaves a lot to be desired. One of the problems is Europe's ambivalence about the role of the European Union and the European Commission in this area. This leads to confusion in Washington about who to talk to in Europe on strategic issues related to the war on terror. Should it talk to each head of state individually? Should it talk to only those represented at the G8? Should it talk to Javier Solana? Should it talk to whatever nation holds the six-month rotating Presidency of the European Council? It is hard from Washington's perspective to just figure out who should we be talking to. Who represents Europe?

Washington wishes to work more closely with Europe on a strategic issues related to terrorism, but really doesn't know who represents Europe on this issue. The institutional structures and the division of responsibilities between the nations and the European Union apparatus in Brussels are simply too complicated for the U.S. to navigate very well. I certainly admit many missteps from the United States and by Washington in dealing with Europe on matters dealing with international operations against terrorism. But I hope that Europeans will understand that their own house is not entirely in order either, and that there are many issues we need to work through. In many cases, unfortunately, the United States simply does not know who to talk to.

Chapter 19

Tackling Terror:
A Transatlantic Agenda

Daniel S. Hamilton

The fight against terrorism has the potential either to drive Europeans and Americans apart or to bring them together. Much depends on leadership. If Europeans and Americans are to be safer than they are today, individual efforts must be aligned with more effective transatlantic cooperation. Neither the framework for the transatlantic relationship nor the way European or North American governments are currently organized adequately address the challenge of catastrophic terrorism. There have been some promising beginnings, but they have been ad hoc achievements rather than integrated elements of a more comprehensive approach.

Individual efforts must now be complemented by a systematic, high profile effort in areas ranging from intelligence, counterterrorism, financial coordination and law enforcement to customs, air and seaport security, biodefense, critical infrastructure protection and other activities.[1]

Four Hurdles

If Europe and the United States are to engage more effectively together, they first need to understand better the different paths each has been on until now. Four hurdles in particular have consistently plagued transatlantic cooperation:

---

[1] This article draws on other work by the author, referenced in additional footnotes, as well as Daniel S. Hamilton, "Transforming Homeland Security: A Road Map for the Transatlantic Alliance," in Esther Brimmer, ed., *Transforming Homeland Security: U.S. and European Approaches* (Washington, D.C.: Center for Transatlantic Relations, 2006).

- differences in risk perception;
- the U.S. tendency to treat the issue as one of war and peace, versus European tendencies to treat the issue as one of crime and justice;
- challenges inherent in the U.S. concept of "pushing borders out;" and
- sheer organizational incoherence on both sides.

Let us review these briefly. The first hurdle is a difference in risk perception. Most Europeans feel significantly less threatened than Americans—despite incontrovertible evidence that Europe is both a base for and a target of international terrorism. Risk perceptions also vary within Europe itself. Many in Europe and not a few in the United States view the 9/11 attacks as isolated incidents. Some in Europe also see terrorism as principally America's problem, one they believe the Bush Administration has exacerbated through its own actions, particularly the war in Iraq. Some see the subsequent Madrid and London attacks through the same perspective—nations were attacked that joined the Americans in the Iraqi war. It is important to note that European governments promptly rejected Osama bin Laden's offer of immunity to any country that would pull its troops out of the Middle East, and that Europe and the United States are working closely to deal with terrorism. But there is still appeal in policies that demonstrate distance from Washington. These divergent risk perceptions tear at both transatlantic partnership and EU solidarity.

A second hurdle is rooted in different approaches to the challenges posed by 21st century terrorism. Whereas U.S. efforts represent a radical break with traditional American approaches to security and reflect a tendency to characterize the issue as one of war and peace, initial European efforts represented an extension of previous efforts to combat terrorism and reflect a tendency to characterize the issue as one of crime and justice.

During the 20th century Americans thought of "national" security as something to be advanced far from American shores. The United States invested massively to project power quickly and decisively to any point on the globe, and invested meagerly to protect Americans at home. September 11 shattered that perspective. Now, Americans share a strange sense that they are both uniquely powerful and uniquely vulnerable. Partisan divisions within the United States are fierce, but they obscure a deeper consensus that the threat of WMD terrorism warrants a reframing of U.S. foreign and domestic policies. Americans disagree intensely whether the U.S. should have invaded Iraq. They disagree over the degree to which public security efforts may intrude on personal liberties. But most agree that America is engaged in a global war on terrorism. And most are willing to project American power abroad to "win" that war.[2] They are far more receptive to radical breaks with traditional thinking, far more inclined to support crash efforts to protect the homeland, and far less concerned with breaking diplomatic crockery along the way.

In the name of this "war" on terror the Bush Administration has justified a number of extraordinary actions, including spying on U.S. citizens without court warrants, the practice of rendition, and detaining terrorist suspects as "enemy combatants" beyond the jurisdiction of domestic or international law. These are controversial in the United States as well as abroad, and have hampered international cooperation even with America's closest allies.

Just as Americans have sought to understand the consequences of September 11 within the context of their own national experience, European views have been colored by the kind of domestic terrorism that has confronted them for the past three decades. During that period, more than 5,000 lives were lost to terrorism in Britain, Ireland, and Spain alone. Whereas U.S. officials are suddenly haunted by the prospect of further—and perhaps even more catastrophic—attacks, European officials have long been taunted by domestic terrorists, who have argued that a government's own zeal to apprehend terrorists would lead it to subvert the very rules of the open society it sought to protect. A number of European countries have adopted laws to confront domestic terrorism while preserving civil liberties. Of course, there are differences within Europe as well, which make generalizations difficult. Recent British anti-terror laws, for instance, go even further than some U.S. efforts.

These perspectives influence the way in which each side has addressed the threat. Whereas the U.S. effort has been waged with the

---

[2] For more on these developments, see Daniel S. Hamilton, "Transatlantic Societal Security: A new paradigm for a new era," in Anja Dalgaard-Nielsen and Daniel S. Hamilton, *Transatlantic Homeland Security* (London: Routledge, 2006), pp. 172-196; "One nation after all," The Economist, September 11, 2004, p. 32.

rhetoric of war, most European efforts have been viewed largely through the perspective of crime. Most Europeans view terrorism itself as a tactic rather than an enemy. These differing perspectives complicate transatlantic cooperation: American critics charge Europeans with complacency, while European critics accuse Americans of extremism.

A third hurdle has to do with the Bush Administration's initiatives to "push the border out." Despite the impact of September 11 on the United States, the natural instinct in a nation bounded by two oceans is still to fight one's enemies abroad so one doesn't need to fight them at home. Washington's "forward defense" mentality, which exerts such a pervasive influence over the U.S. military, is also being applied to homeland security. The result has been a series of U.S. efforts to "externalize" the nation's domestic security by "pushing borders out"—essentially to move the focus of the anti-terrorism campaign abroad.

Aspects of this effort are controversial and problematic for transatlantic relations, for instance the Bush Administration's attempts to justify its war in Iraq through its war on terrorism; the notion enshrined in the Patriot Act that non-citizens have fewer rights to privacy and due process than U.S. citizens; or the "Guantanomo" practice of holding non-citizens indefinitely outside the jurisdiction of U.S. courts and without status in either domestic or international law. Tremendous European goodwill towards the U.S. after 9/11 has essentially been squandered by various manifestations of the externalization policy. It is important to note that much of the Guantanamo system remains controversial in the U.S. itself, and is currently under review by the courts.

Other "externalization" initiatives have simply caught European partners flatfooted, since such initiatives either require greater coherence among EU member states than they have been able to muster on such issues as customs, or collide with prevailing European regulations, for instance regarding data privacy.

Despite these difficulties, in select areas "externalization" has formed the basis for practical transatlantic agreements. Such U.S.-led initiatives as the Proliferation Security Initiative, the Container Security Initiative, Operation Safe Commerce or the Customs-Trade

Partnership Against Terrorism (C-TPAT)[3] are all examples of "pushing borders out" in ways that have included European partners. The basic premise should be acceptable: it is safer to interdict potentially nasty people or items before they ever reach one's territory rather than trying to find them once they've arrived, even while safeguarding the free flow of people, goods and ideas upon which open societies depend. But "pushing borders out" will require unprecedented international cooperation tied to a major transformation of national customs and immigration agencies into the equivalent of diplomatic services. The resource implications are serious, and as indicated there is potential for abuse—such as conflating anti-terrorist efforts with immigration control efforts in ways that might lead to serious violations of human rights; or paying inadequate attention to the international legal ramifications of extraterritorial initiatives.[4] Moreover, such efforts may be self-defeating unless they establish a level playing field for all stakeholders. But the core principle offers important insights into new forms of international collaboration.

A fourth hurdle has been the sheer organizational incoherence of anti-terrorist efforts in the U.S. and in Europe. The Bush Administration's approach has represented little more an aggregation of discrete elements, ranging from counterterrorist intelligence, border security, risk management and cargo screening to health and other issues. The sum is less than the parts, and many parts are still moving to their own beat. For most of these missions, the bipartisan 9/11 Commission in December 2005 gave the Administration failing grades.

---

[3] For details on the Proliferation Security Initiative, see the U.S. Department of State fact sheet at http://www.state.gov/t/np/rls/other/46858.htm. For information on C-TPAT see http://www.customs.treas.gov/linkhandler/cgov/import/commercial_enforcement/ctpat/ct pat_strategicplan.ctt/ctpat_strategicplan.pdf. For a description of the Container Security Initiative, see http://en.wikipedia.org/wiki/Container_Security_Initiative. Operation Safe Commerce builds on C-TPAT and CSI by (1) building a greater understanding of vulnerabilities within global supply chains, and (2) ensuring that new technologies and business practices designed to enhance container security are both commercially viable and successful. For a critique of some of these efforts, see Stephen Flynn, "Addressing the Shortcomings of the Customs-Trade Partnership Against Terrorism (C-TPAT) and the Container Security Initiative," Testimony before a hearing of the Permanent Sub-Committee on Investigations, Committee on Homeland Security and Governmental Affairs, United States Senate May 26, 2005, available at http://www.cfr.org/publication/8141/addressing_the_shortcomings_of_the_customstrade_partnership_against_terrorism_ctpat_and_the_container_security_initiative.html.

[4] For a critique, see Tom Barry, "Pushing Our Borders Out," http://americas.irc-online.org/ pdf/briefs/0502immigration.pdf.

U.S. efforts are matched by a byzantine collection of efforts on the other side of the Atlantic. The European Union, having expanded to 25 nations, must now address the domestic security needs of 456 million people, with more to come in the next few years. But preventive and protective efforts still consist of a patchwork of contributions by the EU, its member states, and individual ministries, agencies, and services within those states. Links to non-EU members are uneven. Civil protection remains primarily the preserve of member states, and there are major turf wars between the European Commission and the European Council. There is no European "Minister for Homeland Security" available to the U.S. Secretary of Homeland Security. The EU Coordinator for Counterterrorism, appointed for the first time in the spring of 2004, has neither line authority over Commission bureaucrats or member state agencies, nor a significant budget to promote harmonization of policies, procedures, standards, or equipment, which vary widely across member states. He cannot prescribe; he can only persuade. He reports to the High Representative for Foreign and Security Policy in the European Council, and thus is of a lower level than the U.S. Secretary, and works out of the European Council rather than the European Commission, and so only has a small staff at his disposal. In the meantime, the EU suffers gaps in intelligence sharing, and interoperability between the police, judicial and intelligence services is questionable. SitCen, the center for intelligence in the Council Secretariat, analyzes information, but operational work remains the exclusive competence of the national security and intelligence services. The Union simply has a long way to go, particularly with regard to networked civilian and military capabilities, civil protection and safeguarding critical infrastructure.

In short, both sides face serious organizational challenges. And the interaction between these unwieldy, multi-jurisdictional approaches on each side of the Atlantic has complicated efforts to boost transatlantic and broader international cooperation.

Finding Common Ground

Despite these hurdles, much has been done on both sides of the Atlantic to make life safer for ordinary citizens. In recent years a considerable number of cooperative intra-European and transatlantic arrangements have been set in place covering such issues as border security, air transport and container traffic to judicial, law enforcement, and intelligence cooperation.

Within Europe, the EU has created an European Arrest Warrant and started joint investigation teams for criminal investigation. It created a common judicial space, named "Eurojust," to improve the coordination of member states' law enforcement activities, to help with assistance and extradition requests and to support investigations. The EU has adopted legislation on terrorist financing and beefed up laws against money laundering. Europol is collecting, sharing and analyzing information about international terrorism and assessing EU member state performance. National legislation was tightened by key EU member states. Following the March 11 attacks the EU adopted a solidarity clause that commits member states to help each other to prevent and protect against terrorist attacks and to assist each other in case an attack happens. Moreover, European nations have agreed to develop an integrated threat analysis capability at the EU level. FRONTEX, the European Borders Agency, has become operational.[5]

The U.S. and the EU have also stepped up their cooperation. Mutual legal assistance and extradition agreements have been signed. Intelligence sharing has improved, especially information about specific individuals suspected of ties to terrorism. The U.S. and EU have signed agreements to improve container security, expand customs cooperation, improve public-private partnerships to ensure transportation security, and transfer passenger name record (PNR) data. They have agreed to enhance information exchange to target and interdict maritime threats, work more closely through Interpol to deal with lost and stolen passports and other border issues, incorporate interoperable biometric identifiers into travel documentation, enhance their policy dialogue on border and transport security, and start a dialogue on improving capabilities to respond to terrorist attacks involving chemical, biological, radiological or nuclear weapons.

A number of these initiatives are also interesting for broader reasons. First, transatlantic efforts have helped to advance deeper European integration. The creation of the European arrest warrant

---

[5] The European Council provides six-month updates of its efforts in this area. See http://ue.eu.int/ueDocs/cms_Data/docs/pressData/en/jha/87254.pdf

204 Terrorism and International Relations

and the formation of Eurojust, for example, would scarcely have come about without intense U.S. pressure.

Second, the U.S. is gradually accepting the EU as a bilateral partner in issues of societal protection. The U.S.- EU mutual extradition and legal assistance treaties represent a significant expansion of traditional bilateral cooperation in law enforcement and modify transatlantic legal assistance in combating transnational crime in 26 countries. They were the first of their kind to be successfully negotiated between the EU and a third party. Given the divergences in European and U.S. legal systems concerning the death penalty, as well as standards in sentencing and for the protection of personal data, these agreements would have been a political impossibility before September 11.

Third, the U.S. is grudgingly accepting EU standards on issues of vital national importance. U.S. cooperation with Europol, for instance, enables the U.S. to share in the EU's growing development of databases and capabilities, based on the EU's own standards for data protection and privacy.

Fourth, transatlantic cooperation on container security, PNR data transfer and biometric passports is very significant because it requires acceptance of mutual constraints on a broad range of state action in the area of border control—one of the defining aspects of territorial sovereignty. The Container Security Initiative, for instance, is reciprocal, meaning not only that U.S. customs officials can operate in such ports as Rotterdam, Le Havre, Hamburg and Algeciras, but European inspectors could be stationed in Boston, Houston, Long Beach or Shreveport. Such a program is perhaps but the harbinger of a coming revolution in border affairs that creates "virtual" borders far from a nation's territory.

Moreover, such efforts are not starting from scratch. Even though terrorism became the overriding focus of transatlantic security discussions after September 11, 2001, a growing substructure of cooperative efforts to combat criminal and financial threats had already developed among the U.S. and the EU, the G-7, and other OECD countries through the 1990's. These initiatives provided a solid platform on which additional counter-terrorism activities could be based.

In short, despite practical, conceptual and political obstacles to deeper transatlantic cooperation in the area of homeland security, both sides have recognized that deeper collaboration is essential if either side of the Atlantic is to be more secure, and are breaking new ground in their efforts to advance their common security. Taken together, the growing array of U.S.-European cooperative ventures provides ample evidence for a rethinking of anti-terrorist efforts to span the transatlantic space. These agreements underscore the resilience of transatlantic partnership even in the face of serious disagreements.

This is important, because there is still much to be done. Compartmentalized approaches to security remain powerful on both sides of the Atlantic. Transatlantic arrangements have largely been ad hoc achievements rather than integrated elements of a more comprehensive approach. Without systematic pan-European and transatlantic coordination, however, each side of the Atlantic is at greater risk of attack. If the transatlantic allies cannot find common ground, there will be little hope for broader global efforts.

A systematic, high-profile effort is necessary, desirable—and now perhaps more possible. A systematic approach could be guided by a few basic propositions.

First, the threat is real—and common. The entire transatlantic space is both a base for and a target of catastrophic terrorism.

Transatlantic squabbles cannot be allowed to distract from a basic fact: the entire transatlantic space is both a base for and a target of international terrorism. Americans are quite focused on this fact. It would be foolhardy to assume that Europe would not be a target of future terrorist attacks. Al-Qaeda and home-grown terrorists inspired by it have directly attacked three European members of NATO—Turkey, Spain and the United Kingdom—and have tried to launch attacks in other parts of Europe as well. Al-Qaeda cells killed European tourists in North Africa. Terrorist cells have been discovered in London, Rotterdam, Milan, Hamburg, and Frankfurt, as have active recruitment efforts by Europe-based radicals in various parts of the world. Plots have been uncovered against the Strasbourg

Christmas market, planes using Heathrow airport, the French tourist island La Reunion, the Russian and U.S. embassies in Paris, the U.S. embassies in Rome and Sarajevo, a U.S. military base in Belgium, and U.S. military facilities in Great Britain. Switzerland and other nations are major hubs for financial transactions by letterbox companies linked to al-Qaeda. Moreover, radicals based in London and Lyon managed to manufacture and test toxins like ricin and botulism, presumably for attacks across Europe, before being arrested by the authorities. France, Germany, Turkey, Italy, Bosnia and the UK have all uncovered terrorist activity linked to al-Qaeda. One of the terrorists who crashed into the World Trade Center once flew a precise flight plan over unprotected nuclear installations and key political and economic institutions along the Rhine and Ruhr. The horrific school massacre in Beslan emphatically underscored the potential for spillover of terrorism related to the situation in Chechnya. There is simply no question that international terrorism constitutes an active threat to both Europe and North America.[6]

Second, we must understand that what we must protect is our connectiveness, not just our territory.

Al-Qaeda and related terrorist groupings are lethal networks, often with global reach. Such networks can be flexible and agile, constantly able to reconfigure themselves to address new challenges and seize new opportunities. They are networks that prey on other networks—the interconnected arteries and nodes of vulnerability that accompany the free flow of people, ideas, goods and services, and the complex interdependent systems on which free societies depend. These range from global electronic financial networks, networked information systems, "just-in-time" food supply chains and business systems, air, sea and land transportation to flows of fossil fuels or nuclear energy. It is our complete reliance on such networks, matched with their susceptibility to catastrophic disruption, that make them such tempting tar-

---

[6] For other assessments and reports, see the Non-confidential report on the terrorism situation and trends in Europe, EU TE-SAT 14280/2/02, pp. 19-27; Joanne Wright, "Terrorism in Europe Since 9/11: Responses and Challenges, accessed at www.cdu.edu.au/cdss2003/papers/Sym3papers/joannewright.pdf; Desmond Butler, "3 arrested over ties to Muslim Militants," *International Herald Tribune*, November 29, 2003; "Die Saudi-Connection," *Der Spiegel*, 14/2003, pp. 70-72; Jon Henley, "Al-Qaida terror plot foiled, say French police," *The Guardian*, January 12, 2004.

gets for terrorists.[7] In the 21st century, **what we are defending is our connectiveness.**

Globalization is causing a shift in conceptions of power and vulnerability from those that are state-centric and territorial-based to those that are stateless and network-based.[8] A transformative approach to security would supplement the traditional focus on *the security of the territory* with a clearer focus on the *security of critical functions of society*.

Terrorists wielding weapons of mass destruction or mass disruption are less intent on seizing and holding our territory than they are on destroying or disrupting the ability of our societies to function.[9] Antagonists wishing to inflict harm upon a society want to find the key nodes where critical infrastructures connect. When al-Qaeda destroyed the World Trade Center towers, it engaged simultaneously in attacks on the global securities markets through simultaneous market manipulation, demonstrating that terrorists understand how interconnected, and vulnerable, the world's collective infrastructures are to attack.[10]

Natural disasters, however, may also threaten our connectiveness. Hurricane Katrina, for instance, disrupted key energy supply lines between the Gulf coast states and other regions of the United States. The 2004 Pacific tsunami became a world-class security disaster for distant Sweden because of the major tourist networks Swedish citizens had established in recent decades.

A security system focused on protecting the connective tissue of modern society would seek to protect critical nodes of activity while attacking the critical nodes of those networks that would do us harm.

---

[7] See Steven Flynn, *America the Vulnerable: How Our Government is Failing to Protect us from Terrorism* (New York: HarperCollins, 2004), p. 86.

[8] See Jean-Marie Guehenno, *The End of the Nation-State* (Minneapolis: University of Minnesota Press, 2000).

[9] See Bengt Sundelius, "From National Total Defense to Embedded Societal Security," in Daniel Hamilton, Bengt Sundelius and Jesper Grönvall, eds., *Protecting the Homeland: European Approaches to Societal Security: Implications for the United States* (Washington, D.C.: Center for Transatlantic Relations, 2005).

[10] See Jonathan Winer, *The Role of Economic Sanctions in Combating International Terrorism (and Its Place in the Trans-Atlantic Alliance)* (Washington, DC: American Institute for Contemporary German Studies, 2001), available at www.aicgs.org/Publications/PDF/Winer.pdf.

It would integrate security considerations into the design and daily operations of such systems—from oversight of food production to the guarding of airport perimeters to the tracking and checking of ships. It would identify potential vulnerabilities linked to the technological complexity of the modern world and seek to transform them into high reliability systems. In would seek to anticipate and prevent possible "cascading effects" of a breakdown or collapse of any particular node of activity. It would ensure that "connectiveness vulnerabilities" are not built into future systems. It would engage the active participation of the private sector, which actually owns and controls most of these networks.[11]

Under concepts such as "resilience" or "total defense," countries such as the United Kingdom, Switzerland, Sweden and Finland have advanced efforts at national, regional and local levels to detect, prevent and if necessary handle disruptive challenges. These could range from floods, through outbreaks of human or animal disease, to terrorist attacks.[12] The advantage of these approaches is that they are capacity-based rather than threat-based, and they align efforts to improve internal security with those to promote external security. The disadvantage is that for the most part these efforts have been advanced on a national basis and yet, given both the interdependence of complex systems and the nature of contagious disease, effective societal security must also include an international dimension.

Focus on reducing risk rather than perfecting security

Efforts to advance societal security at home and abroad must proceed from the recognition that in an age of catastrophic terrorism there is no such thing as perfect security. It is impossible to stop every potential type of terrorist violence. We cannot protect every possible target, all the time, from every conceivable type of attack. The campaign will never entirely be "won." Terrorism is a threat that we must constantly combat if we are to reduce it to manageable levels so that

---

[11] Some corporate leaders may resist, but many realize that safety makes sense for the bottom line. The 24-hour manifest rule in the cargo industry, for instance, has actually increased productivity. Remarks by Eugene Pendimonti, Vice President of Maersk Sealand, to the Center for Transatlantic Relations, September 13, 2004.

[12] For basic information on UK efforts, see the CCS website, www.ukresilience.info/home.htm. For details and case studies of European national efforts, see Hamilton, Sundelius and Grönvall, op. cit.

we can live normal lives free of fear.[13] Anthony Cordesman summarizes the challenge:

> "Victory cannot be defined in terms of eradicating terrorism or eliminating risk. This war must be defined in much more limited terms. It will consist of reducing the threat of terrorism to acceptable levels—levels that allow us to go on with our lives in spite of the fact that new attacks are possible and that we may well see further and more serious tragedies."[14]

By focusing on preventing attacks that can cause large casualties, major economic or societal disruption, or severe political damage, nations can approach issues of societal security systematically and with a better chance of preventing future attacks.

Don't destroy what you are trying to protect

Thirty years ago, the Baader-Meinhoff terrorist gang goaded German authorities to hit back at them in ways they believed would break the law and undermine Germany's hard-won democracy. They reasoned that the quickest way to wound the German government would be to force it to break its own rules, corrupt its own nature and generate mistrust between the government and the governed. German leaders had to find the difficult balance. The anti-terrorist legislation that resulted sought to find this balance.[15]

This challenge is perhaps of even more relevance to democratic governments fighting international terrorism today. A number of the measures introduced to combat terrorism raise serious civil liberties concerns. In addition, abuses at Abu Ghraib and Guantanamo have undermined confidence in the U.S. Administration and international support for the anti-terrorism campaign. If the campaign is not per-

---

[13] Flynn, op. cit.; Bruce Hoffman, Presentation to Open Road 2002, Atlantic Command Transformation, Norfolk, VA, January 2002.

[14] Anthony Cordesman, *Biological Warfare and the "Buffy Paradigm,"* (Washington, D.C., Center for Strategic and International Studies, 2001) p. 4.

[15] For a review of German efforts to confront terrorism then and now, see Oliver Lepsius, *The Relationship between Security and Civil Liberties in the Federal Republic of Germany After September 11* (Washington, DC: American Institute for Contemporary German Studies, 2001), available at http://www.aicgs.org/Publications/PDF/lepsiusenglish.pdf.

ceived to be legitimate, it is unlikely to be effective. If efforts to protect our societies from catastrophic disruption are not aligned with the
freedoms of those societies, we endanger that which we are trying to
protect. At the same time, the U.S. is finding that judicial cooperation
is particularly important for dealing with terrorism. The unique
nature of terrorism means that maintaining the appearance of justice
and democratic legitimacy will be much more important than in normal wars or struggles. Ad-hoc anti-terrorist measures that have little
basis in societal values and defined legal procedures provide little
long-term bases for the necessary cooperation with other countries.

The U.S. and Europe can each learn from each other's experience
with mechanisms that seek to advance security and liberty, such as
sunset clauses and provisions for legislative oversight and judicial
review. If the U.S. and Europe can help each other live up to their
own standards, together they can help set human rights standards for
the broader anti-terrorist campaign. On the other hand, if concerns
about civil liberties are widespread even in the West's most sophisticated and oldest democracies, how much worse are they likely be in
countries without such strong traditions who are also cracking down
on suspects? Failure to advance security with liberty has the potential
to subvert other key priorities, such as transformation of the Broader
Middle East, where the overall trend throughout the Arab world has
been a decline in social, political and cultural freedoms in the name of
greater security against terrorism.[16]

Recognize that crime and war are merging

The tendency in European to cast the challenge as one of crime
and justice and the tendency in America to treat it as one of war and
peace are each dangerously myopic. As Catastrophic terrorism has
blurred the lines between crime and war, and poses a new threat that
requires the orchestration of efforts in both domains. A decade before
September 11 military historian Martin van Creveld anticipated these
developments:

---

[16] See Alyson Bailes, "Have the Terrorists Already Won?" Speaking Notes, Scanbus
Conference, Riga, September 14, 2004.

"Terrorist organizations and operations will be profoundly affected by information age technologies, which will provide these non-state actors with global reach. Modern communications and transportation technologies will have a profound impact on this new battlefront. There will be no fronts and no distinctions between civilian and military targets. Laws and conventions of war will not constrain terrorists and their state sponsors from seeking innovative means, to include WMD, to attack non-military targets and inflict terrible carnage. . . . Once the legal monopoly of armed force, long claimed by the state, is wrested out of its hands, existing distinctions between war and crime will break down"[17]

Most of the crucial battles in the campaign against terror around the world are not being fought by the military but by police, judges, border officers, intelligence officers, and financial and banking officials. But military force may be required at times, and in many circumstances military power may indeed need to be considered as an extension of law enforcement. Brian Jenkins suggests that this is likely to lead to new categories of law enforcement and precision warfare and new rules for operations, custody, and possible prosecution where law enforcement and armed conflict overlap.[18]

Tackling Terrorism: A Transatlantic Agenda

During the late 1940s and early 1950s Europeans and American responded together to the challenges facing their generation. The potential of catastrophic terrorism now challenges a new generation of Europeans and North Americans to reshape and reposition existing structures, and to devise new approaches that can help us respond more effectively to current threats. We should not settle for incremental, ad hoc adjustments to a system designed generations ago for a world that no longer exists. Instead, we should supplement traditional efforts, which focused either on territorial security or emergency response, with a third layer of "societal" security as an integral component of our relationship. In the first instance, of course, each nation must look to improve its own capabilities. But cooperation for societal

---

[17] Martin van Creveld, *The Transformation of War* (New York: The Free Press, 1991)

[18] See Brian Jenkins, "Intelligence and Homeland Security," in Dalgaard-Nielsen and Hamilton, *op. cit.*

security has become an urgent addition to the wider transatlantic agenda, and can be advanced on multiple tracks.

National Efforts

Nationally, the U.S. has yet to overcome the artificial distinctions between domestic and national security that continue to plague efforts in this area. The 9/11 Commission has made various proposals in this regard.

Within Europe, national efforts are uneven, given differing traditions. European countries have yet to ratify and implement all UN counterterrorism conventions and protocols. Not all have criminalized material and logistical support for terrorism (and in some cases, terrorism itself). Laws against document fraud need to be strengthened. Not all the ability to freeze terrorist assets. Legal or technical impediments to closer cooperation among countries on intelligence and information exchanges must be removed. Some countries have legal impediments to taking firm judicial action against suspected terrorists, often stemming from asylum laws that afford loopholes, inadequate counterterrorism legislation, or standards of evidence that lack flexibility in permitting law enforcement authorities to rely on classified-source information in holding terrorist suspects. The U.S. is concerned that some European states have at times demonstrated an inability to prosecute successfully or hold terrorists brought before their courts. Moreover, new EU and NATO members have quite uneven capabilities when it comes to societal security. Many need assistance to strengthen their legal framework and develop their capabilities to counter terrorism.[19]

Finally, nations on both sides of the Atlantic need to mainstream societal security and counterterrorism into foreign policy, including through better coordination of development assistance to address root

---

[19] The EU has earmarked more than 1 billion euro to continue assisting the new member states in the field of internal security during the period 2004-2006. See Gijs DeVries, European Union Counter-Terrorism Coordinator, to the hearing by the Subcommittee on Europe of the House Committee on International Relations, September 15, 2004. For an official U.S. view of European shortcomings, see the testimony by William Pope, Principal Deputy Coordinator for Counterterrorism, U. S. Department of State, at the same hearing.

causes of terrorism; pursuing terrorists and those that sponsor them wherever they may be; and cooperating on various efforts at non-pro-liferation, including significant "internationalization" and expansion of Nunn-Lugar programs.

Bilateral efforts

Bilateral cooperation between the U.S. and individual European nations will remain important despite more ambitious EU efforts, because even within the EU most of the instruments and competen-cies in the fight against terrorism remain in the hands of member states. Although the EU can do a lot to help national authorities work together internationally, the hard work of tracking down potential ter-rorists, preventing attacks and bringing suspects to justice remains the preserve of national authorities. Operational decisions are still national decisions. Even if the EU were to assume more authority in this area, the United States is unlikely to abandon its important bilat-eral national relationships. Whatever intelligence function would be created at the EU level would most likely coexist with national intelli-gence services.

Intelligence cooperation against diverse terrorist networks has to be advanced at three levels of "operation:" synchronizing and pooling intelligence products efficiently among different national services; coping with different judicial procedures and legal systems, and man-aging the risks of intelligence sharing, at both the European and transatlantic level; and global cooperation regarding terrorism and organized crime.[20]

U.S.-EU cooperation

The U.S. can work not only with individual European nations but with at EU level as well. The depth of that cooperation depends in part on the nature of the EU's own competencies in this area. U.S.-EU cooperative mechanisms are likely to evolve as the EU itself evolves. Transatlantic efforts in law enforcement, intelligence and other areas that operate at the member state level need to be coordi-

---

[20] See Yves Boyer, "Intelligence Cooperation and Homeland Security," in Brimmer, *op. cit.*

nated with efforts at infrastructure protection, health security and other areas that are gradually beginning to be coordinated at the Community level. Information sharing will remain a critical yet difficult issue, given different legal regimes and political perspectives. As in so many other fields of policy, the key is to keep each other informed at an early stage of new policy proposals which might have an impact on the other so that potential differences can be resolved before legislation is enacted.

More can be done together, however, not only to protect European and American societies directly, but to help third countries in their fight against terrorism—in essence to "project resilience" to neighboring countries. Europeans and Americans could engage more effectively together in security sector reform in third countries, and better coordinate external assistance to address conditions in which terrorism can grow. A strong homeland security system in one country may mean little if neighboring systems are weak. Terrorists in Europe, for example, have shown themselves to be far more pan-European than most of Europe's security agencies. They plan attacks in one country and execute them in the next.[21] Health issues, to take another example, have become integral elements of national security in a world of potentially catastrophic bioterrorist threats. In this regard, developed countries are only as secure as the world's weakest public health system.

NATO and its Partners

In past years NATO reforms have focused on projecting force and coping with threats beyond the NATO area. But NATO's nations—and their partners—must be prepared not only to project power beyond Europe but also to prevent, deter and, if necessary, cope with the consequences of WMD attacks on their societies—from any source. Territorial defense in the Cold War sense of protecting sealanes from Soviet submarines or guarding the Fulda Gap from Soviet tanks must give way to a new common conception of societal protection from WMD attacks from any source. If Alliance governments fail to defend their societies from a major terrorist attack, potentially involv-

---

[21] See John L. Clarke, "European Homeland Security: Promises, Progress and Pitfalls," in Bertelsmann Stiftung, (ed.), *Securing the European homeland: The EU, terrorism and homeland security* (Gütersloh, August 2005).

ing weapons of mass destruction, the Alliance will have failed in its most fundamental task. It will be marginalized and the security of Europe and North America will be further diminished.[22]

In most countries these issues are primarily civilian, national and local priorities. But NATO has a role to play, particularly in civil-military planning capabilities, security sector reform, intelligence-sharing, political consultations and consideration of missile defense. NATO's civilian disaster response efforts are still largely geared to natural disasters rather than intentional attacks, and remain very low priority. It is time to ramp up these efforts to address intentional WMD attacks on NATO territory, to develop more serious transatlantic efforts to protect critical infrastructure, to work with partners such as Russia to develop new capabilities and procedures for collaboration with civilian authorities, and to tap the expertise of partners who have had decades of experience with "total defense."

In fact, the area of "transatlantic societal security" could be an attractive new mission for a rejuvenated Partnership for Peace and its political umbrella, the Euro-Atlantic Partnership Council. A bioterrorist attack of contagious disease, for instance, will not distinguish between "allies" and "partners," and a number of partners have more experience mobilizing for societal security than do many allies. Following the last round of NATO enlargement the Partnership for Peace is a strange mix of prosperous, non-aligned Western countries such as Sweden, Finland, Austria, Ireland and Switzerland, and a number of Central Asian nations. It is precisely some of these non-aligned countries, however, which have decades of experience with approaches to societal defense, and it is precisely the area of Central Asia in which forward defense, security sector reform and preventive efforts against WMD threats are critical. NATO's special partnerships with Russia and Ukraine could also be utilized to good effect in this area.

Joint work on societal security could also infuse NATO-EU relations with a new sense of common purpose and lend substance to the "strategic partnership" each has declared yet neither has achieved. While both organizations are exploring how to strengthen their coop-

---

[22] See Daniel S. Hamilton, "Renewing Transatlantic Partnership: Why and How, Testimony to the House Committee on International Relations, European Subcommittee, June 11, 2003; and Daniel S. Hamilton, *Transatlantic Transformations, op. cit.*

eration, they have little to show for it except for some successes in the Balkans. A joint focus on societal security, including consequence management, could inject new energy into their efforts, and both organizations have tools to offer.

Transatlantic efforts can be the motor of effective global efforts

Given the nature and scope of the threat, many solutions will ultimately have to be global. There is some recognition of this on both sides of the Atlantic. The 9/11 Commission reports that America's homeland is, in fact, "the planet." Javier Solana speaks of "global homeland security."[23] And yet any "global" solution must be built by a coalition of nations committed to the effort, and the core to any effective global coalition is most often the transatlantic community. Close transatlantic cooperation is thus likely to provide the backbone to any effective multilateral action.[24] Jonathan Winer and Ann Richard provide a good example of how the Financial Action Task Force has advanced universal and global adoption of standards that were derived from cooperation between Europe and North America.[25] There are many other such examples in many different fields. More often than not, transatlantic cooperation is a stepping stone, not an alternative, to broader global cooperation, not only in the UN Security Council but in such specialized fora as the World Customs Organization or the International Civil Aviation Organization. Moreover, multilateral agreements and global standardization may take considerable time to achieve. Deeper transatlantic cooperation allows for quicker action while providing an important means to set the stage for broader global cooperation.

---

[23] On November 4, 2002, during a visit to Brussels, DHS Secretary Ridge stated '[o]ne of the conclusions we drew early on—and I think it's one that our friends in Europe concluded, perhaps before much of the world—was that the reach of terrorism is global, that targets are global in nature, and that at the end of the day the 21st century world needs to find global solutions to global vulnerabilities.' 'Homeland Security Advisor Ridge in Brussels for EU, NATO meetings—November 4 2002' accessed via http://www.useu.be/Terrorism/EUResponse/

[24] See Daniel Hamilton, Renewing Transatlantic Partnership: Why and How? Testimony to the House Committee on International Relations, June 11, 2003.

[25] See Jonathan Winer, "Cops across borders: the evolution of transatlantic law enforcement and judicial cooperation," in Dalgaard-Nielsen and Hamilton, op. cit.; Ann Richard, Fighting Terrorist Financing: Transatlantic Cooperation and International Institutions (Washington, D.C.: Center for Transatlantic Relations, 2006).

It takes a network to beat a network

Repositioning existing structures will be important. But traditional alliance mechanisms or government-to-government relationships are inadequate to the challenge of globally networked terrorism. It will take a network to beat a network. A key premise of the anti-terrorist campaign must be networked defense: traditional structures must be supplemented by an overlay of informal networks that offer a denser web of preventive efforts. Since most of the critical infrastructures that terrorists might want to destroy or disrupt are linked to global networks, it is vital to include citizens and companies in any new regime.[26] This will require governments to define national security more in societal than statist terms and to move beyond traditional "public diplomacy" and "outreach" activities for NGOs toward more effective public-private networks. Traditional alliance mechanisms may be the densest weave in the web, but other connections will be needed to make the overall effort more effective.

During the 1980s and 1990s, military planners moved defense establishments into network-centric warfare, while business executives moved away from vertical hierarchies to flat structures and networked operations. Foreign ministries and other agencies of government, however, remain caught in state-centric approaches and organizational stovepipes. They need to undergo the same type of network-centric reforms. The 9/11 Commission has proposed unifying the many participants in the U.S. domestic counterterrorism effort and their knowledge in a network-based information-sharing system that transcends traditional bureaucratic boundaries. An international dimension to such an effort would also be essential, and if it were to be launched it would most likely begin with America's closest allies.

Of course, governments are not starting from scratch. In a number of areas relevant to societal security the rigid trappings of state-to-state diplomacy have been giving way, gradually and unevenly, to new forms of interaction among state and non-state actors. Beyond the media glare on transatlantic squabbles the United States and its European allies have been forming their own complex, almost invisible and somewhat unconventional networks of cooperation that have

---

[26] Flynn provides a variety of proposals, *op. cit.*, p. 166.

become the foundation of joint efforts to freeze terrorist funds, toughen financial transparency measures, and bring aggressive threats of sanctions to those not cooperating. National governments are linking with their regulatory counterparts and the private sector across the globe to tackle thorny transnational issues such as money laundering, securities fraud, and drug trafficking. Governments are finding that such networks can be fast, flexible, cheap, and effective. They can lower the cost of collective action and enable large and disparate groups to organize and influence events faster and better than before. They can build capacities without building bureaucracies.

Effective anti-terrorism efforts will depend increasingly upon new forms of cooperation among state and non-state actors. In the international sphere, such efforts have been led almost entirely by institutions that are neither nation states, regional unions, multilateral organizations, or international organizations, but rather informal networks of law enforcement agencies, regulators, and the private sector. Such "international non-organizations" such as the Financial Action Task Force (FATF), the Egmont group or the Lyon Group can make a difference by setting standards and attacking nodes of terrorist or criminal activity. These structures developed in response to particular crises in the global financial system, as stakeholders came to realize from painful experience that transborder financial crime, including money laundering, terrorist finance, the theft and sequestration of national patrimonies by corrupt officials, stock market and investment fraud, contributed to such serious domestic problems as drug trafficking, immigrant smuggling, insurance crime and terrorism. By naming and shaming miscreants and threatening to block their access to the world's two most important markets, the Europeans and North Americans at the core of such networks began to produce practical results.[27] Such groups might offer models for similar networked cooperation in related fields.

Such networks aim to protect the critical nodes of activity that connect modern societies while attacking the critical nodes of those networks that would do us harm. Nodal strategies give higher priority to creating an environment hostile to all antagonists than to invest inor-

---

[27] See Jonathan Winer, "Cops across borders: the evolution of transatlantic law enforcement and judicial cooperation," in Dalgaard-Nielsen and Hamilton, *op. cit.*, pp. 106-125.

dinate resources in chasing any particular offender. In each relevant sector the ultimate objective must be to create a loose, agile but muscular public-private network capable of responding to the terrorists' own transnational networks.

Needed: New mechanisms and new approaches

The world is on the cusp of exponential change in challenges posed by pathogens and their accessibility to state and non-state actors. These challenges require actions beyond piecemeal extensions of current policies. They require something more holistic than disease-specific stockpiles of medicines or vaccine. They require us to integrate public health and national security communities in ways that allow us to deal with an unprecedented challenge. Key multilateral frameworks such as NATO and the EU are limited in their ability to cope with the unique challenges posed by a bioweapon-induced spread of epidemic disease. Would a bioweapon attack that threatens a nation's health rather than its territory warrant a collective response under NATO's mutual defense clause or the EU's "solidarity clause?" What might such a response entail, and is either institution equipped for such action? Joint planning for traditional international security contingencies has occurred in NATO for decades. Planning with that degree of rigor and strategic and operational detail, but now for international response to epidemics, is but one example of what is needed to cope with potential threats to the European or North American homelands.

Conclusion

Europeans and Americans again face a new era. The open question is whether we are prepared to face it together. Our economies and our societies are too deeply intertwined to allow transatlantic divorce, but we do face the very real possibility of transatlantic dysfunction in the face of terrorist dangers that blur the lines between domestic and international security and between crime and war, and that neither Europeans nor Americans will be able to tackle alone.

Separate or competitive approaches will prove inadequate to the common challenge of catastrophic terrorism. A broad transatlantic campaign to confront this threat will require comprehensive cooperation among intelligence officials, police, diplomats, military, medical doctors, public health authorities and first responders, customs and financial institutions, the private sector and individual citizens. It will force us to understand more clearly where and why we agree and where—due to different national experiences and perspectives—our approaches may need to be reconciled. It will mean aligning Europe's grand yet difficult experiment of integration with a reorientation and strategic transformation of transatlantic relations to create new models of Atlantic partnership. Victory will be piecemeal and incremental. In President Bush's words, it will require a "patient accumulation of success." The alternative could be tragedy on a scale exceeding even the horrors of the bloody century we left behind.

Conclusion

Democracy and Terrorism

Fernando Gil

I want to thank all the authors for the quality of their contributions. The first conclusion one can draw from these analyses is that we find ourselves at the beginning of the problem and that no country is protected from terrorist acts. The second conclusion, equally obvious, and for the very same reason, is that international cooperation is required on a considerable number of levels: information, coordination, military and police means, legal arsenal, prevention, repression. Terrorism negates the very concept of international relations.

Perhaps it is best to conclude such a volume with a simple note of reflection, and that is that the very nature of democracy makes the fight against terrorism very difficult. More precisely, what basically characterises democracy is an historical and evolutionary perspective: democracy defines itself as the way to progress for humanity as whole. Enlightenment remains its ideological substructure. From the perpetual peace of Kant to the law of the three States of Comte and to the open society of Popper or to the theory of justice of Rawls, Western reason sees itself as an almost natural solution with a universal vocation. It is difficult for it to admit that all peoples and all individuals do not aspire to the values that have proved their worth, from Athenian democracy to the English and French revolutions, and for which a high price has always been paid. Across the centuries Western reason has acquired a weight of experience that is often very heavy. Neither dark hours nor enormous tragedies have been lacking: wars of religion and of nations, totalitarianism, genocides, colonial depredations.

Terrorism attacks where western reason is most at its mercy. A list of the weaknesses would be long and I limit myself to indicating some directions. They seem to me to be *prior questions* to the dialogue and to the recognition of otherness. I fear that they may be absolute conditions.

The first direction is that the history of the West led us to consider that the *religious* and the *theological* elements must be absolutely dissociated from *the political*. Besides, it is on this point that a dividing line separates the positions of the "old Europe," on one side, and the United States and Israel, on the other. The relation to God of the Constitution of the United States and of a certain type of American political discourse, just as much as the Jewish nature of the State of Israel, can appear as a leftover in relation to a secularization *a priori* unstoppable and without faults. In other words, when Islamic terrorism invokes Allah, the Koran, Sharia law, the Jihad against the infidels, democratic principle has difficulty in admitting that this might be able to build a political principle. The West tends to think that God is a private matter and that, in the final analysis, belonging to a religion relates to a pleasant family tradition. Democracy is based on a secular moralization of the religious sphere, as if progress might imply abandoning churches.

The second direction is that of *hate*. Democracy has generalized the Judaeo-Christian love of one's neighbor, transforming it into brotherhood and social solidarity. These two ideas are not only compatible but find themselves insolubly linked to the development of the individuality of people. "Rousseauean" self-love functions as a type of guarantee of the love of others and of the understanding that can come from them. Hate is, in consequence, something exclusively negative (as Espinosa reminds us), and what survives of hate in democratic societies is tolerated exclusively *as hate for its own sake* that, on a psycho-moralist level shows itself frequently in the posture of acceptance of guilt. The acceptance of guilt is not necessarily the index of true responsibility.

On the contrary, terrorism expresses itself as *pure and total hate*, massively. Western reason tries desperately to idiomatize this bloc, probably to reduce its archaic force. In a certain way, concepts such as humiliation, oppression, racism, or colonization are intermediary openings—the West uses them as an interpretative grid. Terrorism uses them too, but leaving the pure hate untouched—these concepts cease to constitute mediations and turn themselves into mirrors of Western guilt.

The third direction is *the link to time*. In democracies, time functions as a mediating factor for action. Democracy is a perpetual process. Never is it given once and for all. It is always seen as a process of democratization, that is, of humanization, civilization, improvement. Continuity is valued as something positive. The past and the present tend towards a future that must be better and is itself open.

For this reason, democracy does not appear to be sufficiently prepared to confront ideologies that, like terrorism, favour rupture, abandonment and eternity. In contrast to the Western relationship with time are the articulations of terrorism with globalization or the idea of a 'network' of terrorism, and the particular exaltation of *sacrifice* when this corresponds to a movement of *spatial extension of time*. Past and future project themselves onto a single point, the here and now of the terrorist act—and in the eternity of death. On the other hand, democratic reason continues to hope, and because of this fights so that its extension remains temporal and gradual. It will give to globalization a utopian force that will secure a better *future* for all peoples. For democracy, time is a factor in the realization of Good.

In conclusion, democracies only have one choice possible: to draw from their own fragility a stimulus capable of reinforcing their vigilance. In view of what they perceive as nihilistic in terrorist behavior, they must protect themselves against their own internal nihilist tendencies. Considering that, in a confrontation between nihilisms, the comfortable nihilism *will always lose* against the nihilism of sacrifice and destruction. Happily, in this confrontation, we can count on forces hostile to the societies that produce terrorism. Here it is important to note that democratic aspirations are also stirring deeply within these societies. Inversely and complementarily, on the Western side we are being invited to reinvest in the history of our values. Its rejection on the part of terrorism is perhaps an opportunity for re-foundation. A certain post-modern conception of modernism makes the "death of God" a new point of departure. Unhappily, up to now it appears to be grievously sterile. Perhaps it might be preferable first to look back: the requirement for liberty must not exclude *a priori* the Judaeo-Christian part of Enlightenment and of Modernity itself. This could in fact be the theme for another book.

About the Authors

Yonah Alexander is currently a Senior Fellow at the Potomac Institute for Policy Studies and Director of its International Center for Terrorism Studies as well as a member of the Board of Regents. He is Director of the Inter-University Center for Terrorism Studies and Co-Director of the Inter-University Center for Legal Studies. Both are consortia of universities and think tanks throughout the world. In addition, Yonah Alexander is the former Director of Terrorism Studies at The George Washington University and the State University of New York, totaling 35 years of service. Educated at Columbia University (Ph.D.), the University of Chicago (M.A.), and Roosevelt University of Chicago (B.A.), he taught at George Washington University, American University, the Columbus School of Law at Catholic University of America, Tel Aviv University, The City University of New York, and The State University of New York. Yonah Alexander is founder and editor-in-chief of TerrorismCentral.com and the International Journal on Minorities and Group Rights. He also founded and edited Terrorism: An International Journal and Political Communication and Persuasion: An International Journal. He has published over 90 books on the subjects of international affairs and terrorism.

Daniel Benjamin is a senior fellow in the International Security Program at the Center for Strategic and International Studies. His scholarly interests include terrorism, American foreign policy, the Middle East, Europe and South Asia. From 1994 to1999, he served on the National Security Council staff. In 1998-1999, he was director for transnational threats. From 1994-1997, he served as foreign policy speechwriter and special assistant to President Clinton. Before entering the government, he was Berlin bureau chief for *The Wall Street Journal* and a foreign correspondent and staff writer for *Time*. In 2000, he was a Jennings Randolph Senior Fellow at the United State Institute of Peace. In 2004, he held a Bosch Fellowship at The American Academy in Berlin.

Monique Canto-Sperber is the Director of the *Ecole Normale Supérieure* in Paris, France. She has published several books about ancient philosophy (*Ethiques gracques*, 2002) and moral and political philosophy (*Dictionnaire d'éthique et de philosophie morale*, 2001; *L'Inquiétude morale et la vie humaine*, 2001). She is considered to be one of the top French specialists on Plato of whom she translated and commented innumerous dialogues (*Euthydème, Gorgias, Ion, Ménon*). Her most celebrated books are *Le socialisme libéral : une anthologie : Europe—Etats-Unis* (2003), *Les Règles de la liberté* (2003) and *Le Bien, la guerre et la terreur. Pour une morale internationale.* (2005)

Gareth Evans has been since January 2000 President of the Brussels-based International Crisis Group, an independent organization with over 100 full-time staff on five continents working to prevent and resolve deadly conflict. He came to Crisis Group after 21 years in Australian politics, thirteen of them as a Cabinet Minister. As Foreign Minister (1988-96) he was best known internationally for his role in developing the UN peace plan for Cambodia, helping conclude the Chemical Weapons Convention, and helping initiate new Asia Pacific regional economic and security architecture. He has written or edited eight books—including Cooperating for Peace, launched at the UN in 1993—and has published over eighty journal articles and chapters on foreign relations, human rights and legal and constitutional reform. He was Co-Chair of the International Commission on Intervention and State Sovereignty, which published its report, The Responsibility to Protect, in December 2001; and a Member of the UN Secretary General's High Level Panel on Threats, Challenges and Change which reported in December 2004. He is currently a member of the Zedillo International Task Force on Global Public Goods and the Blix Commission on Weapons of Mass Destruction.

Richard Falkenrath is a Senior Fellow in the foreign policy studies at the Brookings Institute. He is also Senior Director of the Civitas Group LLC, a strategic advisory and investment services firm serving the homeland security market, a security analyst for the Cable News Network (CNN), a member of the Aspen Strategy Group, and a member of the Business Advisory Board of Arxan Technologies. He left the White House in May 2004. His last position was Deputy Assistant to the President and Deputy Homeland Security Advisor, a position he had held since January 2003. Previously, he served as Special Assistant to the President and Senior Director for Policy and Plans within the Office of Homeland Security since October 2001. He also served as Director for Proliferation Strategy on the National Security Council staff from January to October 2001, and was a member of the Bush-Cheney Transition Team for the National Security Council. He was Assistant Professor of Public Policy at the John F.

Kennedy School of Government, Harvard University, before entering government. From 1995 to 1998, he served as Executive Director of the Belfer Center for Science and International Affairs (BCSIA). He is the author and coauthor of *Shaping Europe's Military Order* (1995), *Avoiding Nuclear Anarchy* (1996), *America's Achilles' Heel; Nuclear, Biological, Chemical Terrorism and Covert Attack* (1998), and numerous journal articles and chapters of edited volumes. Dr. Falkenrath was also a Visiting Research Fellow at the German Society of Foreign Affairs (DGAP) in Bonn in 1995. He holds a Ph.D. from the Department of War Studies, King's College, London, where he was a British Marshall Scholar, and is a *summa cum laude* graduate of Occidental College, Los Angeles, with degrees in economics and international relations.

Bruno S. Frey is Associate Professor in the University of Basel since 1969, was Full Professor in the University of Constance 1970-77, is Full Professor in the University of Zurich since 1977, was awarded an Honorary Doctor of Economics in the University of St. Gallen in 1998 and an Honorary Doctor of Economics in the University of Göteborg in 1998. His most recent books are *Not Just for the Money. An Economic Theory of Personal Motivation*, 1997, *Economics as a Science of Human Behaviour*, Extended 2nd Edition, 1999, *The New Democratic Federalism for Europe. Functional, Overlapping and Competing Jurisdictions* (with Reiner Eichenberger), 1999, *Arts & Economics. Analysis & Cultural Policy*, 2000, *Successful Management by Motivation. Balancing Intrinsic and Extrinsic Incentives* (with Margit Osterloh), 2001, *Inspiring Economics. Human Motivation in Political Economy*, 2001, *Happiness and Economics: How the Economy and Institutions Affect Human Well-Being* (with Alois Stutzer), 2002, and *Dealing with Terrorism—Stick or Carrot?, 2004.*

Fernando Gil, born in 1937, passed away in 2006. As a Full Professor of the *Faculdade de Ciências Sociais e Humanas* of *Universidade Nova de Lisboa* since 1988, he lectured Knowledge Philosophy. He was also, since 1989, *Directeur d'études* of the *École des Hautes Études en Sciences Sociales* (EHESS) in Paris, Visiting Professor at the Johns Hopkins University, in Baltimore, and Visiting Professor and Conferencist in several universities in different continents. At *Universidade Nova de Lisboa* he was equally the Interdisciplinary Network Coordinator for the Research Centres (RICI), created in

2003, where he organized a series of interdisciplinary conferences. He had a Law degree at *Universidade de Lisboa* and a degree in Philosophy at Sorbonne, where he also took his PhD in Logics with the thesis *La Logique du Nom*, published in France, in 1972. He published a vast number of scientific papers such as *La logique du nom* (1972), *Traité de l'evidence* (1993) *Mimésis e negação* (1984), *Provas* (1988), *Modos da Evidência* (1998) *Viagens do Olhar* (1998), *La conviction* (2000), *Mediações* (2001), *Impasses* (2003), or *Acentos* (2005) and coordinated joint works. He also translated into Portuguese works from authors like Karl Jaspers, Romano Guardini, Cesare Pavese and M. Merleau-Ponty. He was awarded the title of *Grande Oficial da Ordem do Infante D. Henrique* in 1992, and was honored with the title of *Chevalier des Palmes Académiques* by the French Goverment, in 1995. He received the Pen Club Essay Award in 1984 (*Mimésis e Negação*), a prize that he would receive a second time with the publication of *Viagens do Olhar* (1998). In 1993 he was granted the *Prémio Pessoa*.

Daniel S. Hamilton is the Richard von Weizsäcker Professor and Director of the Center for Transatlantic Relations at Johns Hopkins University's Paul H. Nitze School of Advanced International Studies. He is also Executive Director of the American Consortium on EU Studies (ACES), the EU Center of Excellence in Washington, DC, and Publisher of *Transatlantic* magazine. He leads the international activities of PACER, the Johns Hopkins-led Center for the Study of High Consequence Event Preparedness and Response, designated a National Center of Excellence in Homeland Security by the U.S. Department of Homeland Security. He previously served as Deputy Assistant Secretary of State for European Affairs; Associate Director of the Policy Planning Staff; U.S. Special Coordinator for Southeast European Stabilization; Senior Associate at the Carnegie Endowment for International Peace, and Deputy Director of the Aspen Institute Berlin. He has authored and edited many works on international relations.

Aboubakr Jamaï is publisher of Morocco's leading weekly newspaper, *Le Journal Hebdomadaire*. His paper has tackled tough topics such as government corruption, corporate impropriety, and other taboo political subjects in Morocco. Jamaï, 37, began his career in finance, co-founding Morocco's first independent investment bank in 1993. After two years advising international emerging market funds with holdings in North Africa, the company, Upline Securities, became the holdings in North Africa, the company, Upline Securities, became the first Moroccan-based bank ever selected to manage a privatization project in Morocco. In 1996 he joined the Executive Secretariat of the Middle East and North Africa Economic Summit as a financial and economic adviser. This organization was set up by the sponsors of the Middle East peace process to foster economic cooperation in the region. His foray into journalism came in 1995, when he began writing a column on the relationship between international financial markets and the Moroccan financial market for a weekly economic newspaper. He co-founded *Le Journal* and *Assahifa* in 1997 and 1998. In 1999 and 2000, the Moroccan government banned temporarily his newspapers. He won the Committee To Protect Journalists' International Press Freedom Award in 2003. He was been selected by the World Economic Forum as a Young Global Leader for 2005. He was a Yale World Fellow in 2004 at Yale University. He holds a BA from The Higher Institute of Commerce and Management at Casablanca, and a M.B.A. from Oxford University's Saïd Business School.

Mark Juergensmeyer is Director of Global and International Studies and Professor of Sociology and Religious Studies at the University of California, Santa Barbara. He is an expert on religious violence, conflict resolution and South Asian religion and politics, and has published more than two hundred articles and a dozen books. His widely-read *Terror in the Mind of God: The Global Rise of Religious Violence* (University of California Press, revised edition 2003), is based on interviews with violent religious activists around the world— including individuals convicted of the 1993 World Trade Center bombing, leaders of Hamas, and abortion clinic bombers in the United States—and was listed by the *Washington Post* and the *Los Angeles Times* as one of the best nonfiction books of the year. A previous book, *The New Cold War? Religious Nationalism Confronts the Secular State* (University of California Press, 1993) covers the rise of religious activism and its confrontation with secular modernity. It was named by the *New York Times* as one of the notable books of the year. His book on Gandhian conflict resolution has recently been reprinted as *Gandhi's Way* (University of California Press, Updated Edition, 2005), and was selected as Community Book of the Year at the University of California, Davis. His most recent work is an edited volume, *Global Religions* (Oxford University Press 2003), and he is working on a book on religion and war, and an edited volume on religion in global civil society. He has received research fellowships from the Wilson Center in Washington D.C., the Harry Frank Guggenheim Foundation, the U.S. Institute of Peace, and the American Council of Learned Societies. He is the 2003 recipient of the prestigious Grawemeyer Award for contributions to the study of religion, and is the 2004 recipient of the Silver Award of the Queen Sofia Center for the Study of Violence in Spain. He received an Honorary Doctorate from Lehigh University in 2004. Since the events of September 11 he has been a frequent commentator in the news media, including CNN, NBC, CBS, BBC, NPR, Fox News, ABC's Politically Incorrect, and CNBC's Dennis Miller Show.

Farhad Khosrokhavar is Professor at the Ecole des Hautes Etudes en Sciences Sociales (EHESS)—Cadis, Paris (France) since 1998. He was previously associate professor at EHESS-Cadis (1991-98) and Rockefeller Fellow (1990-91). His research interests include political sociology, sociology of religion, contemporary Islam, Iran. He has published extensively on Iran and Islam in Europe: *Les nouveaux martyrs d'Allah* (Paris, Flammarion, 2002); "Postrevolutionary Iran and new social movements," in *Islamic Revolution, political and social transition in Iran since 1979* (Syracuse University Press, 2002, pp.3-18); *La recherche de soi, dialogues sur le sujet* (with Alain Touraine) (Paris, Fayard, 2000); *L'islam des jeunes (en France)* (Paris, Flammarion, 1997); *Le Foulard et la République* (with Françoise Gaspard) (Paris, La Découverte, 1995); "Attitudes of teenage girls to the Iranian Revolution," in Elizabeth W. Fernea (ed.), *Children in the Middle East* (Austin, University of Texas Press, 1995, pp.392-409).

Simon Luechinger was born on July 5, 1975 in Zurich, Switzerland. In 2004 he attended Summer School at the London School of Economics: Advanced Microeconomics. He received his Masters degree in History (Lizentiat, summa cum laude) in 2003. Between 1996 and 2003 he attended History, Economics and Political Sciences at the University of Zurich. Between 1991and 1996 attended Freies Gymnasium Zürich, Matura Since 2003 he is an Assistant at the Institute for Empirical Research in Economics, at the University of Zurich. His research interests are political economy, economics of terrorism, economics and psychology. He was awarded with a price by the history department of the philosophical faculty for the best seminar paper written by a student in the summer semester 2001.

Sergio Marchisio is the Director of the Institute for International Legal Studies of the Italian National Research Council (CNR). Full Professor of Law of International Organizations at the University La Sapienza of Rome. Secretary General of the Italian Society of International Law. Chairman of the Legal Subcommittee of the United Nations Committee on the Peaceful Uses of Outer Space (COPUOS, Vienna). Member of the Committee of Experts on Nationality of the Council of Europe. Legal Counsellor at the Italian Ministry of Foreign Affairs. He acted as representative of the Italian government in a number of international conferences and negotiations, including the Conference for the Establishment of an International Criminal Court. Member of the Italian Consultative Committee on Human Rights and of the National Commission for Promoting the Italian Culture abroad (Italian Ministry of Foreign Affairs). He published several monographs, essays and articles on different International law and European Union law topics. Editor of the eight volumes of the Third Series of the Italian Practice on International Law (Rome, 1995). Author of the chapter on "Counter-Terrorism in Italy" for the research on "Counter Terrorism Strategies in the 21st Century," International Center for Terrorism Studies of the Potomac Institute for Policy Studies, Arlington.

Brigitte L. Nacos, a long-time U.S. correspondent for newspapers in Germany, received a Ph.D. in political science from Columbia University, where she teaches courses in American politics and government in the Political Science Department for more than 15 years. Her research concentrates on the links between the media, public opinion, and decision-making and on domestic and international terrorism and counterterrorism. Besides publishing many articles and several book chapters, she is the author *of The Press, Presidents, and Crises* (Columbia University Press, 1990); *Terrorism and the Media:From the Iran Hostage Crisis to the World Trade Center Bombing* (Columbia University Press, 1994); *Terrorism and the Media: From the Iran Hostage Crisis to the Oklahoma City Bombing* (Columbia University Press, 1996), and *Mass-Mediated Terrorism: The Central Role of the Media in Terrorism and Counterterrorism* (Rowman & Littlefield, 2002).She is co-author (with Lewis J. Edinger) of *From Bonn to Berlin:*

German Politics in Transition (Columbia University Press, 1998), and co-editor (with Robert Y. Shapiro and Pierangelo Isernia) of *Decisionmaking in a Glass House* (Rowman & Littlefield, 2000). Her most recent book, *Terrorism and Counterterrorism: Understanding Threats and Responses in the Post-9/11 World*, was published by Longman in July 2005.

Stefan Oeter is Full Professor with the Chair for Public Law and Public International Law and Managing Director of the Institute of International Affairs at the University of Hamburg Law School; member of the Independent Committee of Experts for the European Charter for Regional and Minority Languages of the Council of Europe; member of the Scientific Advisory Board of the Federal Ministry of Transport; President of the Historical Commission of the International Society for Military Law and the Law of War. 1997-1999 he was Visiting Professor for Public Law at Europa-Universität Viadrina, Frankfurt/Oder. 1997 he was Acting Professor for Public Law at Heidelberg University Law School and in 1996 completed his Habilitation at the Law Faculty of the University of Heidelberg. 1990 graduation as Dr. iur. utr.; expert for Council of Europe and OSCE in judicial reform projects in Eastern Europe. 1987-1997 research fellow at the Max Planck Institute for Comparative Public and Public International Law, Heidelberg. 1984-1987 practical training as ´Referendar´ at courts, law firms and administrations in Heidelberg, Mannheim, Karlsruhe and as an intern at the UN Office of the Legal Counsel in New York; 1979-1983 studies in law at the Universities of Heidelberg and Montpellier. His research priorities include protection of minorities, comparative federalism, European and international economic law, international humanitarian law: theory of international law and international relations.

Christine Ockrent is producer and anchor of the weekly current affairs program France Europe Express on France 3 Television. She is also president of the advisory board of METRO International France, and a columnist for various French and Swiss newspapers. Previously she was editor in chief of the weekly news magazine, *L'Express*. She has had an outstanding carrer in television, both as producer of documentaries and anchor of the evening news, where she shaped a style as the first woman presenter and editor. Ms. Ockrent was also deputy director general of TF1 Television and an editor with RTL Radio. She began her career in broadcast journalism at NBC News and worked for eight years at CBS' 60 Minutes. She has been awarded several French and international distinctions for her work in TV journalism. She is a graduate of the Institut d'études politiques in Paris and studied at Cambridge University. She has written eight books, one of which translated in German ("*Wie Julius Caesar den Euro erfand*" Rowohlt). She is on the board of Reporters sans frontières, Aspen France and International Crisis Group (ICG). She has been awarded the French Legion d'Honneur.

Magnus Ranstorp is Research Director of the Center for Asymmetric Threat Studies at the Swedish National Defense College, Stockholm, where he is leading a major funded project on strategic terrorist threats in Europe, including radicalization and recruitment of jihadists. Until recently he was Director of the Center for the Study of Terrorism and Political Violence (CSTPV) at the University of St Andrews, Scotland. He is the author of *Hizb'Allah in Lebanon: The Politics of the Western Hostage Crisis* and numerous articles and monographs on terrorism and counterterrorism. He is a member of the International Editorial Advisory Board of the academic journal, *Studies in Conflict and Terrorism*. He is currently completing a book on *Mapping Terrorism Research: Achievements, Gaps and Future Directions*. He is internationally recognized as a leading expert on Hizb'Allah, Hamas, al-Qaeda and other militant Islamic movements. He has conducted extensive fieldwork around the world, interviewing hundreds of terrorists as well as members of militant Islamic movements. In March 2000, the Israeli media recognized his research on the behaviour of the Hizb'Allah movement as among the contributing factors leading to the Israeli government's decision to withdraw from southern Lebanon. Dr Ranstorp has briefed many senior government and security officials from around the world and lectures regularly at major universities, think tanks and intergovernmental organizations. In 2003, he was invited to testify before The National Commission on Terrorist Attacks Upon the United States in a panel on "The Attackers, Intelligence and Counterterrorism Policy." In 2004, he also assisted the Scottish Police College with curriculum development and delivery of lectures in the *Leadership in Counterterrorism (LINCT) Course*, involving the FBI, Police Service Northern Ireland, and the Royal Canadian Mountain Police. Over the last ten years, Dr Ranstorp has engaged in Executive Education modules on *Terrorism* *and Counter Terrorism* worldwide in Europe, North America and the Middle East. He was a principal consultant on terrorism for CNN before and after 11 September 2001.

Daniel Sibony was born and grew up in the "médina" of Marrakech amidst Jewish, Arab and French culture. He emigrated to France when he was 14 years old. He rapidly became a *researcher in mathematics*; then a professor at the University of Paris (after a state Doctorat in mathematical analysis). Then, a state doctorate in philosophy (with Emmanuel Levinas). At the same time, he discovered *psychoanalysis* and became a psychoanalyst. He clearly demonstrated his independance from present psychoanalytic institutes with the publishing of his first book *The name and the body* (1974). He has a teaching position at the University of Paris VIII but is also a psychoanalysis practitioner, a writer and a lecturer. He has published thirty books. His last yearly seminars were on: *Ethics of being* (1999), *Thinking in act* (2000). Sibony has elaborated a new theory on religion, beside his clinical works. His latest book (2005) is *CREATION. Essay on contemporary art.*

Paul Wilkinson is Professor of International Relations and Chairman of the Advisory Board of the Centre for the Study of Terrorism and Political Violence (CSTPV) at the University of St Andrews. Prior to his appointment at St Andrews in 1989 he was Professor of International Relations, University of Aberdeen 1979-1989. He was visiting Fellow at Trinity Hall, Cambridge in 1997—1998 and is Honorary Fellow of University of Wales, Swansea. His publications include *Political Terrorism* (1974); *Terrorism and the Liberal State* (1977/1986); *The New Fascists* (1981/1983); *Contemporary Research on Terrorism* (as co-editor, 1987); *Aviation Terrorism and Security* (as co-editor, 1999) and *Terrorism versus Democracy: The Liberal State Response* (2001). He co-authored with Joseph S. Nye Jr. and Yukio Satoh the report to the Trilateral Commission (May 2003) *Addressing the New International Terrorism; Prevention, Intervention and Multilateral Co-operation*. He is co-editor of the academic journal *Terrorism and Political Violence*. He is currently director of a research project funded by the ESRC on the domestic management of terrorist attacks in the UK. He served as Adviser to Lord Lloyd of Berwick's Inquiry into Legislation Against Terrorism, and authored vol. two, the Research Report for the Inquiry (1996).

Florence Taubmann has been Pasteur de l'Eglise Réformée de Frnce since 1992, with a bachelor degree in « Lettres Modernes » at the Sorbonne University and a master degree at the theology protestant faculty of Paris-Montpellier. She is member of the « Association française du protestantisme libéral « Evangile et liberté » and the director committee of the « Amitié judéo-chrétienne de France."

Jorge Sampaio was President of the Portuguese Republic from 1996 to 2006. Mr. Sampaio has been a member of the Socialist party since 1978, and was first elected to parliament in 1979. Since then he has been reelected four times. He headed the Socialist party from 1989 to 1992. From 1989 to 1995 was the Mayor of Lisbon.

Emílio Rui Vilar is President of the Board of Trustees of the Calouste Gulbenkian Foundation, Chairman of the Board of Directors of Partex Oil and Gas (Holdings) Corporation, Guest Professor at the School of Economics and Management (Portuguese Catholic University, Porto) and Chairman of the Audit Commission of the Bank of Portugal. He was Director General at the European Union's Commission (1986 to 1989), Chairman and CEO of Caixa Geral de Depósitos (1991 to 1996), in 1996 he was co-opted trustee of the Calouste Gulbenkian Foundation. He was Secretary of State for External Trade and Tourism (1974), Minister of the Economy (1974 to 1975), Minister of Transports and Communications (1976 to 1978), and Deputy Governor of the Bank of Portugal (1975 to 1984).

Conference Program

Conflict and Cooperation in International Relations Cycle

International Conference

Terrorism and International Relations

October 25-26, 2005
Calouste Gulbenkian Foundation, Lisbon, Portugal
Program

Tuesday, 25th October 2005

9.30h *Introduction*

H.E. The President of the Portuguese Republic, Dr. Jorge Sampaio

Emílio Rui Vilar, President, Calouste Gulbenkian Foundation

10.30 Keynote Address

Chairman: **Teresa Gouveia**

Gareth Evans, *The Global Response to Terrorism*
President, International Crisis Group

11.30h *Terrorist Itineraries: causes, networks and biographies*

Chairman: **José Manuel Fernandes**

Aboubakr Jamai,
Director of *Journal-Hebdomadaire*, Casablanca

Daniel Sibony,
Université de Paris VII

Farhad Khosrokhavar, *Islamic terrorism, European style*,
EHESS, Paris

13.00h Lunch

15.00h *Costs of terrorism and defence strategies*

Chairman: **Loureiro dos Santos**

Richard Falkenrath,
Elements of a comprehensive strategy against terrorism
Senior Fellow, The Brookings Institution

Bruno S. Frey and Simon Luechinger,
Costs and Benefits of anti-terrorism politics.
Zurich University

Jean-Louis Bruguière,
Vice-president, Tribunal de Grande Instance, Paris

18.00h *Keynote Address*

Chairman: **Artur Santos Silva**

Paul Wilkinson,
The Threat from the al-Qaeda Hydra: The Liberal State Response
Director, St. Andrews Centre for the Study of Terrorism and
Political Violence

20.00h Dinner

Wednesday, 26th October 2005

10.00h *The Internationalisation of terrorism*

Chairman: **Rui Pereira**

Brigitte L. Nacos,
Terrorism and Media in the Age of Global Communication
Department of Political Science, Columbia University

Mark Juergensmeyer,
Director of the Global and International Studies,
California University, Santa Barbara

Magnus Ranstorp,
Al-Qaeda—An Expanded Global Network of Terror?
Research Director, Centre for Asymmetric Threat Studies, Swedish
National Defence College, Stockholm, Sweden

11.30h *Law and Terrorism*

Chairman: **António Vitorino**

> **Sergio Marchisio,**
> *Recent Developments in Anti-Terrorism Law: How to Fill Normative Gaps*
> Università di Roma La Sapienza,
>
> **Stefan Oeter,** *Terrorism as a Challenge for International Law*
> Institute for International Affairs, Hamburg University.
>
> **Yonah Alexander,**
> *Counter Terrorism Legal Training: Uncharted Territory*
> Senior Fellow, Director of International Center for Terrorism
> Studies, Potomac Institute for Policy Studies, Washington DC, US

13.00h Lunch

15.00h *Religion and Civilisation*

Chairman: **Diogo Pires Aurélio**

> **Monique Canto-Sperber,** *Terrorism and Just War*
> Centre de Recherches Politiques Raymond Aron
>
> **Florence Taubmann,** *Dieu: Mot dangereux, mot necessaire!*
> Minister of the protestant reformed Church of France
>
> **Daniel Benjamin,** *Religion and Civilization*
> Senior Fellow, Center for Strategic and International Studies, US

18.00h *Keynote Address*

Chairman: **André Gonçalves Pereira**

Christine Ockrent, *Media and Terrorism*

19.00h *Closing Session*

> **Emílio Rui Vilar,** President, Calouste Gulbenkian Foundation
>
> **Fernando Gil,** Conference Commissioner
>
> **Diogo Freitas do Amaral,** Portuguese Foreign Affairs Minister